NOTRE-DAME
DE PARIS

NOTRE-DAME DE PARIS

Alain Erlande-Brandenburg

Photographs by Caroline Rose

Translated by John Goodman

Abradale Press
Harry N. Abrams, Inc., Publishers

For Brice

The following abbreviations are used in the captions:
B.F.C.E. Banque Française du Commerce Extérieur
B.H.V.P. Bibliothèque Historique de la Ville de Paris
C.N.M.H.S. Caisse Nationale des Monuments Historiques et des Sites
C.R.M.H. Centre de Recherches sur les Monuments Historiques

Art Director: Jean-Louis Germain
Photo Research: Gisèle Namur
Editor, English-language edition: Diana Murphy
Designer, English-language edition: Carol Robson with Gilda Hannah

The Library of Congress has cataloged the Abrams edition as follows:
Erlande-Brandenburg, Alain.
    [Notre-Dame de Paris. English]
    Notre-Dame de Paris / Alain Erlande-Brandenburg ; photographs by Caroline Rose.
        p.   cm.
    Includes bibliographical references and index.
    ISBN 0–8109–1394–1 (clothbound)
    1. Notre-Dame de Paris (Cathedral) 2. Architecture, Gothic-France—Paris.
3. Paris (France)—Buildings, structures, etc.
I. Title.
NA5550.N7E7413   1998
726.5 ' 0944 ' 361—dc21   97-35370

Abradale ISBN 0–8109–8179–3

Abradale Press
Harry N. Abrams, Inc.
100 Fifth Avenue
New York, N.Y. 10011
www.abramsbooks.com

Contents

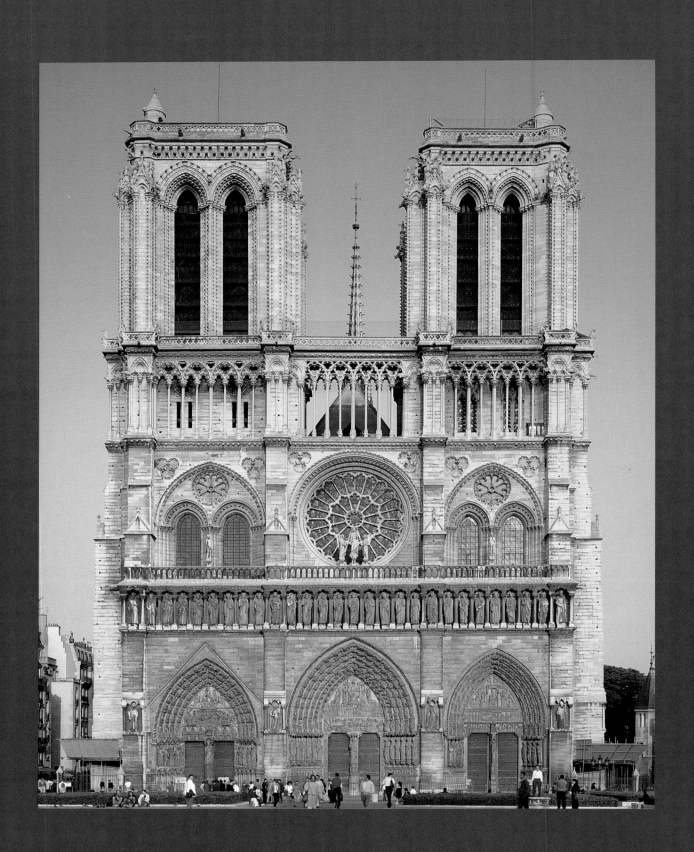

The Cathedral of Notre-Dame

So simple and harmonious is the imposing mass of Notre-Dame de Paris that it can be taken in at a single glance. The facade is solemn and serene but not austere. Its composition, based on a judicious balance of horizontals and verticals, honors the plane of the wall: both projections and indentations are discreet. The buttresses at first rise assertively but in the end shrink back to avoid brutal disruption of the pervasive planarity. Likewise, the three portals, rose window, and lancets scarcely seem to compromise the integrity of the wall. The Gallery of Kings becalms the strong vertical thrust by establishing an emphatic horizontal accent, as does the second gallery at the base of the towers, but to an even greater extent, thanks to its height, its independence from the supporting wall, and its transparency across the central bay. The light of the Île-de-France glides over the spare surfaces, penetrates the voids, is caught on the projections to produce nuanced shadows. In the upper register, the sky slips between the two towers, sweeping all before it.

The side elevations preserve this equilibrium by means of their three superimposed envelopes. The first, firmly articulated, continues—thanks to walls built flush with the buttresses—to enclose the apse. It is interrupted by the transepts, which rise to underscore the building's cruciform plan. The two upper envelopes adhere to an identical schema. They establish an even more assertive horizontal emphasis, reinforced visually by the balustrades mounted along the gutters. These three masonry masses, superimposed and progressively set back, are pacified by the buttresses, which take on individual identities as they escape from the lower envelope, assertively along the nave, more subtly around the apse. The flying buttresses establish vertical links between these contrapuntal lines, bestriding the side aisles and the tribunes. Their audacious leap toward the upper nave walls crucially shapes perception of the masses. Their boldness seems to defy technical logic around the chevet, for the arch spans are immensely long yet are reduced to the thinnest possible width. The resulting visual dynamic continues into sloping roofs that intersect below and culminate in the spire. Notre-Dame, then, obeys a double movement: it both hugs the ground and breaks free of it through the play of pronounced verticals.

The interior is conceived along similar lines, both in plan and in elevation. The chevet is separated from the nave by a transept whose arms do not extend beyond the lower envelope but whose vault rises to the height of the central nave, giving the transverse aisle a pronounced visual presence. The five perpendicular aisles along the main axis—the nave and two pairs of side aisles—continue on their course unaffected by this interruption, which becomes apparent only as one advances through the building. The use of identical elevations in the nave and the transept arms accentuates the effect of overall harmony, establishing rhythms of great beauty and elegance

Opposite:
The west facade rises above an immense square cleared in the nineteenth century. Its sober grandeur derives from a judicious balance of vertical and horizontal lines and a wall whose planarity is only slightly compromised by the shallow insets of the portals, rose window, and lancets.

The chevet rises from a nineteenth-century garden. Its curving forms generate a superb upward dynamic that culminates in the spire.

that pull the visitor forward. The doubling of the side aisles creates transverse openings that counter the pronounced axial dynamic. The identical heights of the side aisles and the calculated reduction of intermediary supports unify these subsidiary spaces. The use of alternation—simple round columns alternate with supports of reduced diameter surrounded by twelve colonnettes—plays an essential role here, establishing rhythms of great subtlety. This enriches the transverse views, despite the darkness of this first level, which was increased in the thirteenth century by the addition of chapels between the buttresses that displaced the windows outward.

This spatial expansiveness, this interpenetration of volumes, is even more emphatic in the apse, not so much in its central aisle (due to the presence of the choir enclosure) as in the aisles of the ambulatory. These are covered by vaults of equal height and supported by columns of narrow diameter. The latter count for little in the articulation of the space but function as directional indicators, helping the eye negotiate the curving movement around the apse. Even more than the nave, this volume is experienced as a unity, a perception augmented by the chapels between the buttresses. The very high, very wide arcade openings and the abundant light, issuing from windows of equal size, tend to integrate these spaces, the relatively small supports serving more as aids to apprehension of the plan than as enclosing elements.

The tribune, too, is spacious and unencumbered. Extending east and west from the transept arms, bending to embrace the chancel, it is largely open to the choir as well as, through still wider openings, to the nave. Thus the dominant longitudinal thrust of its volumes is countered by these lateral openings. In marked contrast with the lower level, here illumination abounds, thanks to the windows, whose forms vary somewhat at the eastern end but are identical toward the west.

Yet again, a rare equipoise is achieved in the nave elevation, where the vertical dynamic of the bays is countered by the moldings that define their three levels. Even so, verticals prevail over horizontals. The upward movement continues from the main arcade through the colonnettes rising from its capitals to the springs of the nave vault. Each bay, clearly delineated, contains, in ascending order, an arch of the large arcade, a tripartite tribune opening, and a tall clerestory window. There are, however, two exceptions to this rule. The bays adjacent to the crossing are differently disposed, incorporating rose oculi between the tribune level and clerestory windows of reduced height; and the first bays of the nave, while having what is essentially a three-level elevation, feature small clerestory windows separated from the tribune level by an expanse of bare wall. The balance between solids and voids and the limited use of projecting elements produce a wonderfully serene effect. At first glance, the consistency of the bay elevations obscures a contrapuntal rhythm established above them by the sexpartite vaults, each of which is almost square and encompasses not one bay but two. The same configuration is repeated in the transept arms.

The serenity of the building is not immediately apparent, revealing itself only with sustained exposure and only after allowances have been made for the major problem posed by the relative darkness of the interior. Despite their large size, the superb rose windows in the transept arms and the openwork galleries below them do not provide sufficient illumination to compensate for this deficiency.

The building we know today is not the one conceived and realized in part by Maurice de Sully. It also reflects a series of significant interior and exterior modifications conceived by architects of immense gifts, each of whom eschewed patchwork solutions in hopes of achieving a new homogeneity. Furthermore, their designs were realized with such care that their respective contributions are difficult to distinguish from one another. Thus reconstruction of the original structure inevitably calls for interpretation. The sensibility of the second architect was already distinct from that of the first, and the two subsequent masters, who succeeded one another early in the thirteenth century, also left their marks on the building. During the 1250s, Jean de Chelles was charged with designing the new transept; he completed its northern arm but not its southern one,

which was completed after his death in 1258 by his successor, Pierre de Montreuil. At the end of the thirteenth century, a new architect added the chapels of the chevet. In the middle of the nineteenth century, Jean-Baptiste Lassus and Eugène Viollet-le-Duc were charged with restoring the cathedral. They undertook to return it to its "original" state, a project that entailed many hazardous interpretive judgments, and it is their revised version of the building that has come down to us. Recovery of the thirteenth-century structure conceived by Maurice de Sully, not to mention the ancient cathedral that preceded it, is itself an act of deciphering.

The southern transept viewed from the left bank. It interrupts the horizontal lines of the nave and the chevet.

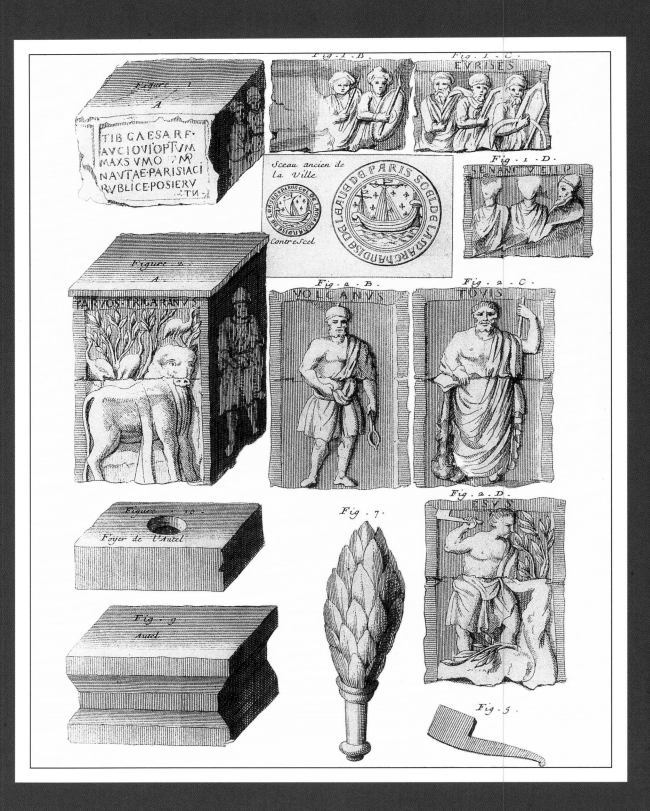

The Ancient Cathedral

The destiny of Paris was set in the course of the fourth century: during this period of great upheaval rose the new structures that were to define the city's future. The upheavals in question were political, administrative, and religious. To be sure, the city took part in the great movement that swept Gaul, one that replaced the world of antiquity with a new one, generally designated late antiquity. This civilization was characterized above all by religious anxiety: the gods gave way to God. In Gaul, this religious trend profited Christianity. In 313, Emperor Constantine declared that Christianity would be "tolerated"; it was recognized as the official religion at the end of the century. No sooner had this pronouncement been made than the Church set about organizing itself, slipping into the administrative structures of the Roman Empire. The Christian community of each *civitas* was headed by a bishop.

Another major development was the urban upheaval provoked by barbarian invasions. At the time, the cities were open, extended in area, and adorned with beautiful public buildings. Violation of the *limes* by the barbarians necessitated defensive measures. In 396, Rome decreed the construction of thick walls to protect these settlements. The effects of this double phenomenon were mixed. First, there was a reduction of urban territory; not all of the city could be enclosed, for this would have entailed a project of gigantic proportions. Engineers were dispatched to define the parcel to be defended and establish its perimeter. Subsequently, the bishop was established within this territory and provided with the buildings indispensable for worship. The resulting new city would be forever marked by these developments, as would Christianity itself.

Overall, Paris adhered to the same model as other cities in Gaul, but it acquired special features due to changes in its status as the fourth century progressed: initially a simple village, it was promoted first to a garrison town, then to nothing less than an imperial residence. There was nothing exceptional about its position within the empire, but attacks on the *limes* lent it strategic importance. The decision to erect defenses proved crucial, and the task was facilitated by the site's topography. The city of the left bank, where the most beautiful structures were located (witness the remains of the northern baths, since the late fifteenth century part of the residence of the abbots of Cluny), was left without protection. Its functions were moved to the Île de la Cité, already sheltered by the two arms of the Seine, which held it in a protective embrace.

Construction of these ramparts was to seal the future of Paris, which gradually shrank to the island alone. Not until the twelfth century did its inhabitants finally dare to break loose of this confining yoke. The builders faced gigantic difficulties due to the low ground level. Infilling was necessary, in certain areas to a height of about twenty-three feet. As a consequence, the island rose to between 115 and 118 feet above sea level. The ground sloped at the northern end, so much so that it descended into the water, and a vast marsh occupied the sites of the present Marché aux

Opposite:
Fragments discovered in 1711 under the choir of the cathedral and incorporated into the eastern portion of the ancient wall enclosing the city. They were originally part of what is now known as the Pillar of the Nautae, the Latin name designating an important professional organization of navigators. The inscription indicates that this monument was erected during the reign of Emperor Tiberius (A.D. 14–37). (Engraving from Félibien, *L'Histoire de Paris,* vol. 1.)

The fourth-century Île de la Cité was very small, covering an area of less than twenty-five acres. The infilled area suitable for construction was contained within a wall whose northern, southern, and eastern courses have been located. (Reconstruction by Berty, Sylvie Legaret, and Alain Erlande-Brandenburg.)

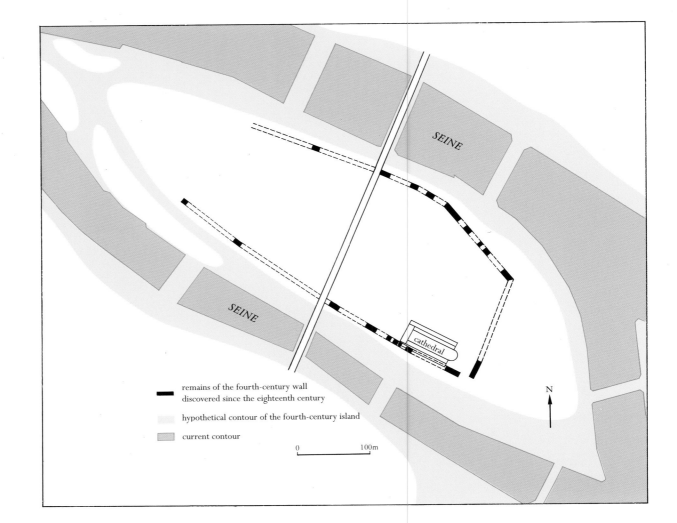

■ remains of the fourth-century wall
   discovered since the eighteenth century

   hypothetical contour of the fourth-century island

   current contour

0   100m

N

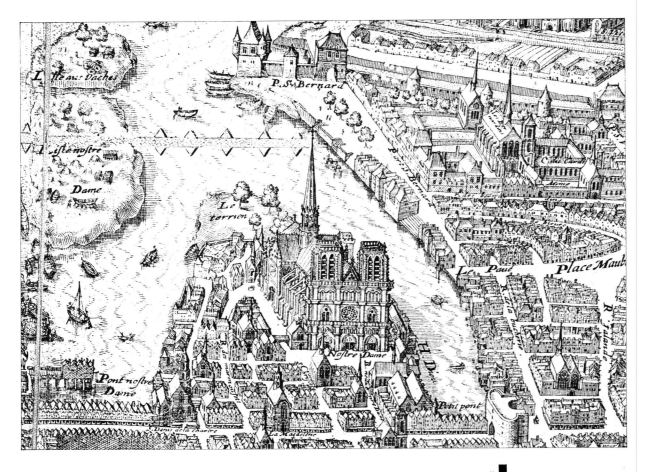

The so-called Tapisserie Plan pictures the state of the Île de la Cité about 1530. The terrain east of the cathedral lacks a protective embankment and slopes into the water. (Musée Notre-Dame.)

When the ancient ramparts were erected in the fourth century, the area within them was infilled and graded, giving the Île de la Cité a higher elevation. (Stratigraphic section based on Berty.)

The Ancient Cathedral

Fleurs and Tribunal de Commerce. These difficulties had to be addressed if foundations for the wall were to be consolidated. Discoveries made in the nineteenth and twentieth centuries have revealed the wall's northern and southern courses, which enclosed an area some 590 feet across at its widest point. By contrast, no traces of its eastern and western courses have been uncovered in these two centuries. The western tip of the island has since been extended by the incorporation of several small islands. The same holds true for the eastern tip. An Île Notre-Dame mentioned in 867—too often confused with the Île Saint-Louis—was absorbed after this date, after the infilling. What's more, we shall see that the whole of the eastern tip, called *le terrain,* has remained unsuitable for building because it consists solely of infill. In fact, while the course of the western wall remains problematic, that of the eastern wall has been determined. We know, in effect, that in 1711, during construction of the archbishops' sepulchral vault, several pieces of carved stone were discovered in the second bay of the choir of the Gothic cathedral and immediately moved for safekeeping to the small cloister of Saint-Denis-du-Pas; these were the blocks from the Pillar of the Nautae, now in the Musée de Cluny. The report of the architect Baudelot, who oversaw the work, is sufficiently precise to preclude all doubt, especially when coordinated with data obtained during subsequent excavations. The foundations, laid directly on the ground, consisted of rough blocks of ashlar posed without mortar to a width of ninety-eight and one-half inches. Many recycled fragments of sculpture were incorporated. As yet, no elements of the superstructure have been discovered, but very likely it consisted, as elsewhere in Gaul, of small rows of regular masonry separated by courses of brick. However that may be, determination of the course of the eastern wall indicates that the area initially contained by the ramparts was relatively small, amounting to less than two and three-quarters square miles. We should remember, however, that the task of grading even this area was a formidable one.

The large scale of this undertaking should be considered in conjunction with the strategic role newly assigned to the city in the defense of the *limes.* It was destined first to house garrisons, then to serve as an imperial residence, under both Julian on two occasions, in 357–58 and 359–60, and Valentinian, in 365–66. Hence the necessity for remodeling and construction. The western tip became the site of an imperial palace, then that of the Merovingian rulers. A large basilica—230 feet long and 115 feet wide—was built on the site currently occupied by the Marché aux Fleurs.

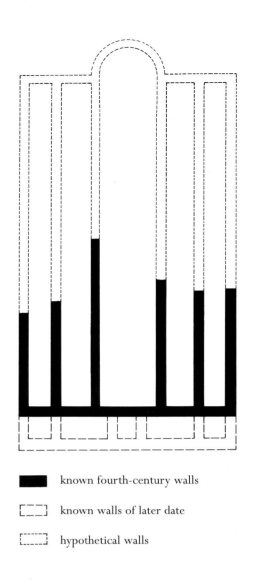

known fourth-century walls

known walls of later date

hypothetical walls

Discoveries made below the cathedral square in the nineteenth and twentieth centuries make it possible to reconstruct the plan of a five-aisle building as large as the basilicas erected by Constantine in the fourth century.

The Cathedral in the Fourth Century

It was over this new urbanistic and architectural complex that the bishop assumed authority in the fourth century. We must address the legend, so often recounted, of a first cathedral *extra-muros* that was subsequently transferred to within the city walls. This opinion originated in Paris based on the later mention of a *senior ecclesia* in the Saint-Marcel quarter. There was nothing of the kind. From the time of the edict of toleration or shortly thereafter, the seat of the bishop was inside the city. Very early on, the city assumed a certain importance in the religious domain. In 362, it hosted a council that condemned the Arian heresy. The cathedral existed at the time and on its present site, protected by the ancient wall. It bore the title *ecclesia parisiaca,* a formula consistent with contemporary custom, for dedications to saints appeared only much later. It was the church of the bishop, whose authority encompassed the entire diocese. The phrase in effect designated the Christian community. As the result of semantic evolution, "community" came to encompass architectural ensembles housing not only the bishop but also priests and the faithful.

We can only imagine the difficulties entailed in liberating the terrain necessary to erect these buildings. Despite a lack of direct evidence, there is little doubt that Constantine and his successors facilitated these delicate operations of acquisition. In Trier, none other than the mother of Constantine, Saint Helena, ceded a sumptuously decorated house, which was immediately demolished to make way for the cathedral complex discovered there after World War II. Elsewhere, the

Early excavations within the square revealed the remains of a cathedral initially thought to date from the Merovingian period and to consist of only three aisles. (Plan based on Théodore Vacquer, in Albert Lenoir, *La Statistique monumentale,* 1867.)

land was simply appropriated. Everywhere, buildings had to be demolished to accommodate new ones intended to house the community. There were usually several such structures. The cathedral itself generally consisted of two adjacent buildings: a baptistry and a *domus episcopi,* or bishop's residence, serving the bishop and the priests assisting him in his pastoral duties. There was also a Hôtel-Dieu, or charity hospice for the poor, of more modest design.

This basic scheme allowed for many variations. One of the most remarkable examples was the complex in Trier, with its two parallel basilicas separated by a baptistry and inscribed within a rectangle 558 feet by 360 feet. The one in Lyon was similar, although not as large, but Trier's had a Constantinian foundation. We know of the hospices only through textual evidence, but the *domus episcopi* in Geneva has been admirably excavated.

The Parisian complex consisted of three buildings: a Hôtel-Dieu, known through texts; a baptistry, known through texts and images; and the cathedral, known through archaeological evidence. In the course of work carried out in front of the Gothic facade in 1847, the substructure of a very large building, razed to ground level, was discovered. Bores sunk in 1907 and 1914 as well as new excavations begun in 1962 for an underground parking garage have completed our knowledge of the western portion of this structure, whose eastern end disappeared completely in the late twelfth and early thirteenth centuries during construction of the facade of the Gothic cathedral. These were the foundations of the early cathedral. Its facade, situated roughly 115 feet in front of the thirteenth-century one, was about 118 feet wide. A rather complex eastern narthex separated it from the nave, which, unusually, featured five aisles of progressively decreasing width: thirty-three feet for the nave proper, sixteen feet for the inner side aisles, and twelve feet for the outer side aisles. We do not know the building's original length, but it could have been as great as 230 feet, making its scale comparable to that of Old Saint Peter's in Rome (328 feet long) or Saint John Lateran (248 feet long), both of which also had five aisles. If so, the apse would have been situated below the third bay of the Gothic nave. The plan itself carried a certain prestige, evoking the grand foundations built in the era of Constantine and his family, and archaeological discoveries indicate that its decor was correspondingly sumptuous: the columns were of antique origin, the capitals were of white marble, and the floor was mosaic.

Interpretive difficulties posed by the nineteenth-century excavations, which were too briefly documented, compel a certain prudence. Furthermore, we shall see that of necessity the structure surviving until 1160 was modified several times over its centuries-long life. Thus the abovementioned eastern narthex, built of thin masonry courses alternating with *opus spicatum,* might be a later addition. Likewise the southern side, which can only have been erected after demolition of the wall over whose course it was built.

This being the case, the correspondence of the building's flat facade, five aisles, and elevation with the Constantinian model becomes even more telling. Four rows of marble columns separated the aisles and were surmounted by beautiful marble capitals supporting arcades or architraves. Above these was a high wall, probably decorated with mural paintings or even mosaics and pierced

Left and below:
Mosaic fragments, columns, and a marble capital hint at the sumptuous decor of the ancient cathedral, which was worthy of comparison with the grandest basilicas of its day. (Mosaic fragments from Albert Lenoir, *La Statistique monumentale,* 1867; column and capital, Musée de Cluny.)

by clerestory windows. A timber-frame roof, left visible or hidden by a coffered ceiling, rested on the thin outer walls.

Exceptional in this region of Gaul, this grandiose monument is difficult to date. Since the discovery of the infrastructures in the mid-nineteenth century it has been believed to date from the Merovingian era; it has even been linked to the reign of Childebert (d. 558). This dating was based on limited knowledge of the origins of Christianity, and especially of Early Christian architecture. In fact, the plan cannot date from this period: we lack evidence of another building of comparable ambition from the era, since by then the number of aisles in basilicas had been reduced to three. The unearthed elements of decor are consistent with a date in the fourth century, and the same can be said for the textual evidence. The famous poem by Fortunatus, *De Ecclesia Parisiaca,* which quite certainly applies to the cathedral and not to another Parisian structure, does not state that King Childebert was responsible for its construction; it only makes the more modest claim that he enriched it, as Dagobert was to do slightly later at Saint-Denis. All indicators suggest that the cathedral discovered in 1847 is indeed the one mentioned by Bishop Prudentius between 375 and 380.

A baptistry remained next to the present cathedral's northern side, immediately east of the narthex, until 1748, when it was demolished to accommodate the western gate of the canonial close. Abbot Lebeuf dated it to the thirteenth century, and its portal to the seventeenth. The earliest mention of such a structure dates from the sixth century: the author of the first *Life of Saint Genevieve,* written shortly after the saint's death in 512, informs us that during Attila's attack on Paris in 451, she sought refuge within the building with the other women of the city to implore divine intervention. These summary indications point to several hypotheses. In all likelihood, the building, originally circular in plan (as indicated by its name, Saint-Jean-le-Rond), was rebuilt in the Gothic period, perhaps after the construction of the new cathedral. It would have retained its initial placement, near the center of the ancient cathedral's northern flank, a situation reminiscent

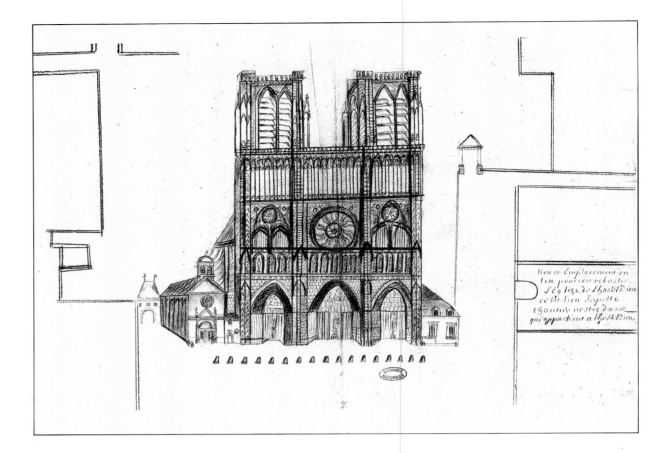

of the configurations in Lyon and, still better, Trier, both dating from the fourth century. Could the scheme here have been comparable, featuring a second cathedral to the north? A hazardous supposition, but one that merits consideration. In such a case, the canonial close established on this site in the ninth century would have replaced the cathedral, demolished to make way for it. In any event, the notion advanced by some that the Paris cathedral cluster was differently configured is to be rejected. The hypothesis that the small apse—some thirty-one feet in diameter— discovered in 1856 by Viollet-le-Duc in the third bay of the chancel corresponds to the eastern end of the second cathedral is untenable, for this location was outside the ancient wall.

It remains to determine the placements of the *domus episcopi* and the Hôtel-Dieu. The bishop's residence might have been situated to the east of the cathedral, between the apse and the wall, a solution adopted in Geneva between the later fourth and early fifth century. As for the charity hospice, it was ostensibly founded by Bishop Landry in 651, but it probably predated him, for the church councils were constantly pressuring the bishops to establish and maintain such services for the poor. In this period, such facilities, overseen by the deacons, were generally housed in subsidiary buildings of the *domus,* from which they separated only later.

By the end of the fourth century, Lutetia, now known as Paris, was no longer a village. Its destiny was in the balance: the political significance it had recently acquired was becoming indistinguishable from its religious life. The one and the other, concentrated within the confines of an island of less than eighteen acres, asserted their strength in exceptional buildings. In this respect Paris differed from other cities in Gaul. However, life was not limited to the island but thrived around it as well, notably on the left bank. Soon large churches would rise, evidence of the increasing importance of the Catholic community.

A century later, the administrative and political structure of Gaul was disturbed. Clovis (d. 511), a barbarian king, triumphed over his enemies, conquering first Syagrius, the last bastion of Roman resistance, in 486, then the Visigoths in Vouillé in 508. The future would be his if he could come to terms with the Romans, of glorious past, and the Catholics, sure of their future. This was achieved at Tours in 508, when he received a legitimizing deputation sent by Emperor

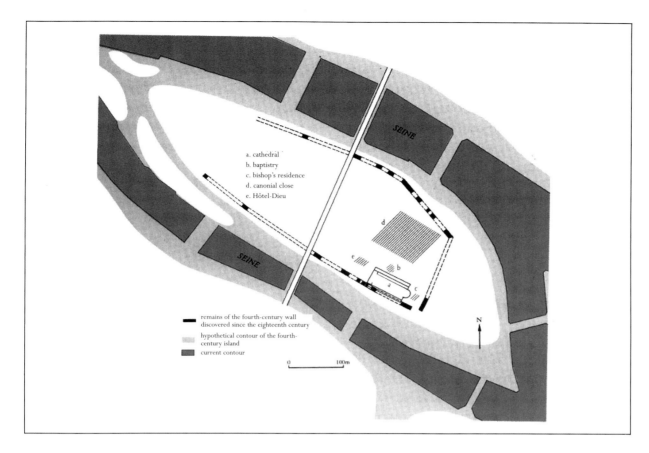

a. cathedral
b. baptistry
c. bishop's residence
d. canonial close
e. Hôtel-Dieu

SEINE

SEINE

N

remains of the fourth-century wall discovered since the eighteenth century

hypothetical contour of the fourth-century island

current contour

0   100m

The canonial close was developed in the eighth century within the confines of the ancient city, to the north of the cathedral. The bishop's residence was situated to the east and the Hôtel-Dieu to the west, near the Church of Saint-Christophe.

Anastasius. His baptism, obtained by his wife, Clotilde, secured his position as a new Constantine. To consolidate his power, he would need a new capital to rival those of the empire: Milan, Trier, Arles, Ravenna. He chose Paris, thereby definitively securing the future status of the city.

THE CANONS: FROM THE EIGHTH CENTURY TO 1160

Although the city evolved considerably under the first Merovingians, the sacred complex, extant for more than a century, was probably little affected. The establishment, at the summit of a hill, of the Church of the Saints-Apôtres by Clovis and that of Saint-Vincent–Sainte-Croix by Childebert points to the privileged nature of the city's destiny in the eyes of its rulers. With regard to the cathedral, one already senses a certain wariness, or rather a mutual respect, between different powers. As noted previously, Childebert contented himself with embellishments, doubtless evidenced by a small marble capital unearthed during excavations in the cathedral square (see page 17). The clearest indication of change comes with its rededication to Saint Stephen in the seventh century. The occurrence was not unique, similar examples being documented in the province of Sens, in both Sens and Auxerre, where, unlike Paris, the dedications were retained.

The most important change introduced into the ancient schema dates from the Carolingian period, when the sacred complex acquired a chapter of canons. In the mid-eighth century, the bishop of Metz, Chrodegang, resolved to reform the life of the clerics in his entourage. His intention was to establish a prayer community among them. At the Council of Vic in 755, Pepin the Short sought to impose this *institutio canonicorum,* which resulted in the establishment of veritable urban monasteries. Very rapidly, these episcopal cities were completed by the addition of new architectural complexes designed to accommodate clerics-cum-canons: canonial closes, consisting of a refectory, a dormitory, a capitular room, and service buildings. There were also individual houses for ill, disabled, and aged monks. To reinforce the monastic profile and strengthen the sense of community, in 816 the Council of Aix-la-Chapelle stipulated that these buildings were to be "enclosed by walls on all sides such that no one can enter or leave except through the gate." True adherence to the spirit of the reform entailed placement of the close near the cathedral.

In 819, the legislator also issued several decrees facilitating acquisition of the necessary land and guaranteeing the livelihood of the canons. Consolidation of the reform was deemed a necessity: even at the council of 816 there was talk of reallocating some of the bishop's temporal revenues.

The reform measures were implemented quite rapidly in Paris. The steady evolution observable in this domain speaks of a resolve to succeed. In 829, Bishop Inchad decreed a division of church goods between episcopal revenues and capitulary revenues. In exchange, the canons were obliged to maintain the buildings thus ceded to them. As early as Charles the Bald (d. 877), the canons strongly objected to living communally: they possessed houses of their own, which entailed the use of a still larger area. We do not know how the necessary lands were found and acquired. Yet again, demolition must have preceded the construction of these important new buildings. The close occupied the northeastern corner of the ancient wall. Even at this time, finding the required terrain within the city wall proved difficult. Thus Bishop Énée, in 867, finagled the "restitution" of an island just east of the cathedral previously owned by the comte de Paris. The first extension was soon joined by a second: in 904, Charles the Simple made a gift to the canons of the bridge linking the island to the right bank. Hence its name, the Pont Notre-Dame.

As in other bishoprics, Chrodegang's reforms entailed significant modifications in the operation of the Hôtel-Dieu, which was plagued by chronic financial difficulties. In 816, the Council of Aix had recommended that bishops allocate to it revenue sources of their own, and in 829, Bishop Inchad set aside a seigneurial tithe for this purpose. Our earliest records of the canons' activities date from this period: among other things, the obligations of their charity work included washing the feet of the poor. The location of the hospice, close to the northeast corner of the cathedral and beside the *memoria* of Saint Christopher from which it took its name, facilitated this task.

Finally, the establishment of the cathedral chapter influenced the dedication of the cathedral, which previously honored Saint Stephen. The name of the Virgin gradually began to appear along with his, and eventually, in the late tenth century, she became the sole dedicatee. Such double dedications were not unusual and do not necessarily suggest the existence of two buildings. In this case, it doubtless reflected the internal configuration of the immense ancient cathedral, with one portion being isolated by partitions for use by the canons. This area would have been dedicated to Our Lady (Notre-Dame), while the portion of the building reserved for the bishop would have been dedicated to Saint Stephen. This duality resurfaced much later, in the mid-thirteenth century, when the two transept arms were built. The northern arm, facing the canonial close, was consecrated to the Virgin, while the southern arm, facing the episcopal palace, was consecrated to Saint Stephen.

Chrodegang's reforms had particularly important consequences in the religious realm, but they also affected the secular one, in effect compromising the power of the bishop. The chapter's prerogatives grew steadily, as evidenced by both semantic developments—already mentioned—and historical ones. In 911, Charles the Simple solemnly reasserted the judicial immunity of the close, which had first been recognized by Charles the Bald. Similarly, the canons of the Hôtel-Dieu became increasingly assertive, to such an extent that the bishop soon had to share his responsibilities, before completely surrendering his authority in 1006. Thereafter, the exercise of high, intermediate, and low justice was the responsibility of the chapter. A final step was taken in 1099, when the bishop ceded the Saint Christopher *memoria* to it.

The cathedral chapter's fantastic rise to power took a new turn in the late eleventh and early twelfth century, when the destiny of Paris finally began to take definitive shape. In effect, it was under the reign of Philip I (d. 1108) that the city recovered the political role that had previously belonged to it, first under Clovis and then under Charles the Bald. Its power continued to increase throughout the twelfth century. Philip Augustus (d. 1223) was to complete this evolutionary trend. At the same time, there appeared on the right bank a new city, industrious and dynamic, that was soon to make Paris one of the realm's most flourishing urban centers. The political capital, whose vitality grew in tandem with the authority of the Capetian line and now took on an

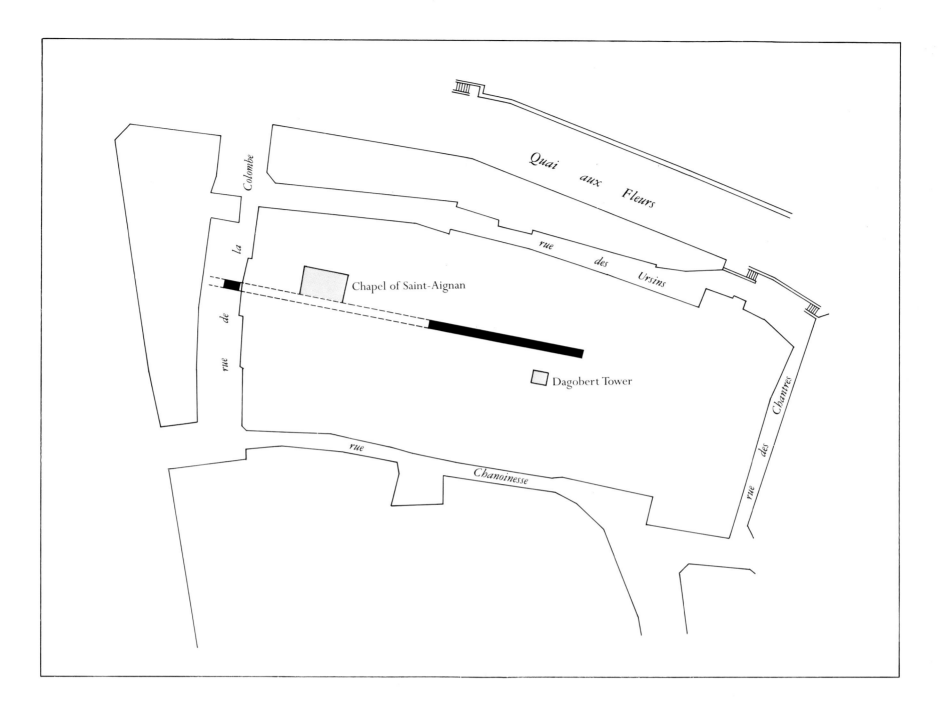

Chapel of Saint-Aignan

Dagobert Tower

Quai aux Fleurs

rue des Ursins

rue Colombe

rue de la

rue des Chantres

rue Chanoinesse

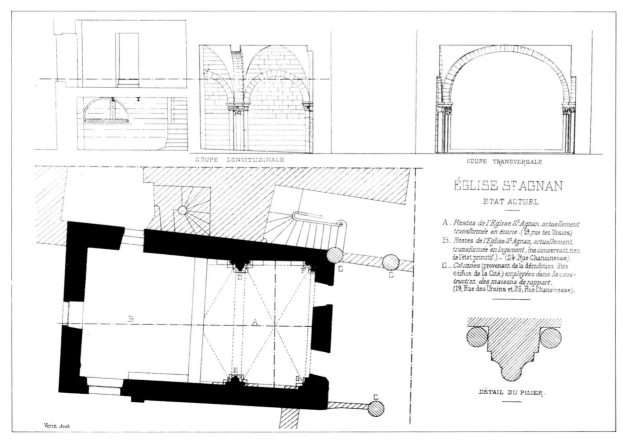

COUPE LONGITUDINALE

COUPE TRANSVERSALE

ÉGLISE Sᵗ AGNAN

ETAT ACTUEL

A. Restes de l'Église Sᵗ Agnan, actuellement
transformée en écurie. (18, rue des Ursins)

B. Restes de l'Église Sᵗ Agnan, actuellement
transformée en logement, (ne conservant rien
de l'état primitif.) - (24, Rue Chanoinesse).

C. Colonnes (provenant de la démolition d'un
édifice de la Cité) employées dans la construction des maisons de rapport.
(19, Rue des Ursins et 26, Rue Chanoinesse).

DÉTAIL DU PILIER.

Vérin Arch

Only in the twelfth century was the ancient
wall broached, with construction of the
Chapel of Saint-Aignan to its north. The
canons needed more space. To obtain it,
marshy areas had to be infilled. (Plan based
on *Procès verbal de la Commission du Vieux
Paris,* 1908. B.H.V.P.)

The Chapel of Saint-Aignan is a rare
surviving example of Parisian architecture
from roughly the 1120s, before the
blossoming of Gothic art. (Plan based on
Procès verbal de la Commission du Vieux Paris,
1908. B.H.V.P.)

economic dimension, became an important religious center as well. In the twelfth century, the episcopal school, which existed previously but was of limited importance, began to rival that of Chartres and soon supplanted it in prestige. Fully cognizant of these general trends, the canons actively sought to foster and reinforce them by collaborating with the Capetian rulers. The dominant personality in this story is Étienne de Garlande, first a cleric at Notre-Dame and then archdeacon there. He also pursued a remarkable career at the court: after becoming the king's chaplain, in 1006 he was named chancellor and then *dapifer* before being given special status in 1128, along with his entire family clan. He profited from his singular position to consolidate the power of the church of Paris. His name appears on many decrees emanating from the chancellory, prior to 1128 as a signatory, and from that point until his death in 1148 as author.

De Garlande focused his attention on three areas: the power of the chapter, the administrative organization of the close, and construction. In 1120, he obtained confirmation of the immunity accorded the close and had it extended to encompass canonial residences outside its walls, to the west of the cathedral. A charter promulgated by Louis VI circa 1112 clarified the bishop's rights of access throughout the eastern portion of the island. In 1127, an agreement was reached between the bishop and the chapter stipulating that students would arrive not via the close but through the palace courtyard, thereby safeguarding the isolation and tranquility of the close. Finally, he effected, for the first time, a breach of the ancient wall, probably to the east and certainly to the north, preparing new landfills for the purpose. This made possible the construction of the small Chapel of Saint-Aignan along and outside of the northern wall. De Garlande had resolved to share his canonial prebend with two canons charged with honoring the memory of deceased canons. The foundation was established under Bishop Gerbert (1116–24) and confirmed by his successor, Étienne de Senlis (1124–42). By this time the building, situated close to his own canonial residence, was complete, which is to say that it probably dates from the 1120s.

Miraculously preserved amid later construction, the Saint-Aignan chapel is a unique remnant of the activity of the canons in the first half of the twelfth century. Rectangular in plan, it is small in dimension: roughly thirty-three feet long by twenty-one feet wide, its vault peaks at almost fourteen feet above the floor, which is now about two feet above its original level. Recent borings have revealed the foundations of an apse to the east.

The chapel decor has disappeared, notably a stained-glass window representing Saint Aignan that was still in place in the mid-eighteenth century, when it was seen by Abbot Lebeuf. However, its carefully constructed rib vaults and walls survive. The supports along the northern and southern walls are contained by colonnettes *en délit* (see glossary), as in the chevet of Saint-Pierre de Montmartre. The major point of interest is the building's sculpted decor: the capitals supporting the vault springs were clearly inspired by capitals carved from Pyrenean marble usually dated to the seventh century. Thus they offer exceptional evidence of a "revival," one that might be explained by the presence of capitals from this period, like those unearthed during excavations in the cathedral square (Musée Notre-Dame). More important is the decoration of the jambs of the recently rediscovered eastern door, which pierced the southern wall. The inner surface of the left jamb, better preserved than its pendant, features a relief of superimposed foliate medallions containing masks. Some of them evoke the medallions at Saint-Martin-des-Champs. While still awkward, in both their disposition and their style these motifs anticipate the jamb decorations that were to become common in the Gothic period, in Paris as well as the surrounding region.

The fourth-century cathedral was in a sufficiently poor state of preservation to occasion concern among the canons, for its condition reflected upon their reputation. Admittedly, documentation relating to this point is scarce, but the few surviving texts point to their concern. A diploma of Louis VI, dated 1123, authorizes the chapter to appropriate a sum of ten livres from the revenues of the bishopric to purchase lathe, nails, and tiles, with the understanding that the canons themselves would provide beams and rafters. This document reveals both the goodwill of the canons and the difficulties they encountered, in the form of an uncooperative bishop whose compliance

The jambs of the portal of the Saint-Aignan chapel are decorated with vertical rows of masks, precious extant examples of Parisian figurative sculpture from the 1120s.

Opposite, top and bottom:
One of the most interesting features of the Saint-Aignan chapel is the style of its capitals, some of which seem to have been inspired by marble examples from the seventh century.

could be obtained only through royal intervention. Clearly what was in question was reconstruction of the roof. Also relevant here is the previously mentioned document concerning access, which refers to the cathedral as having been "in ruins." Yet again, de Garlande appears as the crucial agent. His obit of June 2 leaves no doubt as to his role in this regard: *"ecclesiam beate Marie decenter reparavit"* (he becomingly repaired the church of the blessed Mary). The work was carried out between 1120 and 1148, the year of his death, after completion of the Chapel of Saint-Aignan. It is unclear whether structural elements other than the roofing and its timber frame were involved. But it is certain that this campaign added two important decorative features, in the form of sculpture and stained glass.

We know that Suger, abbot of Saint-Denis (1122–51), presented a stained-glass window to the cathedral. This is believed to have been the Triumph of the Virgin, which the master glazier Le Veil removed in the mid-eighteenth century; it had been salvaged from the ancient cathedral in 1160 and reinstalled in the new building.

THE ANCIENT PORTAL OF THE VIRGIN. Luckily, the carved portal, likewise dismantled in the early thirteenth century for reincorporation into the new western facade, survives, although it was damaged during the French Revolution. Thanks to recent discoveries, its original appearance can now be largely reconstructed. In 1793, the trumeau was mutilated: the face of Saint Marcel was destroyed and the florets of the crowns were removed. In 1793–94, the eight column statues from the jamb were removed. Many fragments of them have since been recovered: the torso of the Saint Peter, found in the rue de la Santé in 1837; two keystones, discovered by Viollet-le-Duc; the Christ of the Apocalypse and the Pascal Lamb, both now in the Musée du Louvre; the head of King David, acquired by the Metropolitan Museum of Art, New York; and finally, a substantial number of fragments of the column statues, whose discovery in 1977 made it possible to partially reconstruct the portal at the Musée de Cluny, incorporating the trumeau removed by Viollet-le-Duc (he replaced it with a copy by Adolphe-Victor Geoffroy-Dechaume). Still more fragments—several bases and capitals reused in the foundations of the second pillar of the nave—were recovered during work within the cathedral in 1983.

The dismantling and remounting of this portal underscore the importance still attached to it half a century after its execution. This delicate operation necessarily entailed modifications, both iconographic—the original portal was consecrated to the Virgin, while the revised one was dedicated to Saint Anne—and material: some of the archivolts were replaced, apparently due to damage incurred during the dismantling; a new tier of archivolt figures was added, as was a lower lintel designed to clarify the portal's new meaning.

Only by reconstructing the portal's initial appearance can we hope to grasp its iconographic program and situate it properly within the development of early Gothic sculpture. The elements added in the early thirteenth century are readily identifiable, despite the effort of some of the sculptors to imitate the older forms in the interest of stylistic harmony. The lower lintel, the two fragments at the extreme ends of the upper lintel, the two angels and the vegetal motifs in the space above the tympanum, and some of the archivolts are thirteenth-century work. The archivolt figures in the lowest tier clearly reveal their later date; by contrast, the figures above, which had to be replaced due to the addition of a new vertical row, were copied from the ancient models, as becomes apparent when one compares the two archivolt figures in the Louvre, the Christ of the Apocalypse and the Pascal Lamb, with those still in place. In all, twelve archivolt figures and the keystones date from the thirteenth century; forty-eight of the archivolt figures are twelfth-century work. To this figure must be added the four original keystones, which produces a final figure of fifty-two surviving elements of the original archivolts to be distributed among four vertical courses. In fact, reconstruction is rendered problematic by our incomplete knowledge of the original iconography, although the elders of the Apocalypse (who carry musical instruments), the kings, and the prophets are all clearly recognizable.

The Pelican Window, now lost, was in the Gothic cathedral but came from the ancient cathedral. This record of its design is the only evidence we have of the important set of windows dating roughly from the 1140s, one of which was presented by Abbot Suger.

Opposite:
Portal of Saint Anne.
The Portal of Saint Anne was made for the ancient cathedral but was remounted on the facade of the Gothic building in the early thirteenth century, when it was altered by the addition of a new lintel and a supplementary tier of archivolt figures. It was originally consecrated to the Virgin. The statues are nineteenth-century copies.
Trumeau: Saint Marcel by Geoffroy-Dechaume.
Left jamb: Saint Peter by Armand Toussaint, Solomon by Jean-Louis Chenillion, Queen of Sheba by Michel Pascal.
Right jamb: Saint Paul by Alexis-Hippolite Fromanger, David by Geoffroy-Dechaume, Bathsheba by Fromanger, a king by Geoffroy-Dechaume.

The jamb figures of the twelfth-century
Portal of the Virgin were, left to right:
Saint Peter, Solomon, the Widow of
Sarepta, Elias, Saint Paul, David, the Sibyl,
and Isaiah. (Engravings from Montfaucon,
Les Monumens de la monarchie françoise,
vol. 1 [Paris, 1755], plate 7.)

Opposite:
The trumeau from the Portal of the Virgin.
(Musée de Cluny.)
The original trumeau with its figure
of Saint Marcel, one of the first bishops
of Paris. In the nineteenth century,
it served as a model—with plaster
additions—for the copy now in place,
by Geoffroy-Dechaume.

The lintel, which reads from left to right, begins with Isaiah, who first prophesied the Messiah; then come the Annunciation, the Visitation, the Nativity, the Annunciation to the Shepherds, a Pharisee and a doctor of the law, Herod, and the three Magi. In the tympanum, the Virgin presents the Child in a way analogous, as we shall see, to the formula later used in the Royal Portal at Chartres, but her presence is magnified by a baldachin, which also isolates her from the two censer-bearing angels. The iconography of the other figures—at left, a standing crosiered and mitred bishop or abbot and a seated companion; at right, a kneeling king unrolling a scroll—is less certain. They have most recently been identified as Saint Germain, bishop of Paris, and King Childebert, believed in the mid-twelfth century to have been the cathedral's founders. They might just as well represent another bishop and monarch whose memories the canons sought to honor in the interests of legitimizing their own power.

Similar considerations influenced the choice of Saint Marcel for depiction on the trumeau. Saint Stephen would have been a likely candidate, but the canons opted instead for this Parisian bishop whose life had been written in the second half of the sixth century, at the bidding of Bishop Germain (d. 576), by Venantius Fortunatus. To be sure, the cathedral housed the relics of this bishop celebrated for his miracles, one of which is here evoked at his feet: he had freed the corpse of a sinning woman from an enormous serpent that had just devoured her and was whisking her away.

But his celebrity does not suffice to explain his prominence in this mid-twelfth-century program. It must have been the result of a preference on the part of the canons—and of de Garlande,

who retained the attachment a century later. The archivolts of the Red Door evoke not only this miracle of Saint Marcel but other episodes from his life as well. The jamb statues flanking the trumeau represented at left Saint Peter, Solomon, the Widow of Sarepta, and Elias, and at right Saint Paul, David, the Sibyl, and Isaiah. Thus Old Testament figures were joined by two from the New Testament and a confessor. The central portal of the Abbey Church at Saint-Denis, consecrated in 1140, already featured a figure of the eponymous saint on its trumeau, but it was surrounded by kings and queens of the old dispensation. In this regard the Portal of the Virgin of the ancient cathedral represented a departure.

The difficulties posed by the overall iconographic program have raised doubts about the portal's homogeneity. Some art historians have suggested that in 1210 several portals were combined into one. This hypothesis is undermined, however, by the fact that, despite the presence of several distinguishable hands, the stylistic harmony of the whole remains striking: the consistency of the column statues, tympanum, lintel, and archivolt figures suggests a unified conception. It is worth repeating that history necessitates a dating prior to 1148, the year of de Garlande's death, as opposed to the later terminus ad quem of 1163 thought to obtain until recently. In other words, the Portal of the Virgin must be situated chronologically between the portals of the western facade of Saint-Denis, dedicated in 1140, and the Royal Portal of Chartres, generally dated 1145–55. It follows that elements long thought to derive from the sculpture of the Royal Portal made their first appearance here, making the Parisian ensemble one of the major monuments of early Gothic sculpture.

To be sure, Saint-Denis had initiated the use of column statues, which immediately became standard. There, as in Paris, columns were completely supplanted by statues that maintained a strong vertical dynamic, despite their horizontal scansion across the width of the jamb. They retained narrow columnar shapes, their draperies being carved so as not to violate their shaft-like forms. The archivolts were designed to reinforce this upward movement, transmitting it to the keystones even as they enclosed the tympanum. The number of column statues, which determined that of the archivolt ranges, was a crucial factor in the perception of Gothic portals, for it shaped the imbrication of the various elements and thus the formal coherence of the whole. In Paris, the thirteenth-century modifications make it difficult to grasp the general configuration of the original portal, but it must have resembled those of the central portals at Saint-Denis and Chartres.

Another important point is the role of relief in each of the constituent elements. We only know the column statues from Saint-Denis through drawings made by Antoine Benoît prior to their destruction, which renders assessment difficult. Comparison of the sculpture in Paris with that in Chartres, however, proves revealing. In Paris, more than in Chartres, the artists allowed the sculpture greater independence from structural elements, letting it project beyond the plane of the wall. The presence of sculpted consoles below the feet of each jamb figure is indicative of this approach. The twelfth-century archivolts are consistent with this conception: the sculptors

eschewed the use of canopies between the figures, thereby accentuating their projection from the stone behind them. The result was a more vigorous and emphatic frame for the portal. The treatment of the tympanum and the lintel also furthers this quest for planar rupture: the seated Virgin is placed within a rigorously sculpted baldachin that projects strongly from the rear surface, and some portions of the figures are vigorously undercut. As for the lintel, it derives much of its effect from an overarching canopy-like element that casts shadows against the rear surface, thereby accentuating the volume of the figures below. Assessment of the original effect remains problematic, not only due to damage wrought during the Revolution but also, and perhaps more decisively, due to modifications introduced in conjunction with the early-thirteenth-century reinstallation. Nevertheless, it is safe to say that an effect of great clarity is achieved by the overall configuration and the planar organization, a factor that did not greatly preoccupy the sculptors at Saint-Denis and Chartres.

Mid-twelfth-century sculptors were especially attentive to the handling of drapery. A key factor in the evocation of volume, it was of vital importance: moving legs, shoulder inflections, and arm gestures were evoked, accentuated, and rendered effective largely by means of patterned fabric folds. Realism was a secondary consideration, especially given that sculptors of the period were most influenced not by other carvings but by repoussé. The importance allotted such metalwork in the twelfth century is crucial. It is as though the stone sculptors of the period had wrought their thin, tight, precise, but sometimes coiled folds with steel punches. Extraordinary rigor is here allied with stunning suppleness, exemplified by the figures of Saints Peter and Paul. The sculptors alternated patterned areas with smooth ones functioning like silences, orchestrating the light so that it glides over them, subsequently becoming lost in a sleeve or below a knee. These nuances result from the high projection of the striations: the folds create hollows, veer away from one another, abruptly form sharp angles, round into drop-like shapes, and seem to disappear

The rationale behind the choice of scenes—made by one of the canons, perhaps Étienne de Garlande—is not understood. On the left is the Visitation; on the right, Joseph from the Nativity and one of the shepherds from the Annunciation to the Shepherds.

Page 30:
The tympanum was surrounded by celestial and Old Testament figures, removed from the original twelfth-century portal and reincorporated into the thirteenth-century Portal of Saint Anne. Here, an angel and a prophet.

Page 31:
The outer archivolt of the Portal of the Virgin was occupied by the elders of the Apocalypse.

The Portal of the Virgin, executed before 1148, was produced by a team of sculptors whose work is extremely homogeneous in style. It is notable for the handling of the drapery folds, reminiscent of repoussé metalwork, as well as for the evocation of movement. This detail is from the angel and the kneeling king in the right portion of the tympanum.

Opposite:
The Portal of the Virgin was the second such ensemble, after Saint-Denis but before Chartres, to incorporate column statues. Here, a fragment of the figure of Saint Peter, discovered in 1839 in the rue de la Santé. (Musée de Cluny.)

only to resurface under raking light. On the figure of Saint Paul, these rays of light first are caught and then slip away, disappearing into the subtle play of lines and folds and coming to an abrupt halt in deep shadows. Such assertive patterning is less prominent in the upper portions of the figures, but there, too, it is discernable in areas that have suffered less from erosion than others. In the poorly protected tympanum, it has largely fallen victim to inclement weather; the present effect, which resembles a photographic negative, must be very different from the one it produced originally. Even so, close examination reveals the same sensibility at work in the kneeling king, the prelate, and the Virgin.

The originality of the portal must have been far more striking in the twelfth century, when the column statues still had their heads. The only one of these to survive is that of David, which is so original that for a time it was thought to date from the nineteenth century (Metropolitan Museum of Art, New York). Rather squashed and haggard, with eyes whose round voids were once filled with glass paste, it wears a crown that is too small for it. The sculptor was an artist of considerable confidence. The playful character of the wayward locks of hair below the crown is remarkable, as is the vigorous articulation of the ringlets. The cheeks project assertively, and the flesh below the eyes, which feature deeply incised sockets, swells forward.

Below:
The column statue of Saint Paul, discovered in 1977 in the rue de la Chaussée d'Antin, was the pendant to that of Saint Peter. The tubular folds tend to elongate the figure. (Musée de Cluny, Gift of the B.F.C.E.)

Right:
The three Magi from the lintel. (Musée de Cluny, Gift of the B.F.C.E.)

Opposite:
The mutilated head of King David was originally even stranger, for its pupils were filled with glass paste. The sculptors had particular difficulty with crowns, which they consistently made too small for the heads below them. (Metropolitan Museum of Art, New York.)

Several sculptors worked on the project, the most gifted of whom executed the jamb figures. Here at least two artists can be distinguished. The first, who carved Saints Peter and Paul, is recognizable by his penchant for deeply incised rectangular folds. The second, responsible for the figure of Solomon, among others, was adept at rendering suppler movements and ampler forms and was more inclined to incorporate large smooth areas. The other column statues could be by either of these sculptors, who seem to have been able to approximate one another's styles. A third hand can be discerned in the archivolts; its style is most pronounced in one of the elders of the Apocalypse, in the fourth tier of the second range on the left. As in some of the column statues of Saint-Denis, he crosses his legs to suggest a dancing movement, which is further amplified by the opposing movements of his arms. This imparts a remarkable vitality to his robe. A fourth sculptor executed the tympanum, which is characterized by a formidable restraint imposed by the solemnity of the iconography. Many of the traits found here also appear in the Saint Marcel figure of the trumeau (Musée de Cluny), notably thin, tightly spaced folds around the neck that continue downward. The artist instilled the faces with a noble, timeless quality that is quite different from the effect sought by the Master of the Head of David. The other sculptures should be distributed among these different artists. The left portion of the lintel is similar in style to the tympanum, although the figures are more elongated. The right portion, with its three Magi whose heads are squashed and who wear crowns that are too small for them, evokes the David. But it is difficult to ascribe many passages to specific hands, which suggests that the portal was produced by artists who worked together as a community and over a very short span of time. This tends to support the idea that it was originally conceived as a unit—and completed, we repeat, before 1148.

Part of the body of King David was discovered in 1977 in the rue de la Chaussée d'Antin. The orphrey of the robe is chiseled to evoke embroidery. The pattern of striations and smooth areas underscores the effect of movement of the figure's right knee. (Musée de Cluny, Gift of the B.F.C.E.)

Opposite:
The same freedom in the evocation of drapery folds characterizes this fragment of the figure of Saint Peter, discovered in 1837 in the rue de la Santé. (Musée de Cluny.)

By this very token, the portal becomes an important benchmark in the development of sculpture during this decade, due less to its relations with Chartres, which remain rather distant, than to its importance for work to the north and closer to Paris. The gisant figure of King Childebert, executed before 1163 for the choir of Saint-Germain-des-Prés (now in Saint-Denis), the Valois Portal of the southern transept of Saint-Denis, reinstalled in the middle of the thirteenth century, doubtless prior to the death of Abbot Suger in 1151, and the portal at Senlis, generally dated to circa 1170 but on tenuous grounds, constitute a homogeneous group that seems closely linked to the artists of the Portal of the Virgin in Paris.

The Ancient Cathedral

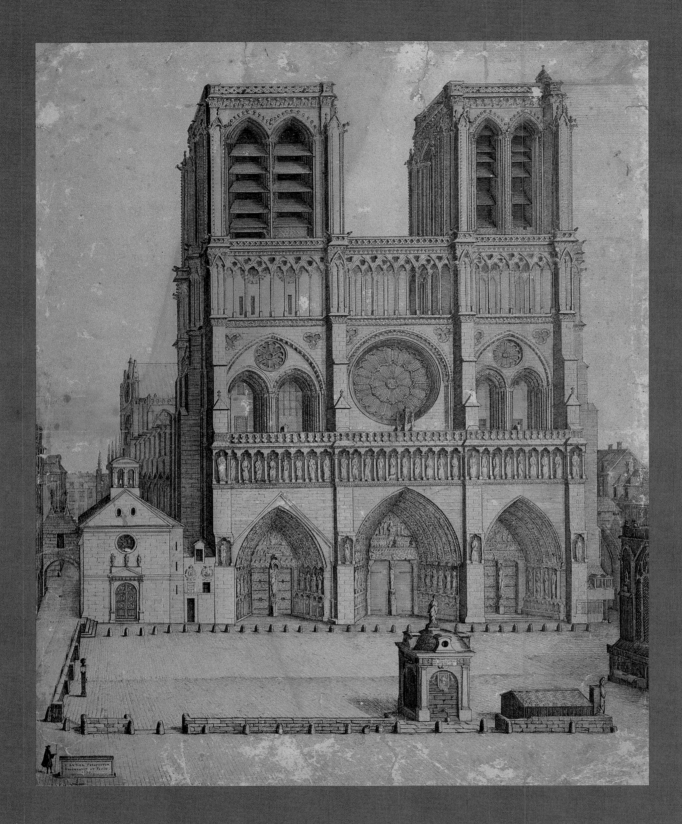

The Grand Design
of Maurice de Sully

I n 1160, soon after a revamping of the ancient cathedral had been completed, there was a sudden change of direction. This manifested itself on two fronts. First, the canons—some of them, at any rate—who had dominated religious, administrative, and political life for more than half a century, and whose power had been consolidated to a considerable degree over a period of two centuries, gave way to the bishops, who became the prime movers. The second front pertains to construction of the cathedral. Given the recent completion of an extensive remodeling campaign, it was probably quite presentable in 1160: even enviably so, given its exceptional size (246 feet long by 115 feet wide at the facade) and, above all, the prestige of its decor, now largely updated. In this respect it was worthy of comparison with the most remarkable of contemporary constructions: Saint-Denis and its three western portals; Chartres and its Royal Portal. To be sure, the Île-de-France had just embarked on the exceptional adventure that was the rebuilding of its large abbey churches and cathedrals. It was initiated by two monks: Abbot Suger and Archbishop Henri Sanglier of Sens. Both had turned to architects whose "modern" approach unsettled traditional schemata inherited from the Roman world. Their ambitions took them in new directions: they envisioned buildings more than 350 feet long (355 for Saint-Denis; 373 for Sens); they transformed their interior spaces thanks to the structural logic of ribbed vaults; they incorporated ensembles of sculpture and stained glass that gave the structures meaning; and, finally, they used the most advanced building techniques to achieve the desired results.

The work completed at Saint-Denis and Sens in the 1140s suddenly made other buildings seem out-of-date. In this context, the ancient cathedral in Paris inevitably came to seem antiquated, poorly adapted to the ambitions of its rapidly expanding diocese. What's more, the momentum to build was spreading. In Angers, Bishop Normand de Doué (1149–53) undertook to rebuild the nave of his cathedral. While remaining faithful to the single-aisle tradition, he covered the bays not with cupolas but with ribbed vaults manifestly inspired by them. Even dioceses far less wealthy and prestigious than that of Paris also took up the challenge: for example, Noyon, due to the resolve of Bishop Baudouin, around 1145–50. This dynamic became even stronger in the following decade. Around 1153, Bishop Thibaud of Senlis did not hesitate to envision rebuilding his cathedral, despite the particularly meager resources of his diocese. In Laon, Gautier de Mortagne (1155–70) dreamed of doing likewise from the moment of his election to the episcopal throne. In Paris, the large abbey churches entered the stakes still earlier: Saint-Martin-des-Champs during the tenure of Prior Hughes (1130–42), and the Abbey of Saint-Germain-des-Prés.

The idea of launching a similar initiative at Notre-Dame must have been on people's minds, even if we have no direct evidence of this. But for a time the bishops seem to have been neither sufficiently strong nor sufficiently interested to have envisioned such a project. Thibaud, elected in 1143, previously the prior of Saint-Martin-des-Champs, remains something of a cipher. The

The wax seal of Maurice de Sully is a conventional image of the bishop in full ceremonial regalia. (Archives Nationales, L.892 P.7.)

Opposite:
The cathedral square in a late-seventeenth-century image, which probably differs very little from the way it appeared in the thirteenth century. In this remarkably precise drawing signed by Antier and dated 1699, the viewer can make out in the lower right corner the "Faster," the cathedral's first trumeau figure; the balustrade above the Gallery of Kings; and the group dominated by the Virgin, which was on axis with the rue Neuve Notre-Dame. (Bibliothèque Nationale, Cabinet des Estampes, Va. 419.)

This eighteenth-century plan, by Abbé Delagrive, clearly indicates the configuration of the Gothic cathedral complex on the eastern tip of the island. The bishop's palace and Hôtel-Dieu, or charity hospice, have been shifted to the south, while the rue Neuve Notre-Dame is squarely aligned with the cathedral's central portal.

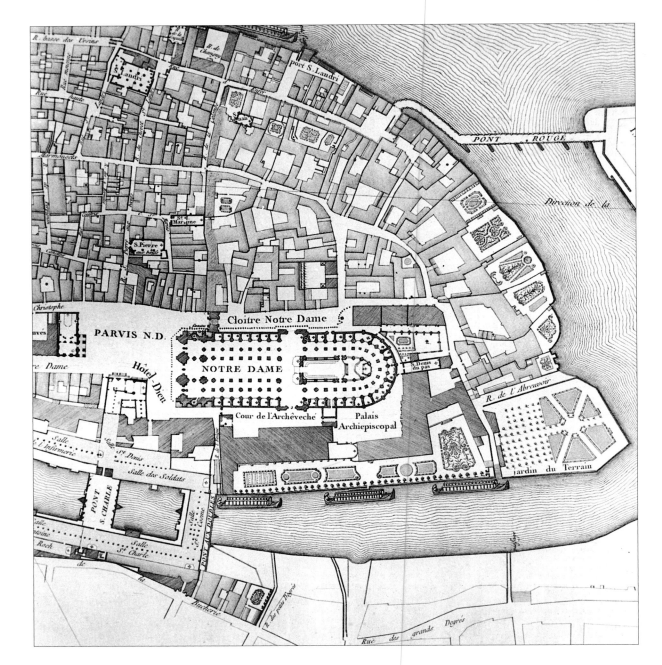

The piercing of the rue Neuve Notre-Dame, begun at the same time as work on the new cathedral, was situated so as to lead directly to the central portal completed forty years later. Maurice de Sully's design was considered a work of urban planning. (From Jean-François Blondel, *Architecture française,* 4 vols. [Paris, 1752–56].)

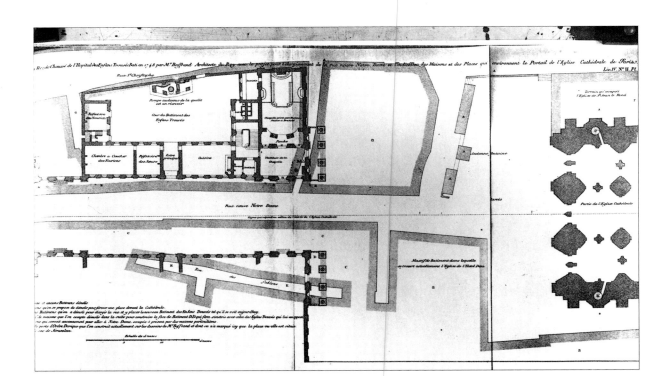

mandate of his successor, Pierre Lombard (June 1159–July 1160), was somewhat fragile, for his competitor for the post had been Philippe, brother of King Louis VII. Of Italian origin, Pierre had gone to Paris to study and subsequently fashioned a remarkable career there. Around 1140, confidence in him was such that he was asked to teach at the school of Notre-Dame. There he had an immense impact, raising the *studium pariense* to a higher intellectual plane than that of competing cathedral schools. His *Quatre Livres de sentence* rapidly became a work of reference for theologians, a status it retained until the sixteenth century. A member of the cathedral chapter from 1145, he seemed destined for a brilliant future. His subsequent election as bishop points to a growing desire—apparent elsewhere as well—to place intellectuals who had shaped contemporary theological reflection in positions of authority. This same resolve led to the election of his successor.

Once again, two exceptional candidates were in the running, both members of the cathedral chapter: Pierre le Mangeur and Maurice de Sully. The canons, unable to decide between them, sought the counsel of Louis VII. The royal response is telling and casts a revealing light on the prelate's future actions: "Choose the one most zealous as regards the governorship of souls; reserve direction of the schools for the most erudite." Maurice carried the day, but his credentials regarding the second point were nonetheless impressive. He had served as regent of the cathedral school, where he was also an authorized professor. Educated as a preacher, he had become famous due to his resolve to address not only clerics, as was customary at the time, but also congregations of the faithful. This put him at odds with the guardians of overly abstract reflection, encouraging him to develop a style in which dialectical discursiveness was replaced by clarity and simplicity.

The cathedral square after the demolition of the "Faster" fountain in 1748 and before that of the baptistry in 1767. The chapel of the Hôtel-Dieu, visible at right, established its southern limit. (Bibliothèque Nationale, Cabinet des Estampes, Va. 419.)

He went so far as to challenge some of the theories of Pierre Lombard that he found heterodox. His views regarding the importance of sermons, pastoral obligations, and ceremony found echo in his projects for the cathedral. In short, they pointed toward the construction of a larger building.

The immense structure that resulted was part of a much larger project whose scope, unique at the time, encompassed religious practice, topographic restructuring of the eastern tip of the island, and the construction, demolition, or reconstruction of many other buildings. One of his first concerns was the reorganization of parish life through clarification of the role specific to the cathedral. A diocesan church intended to serve the community as a whole, it also functioned as a parish church for congregants living within the island's ancient walls. Christians living on reclaimed land along the banks of the Seine belonged to parishes whose churches were situated across the river: residents of the quai aux Fleurs (rue de la Pelleterie), for example, were assigned to Saint-Jacques-la-Boucherie. Around 1183, Maurice de Sully created twelve parishes on the island that disregarded the ancient configuration, transforming some places of worship, including many chapels, into parish churches. The synagogue close to the cathedral, on the rue de la Juiverie, useless after the expulsion of the Jews by Philippe-Auguste in 1183, was ceded by the king to the bishop, who transformed it into a church dedicated to Mary Magdalene. It became the seat of the archpriest who had previously officiated within the cathedral. Maurice completed this administrative reorganization by creating a second archpriestship before the end of the century, this time at Saint-Séverin. The result was a clearer allocation of ecclesiastical authority in Paris, with the cathedral recovering its initial role as a building serving the entire diocese. Ties between the bishops and the parish churches were assured thanks to an obligation imposed on the thirteen principal vicars of the oldest parishes to assist the bishop on important religious feast-days.

TOPOGRAPHIC MODIFICATIONS

In addition to this reorganization of parochial administration, whose results survived largely unchanged until the Revolution, there were also modifications of a topographic order, necessitated

Realization of the bishop's grand design entailed new construction on marshy ground outside the ancient walls: to the east for the chevet of the new cathedral; to the south for the bishop's palace and the charity hospice. The canonial close developed to the north. The church of Saint-Denis-du-Pas and the small cloister were built to the east of the chevet.

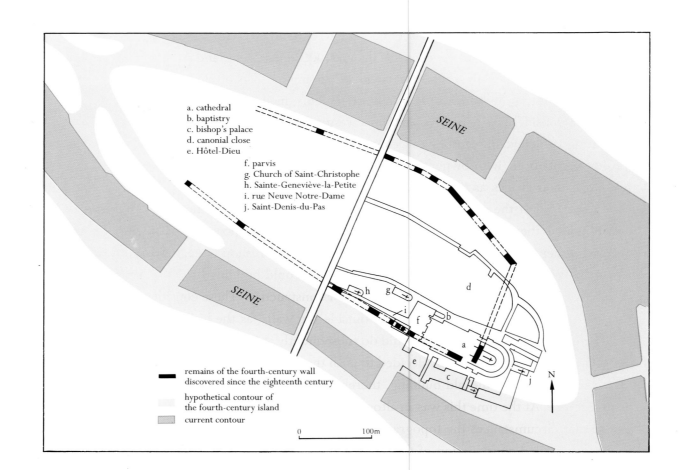

a. cathedral
b. baptistry
c. bishop's palace
d. canonial close
e. Hôtel-Dieu
f. parvis
g. Church of Saint-Christophe
h. Sainte-Geneviève-la-Petite
i. rue Neuve Notre-Dame
j. Saint-Denis-du-Pas

SEINE

SEINE

remains of the fourth-century wall discovered since the eighteenth century

hypothetical contour of the fourth-century island

current contour

0   100m

N

The Grand Design of Maurice de Sully

by the construction of the Gothic cathedral. The new building, with its 402-foot length and its facade 131 feet across, was to cover more than 59,000 square feet, and somehow the necessary land had to be freed. Like most other prelates envisioning projects on such a grand scale, Maurice de Sully now had to grapple with topographic problems, made all the more vexing by the development of a considerably denser urban fabric resulting from the demographic growth that had begun in the late eleventh century and continued unabated. Expansion to the west would entail laborious negotiations with owners reluctant to sell their well-placed land or houses, and who would raise their prices as a result. Eastward expansion would be much easier, for the land between the apse of the cathedral and the ancient walls belonged to the clergy: destruction of extant buildings there—perhaps the bishop's residence—could pose few problems. There was probably another incentive as well. We have already seen that Bishop Énée, in 867, obtained from Charles the Bald an island close to the cathedral. This could be joined to the Cité by landfill, a development that would create new possibilities for construction. These considerations prompted Maurice de Sully to situate the new chevet outside the walls, as the bishop of Noyon had done shortly before, and as other prelates would do subsequently at Bourges, Le Mans, and many other cities. In addition, Maurice de Sully decided to push the facade of the new cathedral about 130 feet farther east than that of the old building, thereby liberating a tract sufficiently large to create a cathedral square. At the time this was an altogether exceptional move, although it must be said that under similar circumstances the topography in many other cities—Noyon, Bourges, Le Mans— would have entailed construction of their new chevets above steep inclines, thereby immensely complicating the work. As early as 1160, then, Maurice de Sully had conceived a square of

In accordance with a common pattern, the bishop's palace was situated on the cathedral's southern flank, counterbalanced by the canonial close to the north. It consisted of a western building of two stories containing the hall and, to its east, an adjacent chapel, also a two-story structure. The square tower rose from an interior court. (Bibliothèque Nationale, Cabinet des Estampes, Va. 419.)

respectable size, but it was cleared only some forty years later, when the facade and first bays of the fourth-century building were demolished (leaving the foundations in place to be unearthed by future archaeologists). From the start, then, Maurice de Sully had boldly addressed a problem that was to vex many prelates seeking to establish narrow strips of land in front of their facades. In Amiens, it was only in 1304 that the bishops authorized the canons to clear a small parvis, or cathedral square, finally making it possible for worshipers to enter via the western facade instead of through a lateral door to the south. Likewise in Cahors, where western access also became possible in the early fourteenth century, making it unnecessary to use the hitherto obligatory northern entry. In Metz, this development did not take place until the eighteenth century; in Bordeaux, not before the nineteenth. As for Narbonne, there the nave was never realized.

Not content with planning such a parvis, Maurice de Sully also sought to improve the circulation system used by the worshipers of the diocese when approaching the facade of their cathedral. There was, of course, an extant network of narrow streets linking the two bridges spanning the Seine (the Pont Notre-Dame to the north, the Petit Pont to the south), but it was not adequate to the scope of so ambitious a project. The prelate traced a new roadway along an east-west axis—at almost twenty feet wide, the broadest in the city—running from the future cathedral portal to the north-south route connecting the two bridges (see page 40). As the Gothic building encompassed more terrain to the north than the earlier cathedral, the axis of its facade was also shifted northward. This complicated matters considerably, necessitating a cut through vital urban fabric that would entail the demolition of several private houses and the relocation of the Hôtel-Dieu. The consequent negotiations were long and arduous, notably with Henri Lionel and his wife, Pétronille, who agreed to surrender several houses in exchange for two others and a plot of land close to the Church of Saint-Christophe. This agreement, negotiated in 1163–64, first by the bishop and then by the chapter, culminated in 1173 in the surrender of three houses, including one that had just been completed, to the Abbey of Saint-Victor. The gift was renewed and expanded in 1182. New difficulties arose some ten years later, when Pétronille demanded further compensation. Only after some thirty years of negotiations was a final agreement reached. Other property owners proved less recalcitrant, although the chronicler d'Anchin reports that they obtained elevated prices for their houses. One of them, Gervais de Tourotte, proved so cooperative that, as a gesture of gratitude, the chapter resolved to pray for his soul as well as those of his wife and son every February 19. The project was finally realized by Maurice de Sully then, but at great cost.

The disparate buildings around the Church of Saint-Christophe that constituted the Hôtel-Dieu, especially those to its south, were even more dramatically affected. Negotiations regarding some of them, situated at the beginning of the rue Neuve, must have been especially difficult. In a notarial act of 1208, the chapter allocated the institution an annuity of twenty-five livres—drawn from the budget of the vestry—by way of indemnity for buildings formerly situated in front of the facade of the ancient cathedral. Seeing these demolitions as an opportunity, Maurice de Sully resolved to construct new facilities for the Hôtel-Dieu in a new location. This move would result in buildings better adapted to emerging needs; situated to the south, the new structures would have more natural light, better heating, and—perhaps most important—ready access to water from the river.

The only surviving evidence of the thirteenth-century appearance of the baptistry is this painting from the fifteenth century, which also offers a glimpse of the chapel of the Hôtel-Dieu. (Master of Saint Gilles, *Saint Leu Healing the Sick Children,* oil on oak, ca. 1480–90. National Gallery of Art, Washington, D.C., Samuel H. Kress Collection.)

Opposite:
The massive form of the cathedral towered over the Cité, whose other thirteenth-century buildings were made of wood, save for its churches and the palace of the kings of France, situated at the western tip of the island. By the mid-fifteenth century, when this illumination was painted, the cityscape had changed considerably, but the cathedral, still visible throughout Paris, remained the dominant architectural presence. The tower of the Louvre rose to a height of only ninety-nine feet. (Jean Fouquet, illumination from *The Hours of Étienne Chevalier,* 1452–61. The Metropolitan Museum of Art, New York, Lehman Collection.)

The new site was outside the ancient walls, on marshy ground bordering the narrow arm of the Seine. Begun in 1164, the work proved arduous, for stable ground was reached only at a depth of thirty feet. The chapel overlooking the square rose first, followed by the Salle Saint-Denis (completed 1195), the Salle Saint-Thomas (ca. 1210), the infirmary (1225–50), the Salle Neuve, and the Chapel of the Petit Pont (1250–60). Admittedly, there is no evidence that Maurice de Sully had originally envisioned buildings extending to a length of 400 feet, but the choice of the site made such expansion possible. In addition to spaces for the sick, there were also to be communal facilities (refectory, dormitory, cloister) and service buildings (infirmary, bakery, and so on). As the land belonged to the Abbey of Saint-Victor, negotiations went smoothly, for the prelate maintained particularly close relations with the convent. Work along the rue du Sablon was completed in 1225, the balance in 1260. From that point until the early sixteenth century, modifications consisted largely of remodeling and reconstruction, the only extensions added being of secondary importance. Here again Maurice's large-scale plans proved prescient, resulting not only in the largest charity hospice of the period but one that was singularly well adapted to its various functions.

The third important project, after the piercing of the rue Neuve and the relocation of the charity hospice, was the construction of a new bishop's palace. We have already noted the paucity of evidence concerning the *domus episcopi* before the election of Maurice de Sully, and this probably tells us something about its relatively small scale. The language used in contemporary documents also points to a complex of modest size: the word *palatium* (palace) appears but rarely; *domus episcopi* (bishop's residence) and s*edes episcopalis* (seat of the bishop) occur far more frequently. So it seems likely that the buildings were by no means sumptuous. A poem by Abbon mentions an *aula* (noble residence), which is not surprising, and in 1179 there is already a reference to it as *vetus* (old), which proves that the new one was already complete. Maurice de Sully was not one to rest content with such a situation, which can only have wounded his pride. We do not know the exact placement of the original complex, but it probably rose between the fourth-century apse and the ancient wall. When deciding to replace it, Maurice opted for a new site: one to the south of the new cathedral and outside the ancient walls, to be reclaimed from marshy ground bordering the narrow arm of the Seine. Thus the sacred city now conformed to the usual schema, consisting of a cathedral flanked by the palace on one side and the canonial close on the other. Construction proved just as difficult as for the Hôtel-Dieu, for stable ground again was located only some thirty feet below ground level. Even so, work proceeded rapidly. There is mention of the *domus nova episcopi* (new bishop's residence) in a text datable to 1168–76, while there are references to the *ostium nove capelle* (new chapel to the east) in 1170 and to the *inferior aula* (lower hall) in 1187.

The new bishop's palace soon came to be regarded by many prelates as a model of its kind, due to its marvelous site as well as to the elegance and configuration of its buildings. Extending along the Seine from east to west, it benefited from full southern exposure and afforded beautiful views. The first building to the east consisted of two stories: a lower hall, whose ribbed vaults were supported by a central row of columns, and an upper hall, an open space spanned by a timber roof. Then came the chapel, also a two-story structure. Access to the cathedral was via a gallery running north-south and issuing into the third bay of the choir, designated in documents of 1185 as the *porticus*. The cathedral treasury was situated on the chapel's second story. In addition, there was a tower known as the *turris,* whose rectangular plan indicates that it must have been intended for residential use; it probably housed the prelate's bedchamber and oratory. This already imposing complex was completed by service buildings, including houses occupied by officers and personnel, namely the bishop's curia. But even this complex was found wanting by Maurice de Sully's successors. Prior to 1288, Renaud de Homblonière envisioned construction of a new *camera,* or chamber, which was finally realized by his successor, Mattifas de Buci (d. 1304).

The canonial close of the first half of the twelfth century must also have been greatly affected by this topographic reconfiguration. It is within the context of the bishopric's initiative that one must situate an act of 1165, in which Pope Alexander III reaffirmed the chapter's property holdings and privileges. In addition, it became necessary to reassure the canons that it would be possible for them to expand their own complex. At the beginning of the thirteenth century, they were fifty-two in number. In the early fourteenth century, the close itself encompassed thirty-seven residences, each endowed with a plot of land and an annuity; the other residences were situated outside its boundaries. The extension, which spread beyond the ancient wall to the east, consisted of communal buildings whose chronology remains elusive: a chapter house containing the capitulary administration, an audience room, and a capitulary room; stables, above which were offices, a library, and a chamber; the small cloister with its ossuary; and, finally, Saint-Denis-du-Pas. This small rectangular building (thirty-nine by twenty-one feet), demolished in 1815, had

already been the object of a *réfection,* or significant reconstruction of some kind, prior to 1164 at the behest of one of the canons, Simon de Poissy. It was early provided with four chaplains who enjoyed the same privileges as the cathedral canons, and its establishment must predate the renovation. Very likely the original chapel was destroyed to make way for the new cathedral and was subsequently rebuilt to the east of the new apse. Despite this move, it retained the reference in its original name to a ford across which one could pass from the Île de la Cité to the Île Notre-Dame. Assuming that these inferences are correct, then the small apse some thirty-one feet in diameter discovered by Eugène Viollet-le-Duc in the choir of the Gothic cathedral might belong to this first oratory, in which case it would slightly postdate the demolition of the ancient wall in the eleventh or twelfth century.

The canonial close continued to evolve throughout the medieval period and even into the eighteenth century. At the time of the Revolution, it boasted many houses with large gardens—to the north—as well as communal buildings of comparable size and other structures whose precise functions have yet to be determined, for example, the Dagobert Tower. The close was then entered through one of four gates: the main gate, situated to the west and erected in 1747 on the site of Saint-Jean-le-Rond; the Marmouzets Gate, on rue de la Colombe; the Gate of the Carré

The canons reclaimed the marshy terrain along the river so as to provide themselves with gardens, which they regarded as indispensable amenities. (Painting by J.-B. Nicolas Raguenet, ca. 1755. Musée Carnavalet, Paris.)

du Pont-Rouge, at the end of the rue de l'Enfer; and, finally, a gate next to the cathedral apse that led to the bishop's palace.

What Maurice de Sully had formulated, then, was a real urbanistic program, a plan that introduced a certain logic into a previously anarchic urban fabric. The new complexes were organized in relationship to an east-west axis that passed through the center of the future cathedral and continued along the rue Neuve. They were situated to either side of the main sanctuary: the canonial close to the north and the bishop's palace to the south. South of the rue Neuve was the Hôtel-Dieu; to its north, small houses of worship like Saint-Christophe and the Madeleine, now designated parish churches.

Maurice de Sully had a rare gift for seeing far into the future, something he did so successfully that the close, the palace, and the Hôtel-Dieu were later able to expand unhampered. Each of these subcomplexes was conceived as an autonomous whole. The canonial close was a protected enclave accessible only through a few gates. The same could be said of the palace, and soon of the Hôtel-Dieu as well, for it created its own square by absorbing the rue du Sablon. Beyond these dispositions, which already evidence an inspired urbanist vision, Maurice de Sully sought to underscore the significance of the cathedral in two ways: by establishing a parvis that would serve as an intermediary space between the secular and civil worlds; and by piercing a broad roadway that, eventually turning north toward the Pont Notre-Dame and south toward the Petit Pont, both integrated the city and linked it to the diocese beyond, thereby reasserting the cathedral's status as a diocesan church.

FINANCING

This urban renovation project, conceived on a large scale, required not only determination but also financial means sufficient to assure its realization with relative speed, before the necessary energy should be exhausted. Instead of deploying his various initiatives in succession, Maurice de Sully launched them all at once and brought them to completion over an extremely short span of time, as though he had doubts about his ambitious plans being honored after his death. God was kind to him, however, granting him an episcopal tenure of thirty-six years, which was exceptionally long for the period. By the time he died in 1196, the rue Neuve had been pierced, the charity hospice had moved into its new quarters, the palace had been built, and the close had been enlarged. The cathedral had not been completed, of course, but it was quite advanced, construction of the nave having begun. Services were already being held in the new choir. There remained only the erection of the facade and its linkage to the bays of the nave before the western portion of the ancient nave could be demolished, thereby freeing the space for the square. Even setting aside for a moment the cathedral, which will be discussed separately, immense sums of money were required to implement this vast project. Where did it come from?

As regards the palace, the answer is unequivocal: Maurice de Sully financed it entirely on his own. The question becomes more complicated with the other projects. If the few surviving documents are trustworthy, the piercing of the rue Neuve was also underwritten by funds provided by the bishop. In principle, expansion of the canonial close to accommodate communal buildings would likewise have fallen under the purview of the chapter. None of the surviving documentation specifically confirms this, but there are many examples in other cities of the bishop's having played the crucial role in the construction of comparable facilities. In the case of the Hôtel-Dieu, however, we must be wary of drawing overhasty conclusions. True, it was under the immediate jurisdiction of the chapter, but this oversight was regulatory in nature and did not necessarily pertain to its funding. We do not know when the institution acquired the civil status that brought with it the authority to acquire, accept, and sell property on its own. Gifts and bequests constituted a substantial source of revenue. It seems unlikely, however, that they would have sufficed to finance the daily operations of such an institution, for it was chronically in debt. We are on firmer ground

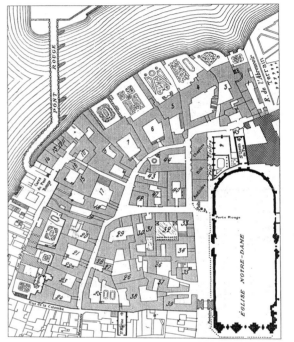

Above:
The canonial close was subdivided into several blocks of buildings separated by streets. The oldest of them rose opposite the northern arm of the transept. The one to its east, bordering the chevet, postdated 1160, while the most recent in date was the oblong configuration situated to the north. (From *Commission du Vieux Paris,* 1908. B.H.V.P.)

Left:
One of the close's most remarkable buildings, whose function has not yet been determined, was the Dagobert Tower, destroyed in 1909. (Musée Notre-Dame.)

regarding external intervention in later periods. In 1234, Blanche of Castille defrayed a considerable portion of the cost of building the Saint Thomas Hall. Similar interventions are likely in the twelfth century as well, despite a lack of concrete evidence. Appeals for private donations to support the construction and/or renovation of facilities for charitable works cannot have gone unheeded.

Regarding the cathedral itself, we must confront the kind of difficulties that habitually complicate attempts to estimate the cost of such undertakings. The chroniclers pay precious little attention to such questions, and the accounting records, which must have existed, are now lost. We should remember that such initiatives were just as audacious in financial terms as they were in structural ones. Our ignorance is even greater than this alone might suggest, for while the persons in authority are generally known to us, we are completely in the dark as regards both the origin of the funds at their disposition and their management. The Paris project provides yet another confirmation of this rule, which holds generally for the second half of the twelfth century.

Maurice de Sully, whose generative role is not open to doubt, would have been obliged to serve as financier as well, presumably along with other contributors. As so often with the great cathedrals, the sovereign played no role in its construction. He turned his attention to less conspicuous enterprises like monasteries, especially those of the Cistercian order. Nonetheless, Louis VII made a gift of 200 livres before his death in 1180, and his third wife, Adèle de Champagne (d. 1206), bequeathed twenty silver marcs, the equivalent of forty livres. Like the king and his family, the gentry of the period also refrained from contributing. Regarding laypersons of lower status, there is mention of a gift of fifty livres from Guillaume de Barres and one of two marcs by Gentil, the nephew of Alexander III. These sums do not add up to much, although at the time each of them must have been gratefully received. One can only be surprised by the scarcity of such contributions from the canons, although periodically they did help defray the cost of ecclesiastical furniture. The chorister Albert contributed twenty "livres parisis" toward the cost of the choir stalls. The dean of the chapter, Barbedor, paid for a stained-glass window that cost fifteen livres. It is not impossible that the chapter also made other contributions on a regular basis, but here the documents are frustratingly silent. Equally delicate is the question of funds raised by other means, for example, offerings, visits to relics, and indulgences. These sums must have been considerable, but nothing indicates that they were all used to underwrite construction. Only in 1209 is there mention of the bishop and the chapter having reached an agreement stipulating that monies collected by custodians of the treasury would be applied against construction costs incurred in connection with the cathedral and the Hôtel-Dieu. In any event, these exceptional sources of revenue were too irregular to have figured prominently in budgetary projections.

Of necessity, Maurice de Sully would have been reasonably sure of his financing before launching this grandiose project. The monk Anchin, who visited Paris in 1182, reported that Maurice used "his own resources as much as those of others" (Ecclesiam . . . propriis magnis sumptibus quam alienis, decentissimo et somptuoso opere renovavit). This statement is consistent with analogous reports concerning other cathedral building projects during the second half of the twelfth century, when underwriting by the bishop himself was usually crucial. This state of affairs changed considerably in the thirteenth century, when the canons began to play a more significant role, establishing an institution charged with managing sums obtained in various ways: the vestry. Unlike his successor, Eudes de Sully (d. 1208), who was allied with the greatest families of the period and thus had considerable revenues at his disposal, Maurice de Sully, of humble social origins, was without personal fortune. Like many prelates of his day, he succeeded in amassing resources through exceptionally skillful management of the revenues reverting to him as bishop. True, Suger had shown him the way during his abbacy at Saint-Denis, having left a detailed account of how he had proceeded; Gautier de Mortagne in Laon and Arnoul in Lisieux had followed his example in the fiscal administration of their respective dioceses. Maurice revealed himself to be equally attentive, managing to secure sufficiently regular sources of revenue not only to launch this building project but also to sustain it over the longer term. Here again, even the most approximate estimate of the specific amounts involved is impossible; we must content ourselves with sharing in the admiration of his contemporaries. The only precise amount recorded in the documents is a bequest of 100 livres, which he stipulated was to pay for a lead roof for the building. His obit, solemnly celebrated on September 16 at the high altar, manifests the canons' acknowledgment of his generosity and his administrative abilities. He was especially generous toward them, leaving them a house close to the gate of the canonial close, several sources of revenue, and a sum—twenty marcs—sufficient to pay for the "golden table" and several other liturgical furnishings. He also bequeathed 190 silver marcs to them for the purchase of land and vineyards.

At his death in 1196, thanks to his unstinting resolve and his exceptional powers of persuasion, the project, while not yet complete, was sufficiently advanced to preclude its being abandoned. The eastern tip of the Île de la Cité—made larger by conquest of the banks of the Seine—had been considerably modified. He had not hesitated to shift the east-west axis substantially northward so as to align it with the new buildings: bishop's palace, charity hospice, cathedral. Eudes de Sully continued the undertaking without notable modification but at a slower pace.

CONSTRUCTION

The decision to rebuild having been made, it was necessary to devise a construction plan. On this point we remain totally ignorant of the problems relating to manpower. Even the architect's name is unknown to us, for all the pertinent written documents have vanished. This, too, is a circumstance that applies consistently during the second half of the twelfth century, with the exception of Canterbury Cathedral, about which the monk Gervais was especially prolix. On the basis of later examples, it seems safe to assume that the Paris project was organized hierarchically in accordance with a system used for all buildings made of stone, with water carriers occupying the bottom rung and the most highly skilled stonecutters the highest. Salaries would have varied accordingly, some being supplemented substantially by additional revenues. We can only guess at the number of people who worked on the project, but it must have risen and fallen along with the funds allotted at any given time: while it was subject to seasonal rhythms, the size of the labor force when work recommenced in earnest each spring would have been sometimes smaller, sometimes greater. We are in possession of rather precise figures for Westminster Abbey from almost a century later, in 1253: between February 1 and April 18 there was a total of 326 workers, inclusive of all craft guilds; between June 23 and 29, this number rose to 428, only to lower to 100 between November 10 and 16. Two suppositions pertaining to this question can be made with regard to Paris. First, construction proceeded at such a rapid pace that the labor force must have been large, always allowing for seasonal and annual variation. The second observation concerns the ease of recruitment and the quality of the labor force. In the early eleventh century, Paris began to be renowned for its building, and its fame in this respect only increased with the passage of time. This reputation was a function of the scale of the demand and the considerable financial resources of the patrons as well as of the quality of the available stone, quarried in Paris itself, and timber, just as easily obtainable in the city's environs. Veritable construction firms capable of satisfying even the most exacting client could be assembled there with relative speed. Paris differed in this respect from cities like Noyon, Laon, and Senlis, where large-scale building projects were hampered by limited manpower and materials. Finally, the standing presence in the city of a high-quality labor force must have lowered costs, for it precluded lodging expenses.

The acquisition of basic building materials—wood and stone—cannot have been the least of the many concerns of the bishop-builders. In the case of timber, a ready supply could be had from the lands owned by the bishops and the canons. Virtually the only related costs would have been those entailed by transport and by allowing the timber to dry. As for stone, there the question is more delicate. To be sure, there were abundant, readily exploitable quarries nearby, most notably in the southern part of the city, on the left bank of the Bièvre. They were probably open to the sky,

Pages 52–53:
The chapter decided to develop the eastern tip of the island only in the seventeenth century, when it built a stone embankment and planted a garden there. But the extant buildings were carefully preserved: the bishop's palace and its tower (to the left of the cathedral in this view), the small cloister and Saint-Denis-du-Pas, and the cloister residences. The complex was still dominated by the apse of the cathedral and its culminating spire. (B.H.V.P.)

for subterranean stonecutting was still rare. Transport from these sites posed few problems, thanks to special boats capable of ferrying loads along the Bièvre and the Seine to the embankment next to the apse, where a port facility was established. Here again, related costs would have been limited, especially as compared with a city like Laon, where the quarries were more than ten miles away and transport entailed a difficult trip up the Arx River. To reduce construction costs still further, bishops generally managed to obtain stone on exceptionally favorable terms, whether by negotiating unlimited quarry rights for the construction period, as in Troyes; by having ownership of the quarry ceded to them outright, as in Laon; or by buying it, as in Amiens. We do not know what the arrangement was in Paris, but everything suggests that the quarries there were already in private hands and that their exploitation was well organized. Doubtless Maurice de Sully negotiated the most favorable terms possible, but, even so, this item must have weighed heavily on the budget, especially given his insistence that only the finest materials be used. Viollet-le-Duc was but the first of many to emphasize this aspect of the building, which some have judged luxurious, especially in comparison with other structures from the period. Generally, the limestone beds in this region are forty-nine to sixty-six feet thick and are composed of superimposed, comparatively dense strata separated by thinner layers of so-called rotten stone. Blocks were cut and chosen in accordance with a rigorous hierarchy, and always with a view to their intended use.

In Paris, as with almost all the great cathedral projects, one is struck by the relative paucity of textual documentation. It is not only a matter of the records directly pertaining to these projects having been lost; contemporary chroniclers also had little to say about them, as though these enormous structures scarcely retained their attention, perhaps because they were deemed too commonplace or because they offered little in the way of anecdotal narrative, judged more exciting and more conducive to stylistic effects. For these authors broke their silence only when difficulties emerged or dramas erupted. It was an absence of conflict in Paris, then, that deprived us of information, for everything suggests that Maurice de Sully maintained calm from the start, establishing a precedent that continued to hold until the project reached completion. This despite the fact that so vast and complex an undertaking inevitably presented many opportunities for strife, especially given the extended timespan involved, which can only have fostered frustration and even confrontation. Such difficulties were further complicated by the building's status as a place of worship. As with many cathedrals, abbey churches, collegiate churches, and parish churches, the reconstruction of Notre-Dame de Paris had to proceed in a way that could accommodate the ongoing presence of at least part of a building already standing on the site, and perhaps in poor condition. Its demolition had to take place incrementally, as portions of the new sanctuary were completed. Of necessity, this entailed imbrication of the two buildings such as can still be seen at the cathedrals of Beauvais and Alet, in the Aude, where construction came to a sudden halt in midstream. It was considered vital that worship services continue without interruption: whatever inconveniences might be entailed by ongoing construction, the Eucharist had to continue at the old high altar until the very day when mass could be celebrated in the new one. Such transfers were always marked by a grandiose ceremony, as indicated by surviving accounts from Cluny in the twelfth century and Chartres in the thirteenth century. The image available to thirteenth-century viewers, then, was complex, for old walls were demolished only upon completion of those replacing them. Thus it must have been difficult to assess the building while it was under construction. Only after completion would it have been fully "legible."

With regard to Paris, yet another difficulty arises: many of the surviving texts considerably postdate the events they recount, making critical acumen indispensable in evaluating them. A source affirming that the first stone was laid by Pope Alexander III during his visit to Paris in 1163, for example, was written in the fourteenth century by Jean de Saint-Victor. If the information he provides is accurate, the ceremony took place between March 24 and April 25. But it seems unlikely that Maurice de Sully would have delayed the launching of his project for so long. He must have begun laying plans in the winter months immediately following his election, on October 12, 1160, so that work could begin with the arrival of fine weather, in March or April of 1161.

Work proceeded with remarkable speed. Robert de Thorigni, the abbot of Mont-Saint-Michel and a particularly well informed contemporary chronicler, carefully noted the following in 1177: "It is already quite some time since Maurice, bishop of Paris, began work, which advances rapidly, on the cathedral in the said city, whose chevet (*caput*) is already finished, save for its roof (*tectorium*)." Eleven years after beginning the project, Maurice de Sully had managed to complete a structure some 125 feet long with a center aisle forty-one feet wide and an anticipated vault some 108 feet high. The choir was not completely finished, for the upper vaults were still lacking—assuming, that is, that Francis Salet is correct in maintaining that the word *tectorium* refers to them and not to the exterior wood-frame roof. In this connection, it is worth recalling that it was customary to add the bay vaults rather late in the construction process, for several reasons. Aesthetics aside, there was no reason for them to be built quickly: protection from rain was assured by a wood-frame roof built over the space as soon as the side walls had attained their full height. Furthermore, Gothic architects, whose use of lancet arches had considerably simplified vault construction, preferred to cover several bays in immediate succession, an approach that maximized efficiency—simplifying construction of the underlying forms—and assured stabilizing thrusts along the east-west axis, it taking some time for the freshly laid limestone to set properly.

Only on May 19, 1182, however, was the new high altar consecrated by a papal legate, Henri de Château-Marcay, with Maurice de Sully assisting. By that time the entirety of the building's eastern portion was complete, including vaults, stained-glass windows, and ecclesiastical furniture, notably stalls for the canons. The monk Anchin left a description of the superb ceremony, in which Maurice presided over some hundred clerics. At the prelate's death in 1196, the nave was incomplete and the lead roof—for which he left a bequest of 100 livres—also remained unrealized.

His successor, Eudes de Sully, continued the work during his brief tenure, which lasted from 1197 to 1208. His election had not been achieved without difficulty, for both his youth—he was thirty-two—and the fact that he was not a Parisian prompted objections. Furthermore, his lifestyle was judged shockingly opulent for a bishop. Unlike his predecessor, he belonged to the highest stratum of society. A cousin of the kings of France and England, and thus possessed of the most prestigious conceivable lineage, he had at his disposal a huge personal fortune, something that Maurice conspicuously lacked. He made his strongest mark as an administrator and jurist. Among other things, he was responsible for promulgating the first synodal statutes. With regard to construction, he did not sustain the rhythms established by Maurice, being content to see the work advance at a more deliberate pace.

Beyond this, the documents remain dramatically silent. None of them provides us with information about the progress of the work.

Beginning with Viollet-le-Duc, and after him Marcel Aubert, attempts have been made to establish a construction chronology by supplementing the sparse information provided by the documents with evidence obtained through careful examination of the building itself. Recently, a new generation of art historians has adopted the same strategy, renewing the field of inquiry in the process. But such an enterprise cannot escape the limits of its own methodology, which is premised on a belief in the logical development of the work. In fact, close study reveals that it sometimes proceeded anarchically, having been shaped by preexisting elements of which the architect had to take account and which he sometimes even reused. Many irregularities in plan resulted from an inability to achieve the desired alignment due to troublesome encumbrances: budgetary constraints sometimes made it necessary to incorporate parts of old buildings into new ones. Who would have imagined, before extensive repair work was undertaken on the piers of the crossing at Bayeux Cathedral in 1857, that they were but skillfully refaced Romanesque supports? Medieval architects displayed a rare genius when it came to this technique at the Cathedral of Nevers; they were also highly adept in the reuse of foundations, as in the choir of the Cathedral

Pages 56–57:
The Master of 1160, like his predecessor the Master of Saint-Denis, sought to express the true function of capitals as elements easing the visual transition between support—in this case a column—and arch spring. Accordingly, he used superimposed registers to generate an upward dynamic leading the eye toward the abacus. The ambulatory features several capital types that reflect this intention; despite their differences from one another, all achieve the desired end.

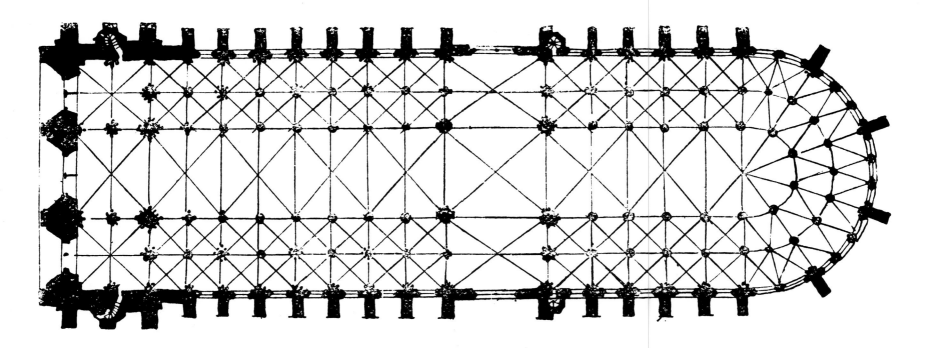

The Master of 1160 devised one of the most rigorous ground plans of the Middle Ages, eschewing all excrescences. Both the ambulatory chapels and the crossing are contained within a continuous envelope, or outer wall. The resulting space is exceptionally unified. (Plan by Marcel Aubert.)

of Meaux, and in the absorption of parts of extant buildings, subsequently demolished, into new ones, as at Saint-Denis. Such working methods must be kept in mind when broaching the history of the Parisian cathedral. Another difficulty exists as well: in the mid-nineteenth century, the building was the object of a gigantic restoration campaign overseen by two extremely gifted architects, Jean-Baptiste Lassus and Viollet-le-Duc. Such was their genius that the interventions they made are not always apparent, even to the practiced eye. Only careful, stone-by-stone examination makes it possible to distinguish their contributions from medieval work. Thus a certain prudence is in order when it comes to extracting clues from the building itself, for conclusions based on details whose dating remains problematic will probably be mistaken. It is preferable to rest content with an account that traces the development of the large masses of the building, an approach that precludes the kind of gross errors likely to result from an ill-advised attempt to be overly precise.

Archaeological analysis is consistent with the historical evidence, indicating that work indeed began with the chevet. It is here that one finds the oldest forms in the profiles of bases and moldings as well as in capital designs. Construction was unaffected by constraints that would become important factors in other areas: being outside the ancient wall, the terrain was either virgin or occupied by light structures that would have been easy to demolish. Thus the architect had a free hand, being able to trace the plan and lay the foundations for the ambulatory exactly as he wished. On the other hand, establishment of solid foundations here entailed deep excavations. South of the choir, Viollet-le-Duc dug to a depth of thirty feet before finding soil sufficiently stable to support the sacristy he envisioned there. The exterior envelope of the ambulatory rose in horizontal blocks to roof level; lengthwise, this first campaign encompassed only the turning bays, as best as one can judge from the style of the surviving capitals: the six groups of three capitals each supporting the outer vault springs constitute a coherent ensemble, suggesting the rapidity with which this part of the work advanced. The capitals of the rectangular bays to the north as well as to the south of the choir are very different in conception, belonging to the "noodle" style, suggesting that they represented a new direction. This shift occurs suddenly in the southern bays and incrementally in the northern ones, where the two styles coexist, the "noodle" capitals occupying the more conspicuous spots along the inner rows of columns. Those placed below the outer springs are in the earlier style; presumably they were used because they had already been carved.

Work continued with erection of the exterior envelope alongside the rectangular bays, culminating on either side in massive elements housing spiral stairs. Then came, in turn, the north- and southeastern piers of the crossing, the inner columns of the ambulatory, and the columns border-

ing the choir, after which rose the exterior and interior envelopes of the tribune. The capitals supporting the double arcade of the tribune are notably archaic in form; unlike those of the lateral vault springs, they are consistent with the initial series of the ambulatory below. Nonetheless, in the second bay of the tribune, to the north as well as to the south, there is a clear shift in style: the capitals of the colonnettes are *en délit* while those of the supports resemble the ones farther west. Only after the walls were in place could these spaces be covered with ribbed arches, a process that began with the two aisles of the ambulatory and continued at the tribune level. Sixteen years were required to complete this portion of the work: as previously noted, in 1177, Robert de Thorigni wrote admiringly of the chevet, specifying that it was finished save for the vault above the choir, then protected by a wood-frame roof. This section of the vault was completed in turn in 1182.

Although its nature remains unclear, a problem confronted the architect when the foundations for the first bay of the choir were being laid: they descend to a depth of almost twenty-five feet, while those of the bays farther east are at most about nineteen feet deep. The difference might be explained by the presence of the spiral stairs, and by the architect's use of narrower bays thereafter. But construction of the choir seems to have been complicated by other factors as well. The remains of an earlier monument uncovered by Viollet-le-Duc in 1857 were situated below this very bay, while the course of the ancient wall traversed the center of the second bay. Finally,

To unify the space of the ambulatory, the Master of 1160, like the architect of Saint-Denis, gave its two aisles vaults of identical height.

we might add that the building was later found to be relatively unstable in this area, a discovery that prompted substantial reinforcement work: the second southern column of the choir as well as the eastern supports of the first bays to both north and south and their lateral vault springs were given new foundations in the first decade of the fourteenth century.

The architect's task was greatly facilitated by the relatively undeveloped character of the terrain to the east, but farther west he had to cope with many encumbrances. Although the buildings were admittedly of light construction, the area within the confines of the wall housed numerous structures: the nave connected to the apse discovered by Viollet-le-Duc, the bishop's residence, and perhaps other buildings as well must have occupied the space between the apse of the fourth-century cathedral and the wall. Completion of the new *domus*—whose existence, as noted previously, is documented between 1168 and 1176—made it possible to demolish the old residence, an operation that must have been undertaken at this time. Farther west, most of the terrain was occupied by the fourth-century cathedral, which apparently extended as far east as the third bay of the nave. Demolition of the earlier structure would have proceeded in step with construction of the new one.

A new architect was responsible for laying the foundations of the outer envelope of the nave, which he then erected to its full height and to a length clearly marked by a sudden change in the design of the eastern supports of the second bay, to the north as well as to the south. Toward the east these supports hug the outer wall, but from a certain point and all the way to the western facade the colonnettes project more markedly than within the two side aisles. Close examination reveals that the southern wall rose before the northern wall. Thereafter, work proceeded rather rapidly with construction, in turn, of the supports of the eastern bays, the tribune, the tribune walls, the central aisle, and the vaults of the side aisles and tribune.

This second building campaign did not follow a halt in the work. It is linked to the arrival of a new architect possessed of a distinctive personality, one who boldly introduced significant modifications into the design devised by his predecessor. He first made his presence felt in the area of the tribune of the choir abutting the southern arm of the transept, with an element characteristic of his style: pilasters, which appear throughout the eastern portion of the nave. He must have succeeded the first architect well before 1182, doubtless even before 1177. Additional proof is provided by some of the keystones: those of the first and second bays of the choir, the transept arm, and the two most eastern bays of the nave are so similar in conception that they must have been designed by the same architect. The vaults must have been realized within a relatively short span of time. Those over the two eastern bays of the nave mark completion of the second phase as well as the disappearance of this architect. Although the date of its beginning is readily determinable, that of its end is more elusive. Its completion must have preceded Maurice de Sully's death in 1196, but probably not by much.

Assuming the hypothetical dimensions of the ancient cathedral are accurate, then the only part of the older building upon which the second campaign would have encroached was its apse, whose demolition it would have entailed. It was in the course of this phase that the nave's orientation was shifted slightly out of true with that of the choir. This development is difficult to explain, especially as there does not seem to have been anything about the terrain that would have impeded accurate surveying. In any event, it became necessary to occlude this discrepancy through skillful manipulation of the transept. And unless one consults a plan, it is indeed invisible.

In the next phase, work moved toward the west. In accordance with a pattern widely favored by medieval architects (many examples could be cited: Reims, Toul in 1460, and so on), the facade block was built and then linked to the nave. For the first time, the ancient cathedral was penetrated so that foundations for the four supports of the two towers could be excavated. Very likely this project commenced before the death of Maurice de Sully. Once the pillars had reached a certain height, work could begin on the bays linking the facade to the nave. This could proceed only after the intervening terrain had been cleared, a process that entailed demolition of the eastern

The Grand Design of Maurice de Sully

bays of the ancient cathedral, which presented serious problems. This linkage was the work of a third architect, who took considerable liberties with the design established by the first master: he abandoned the use of simple columns along the center aisle in favor of more complexly articulated supports, renounced the use of colonnettes along the exterior envelope of the side aisles, added intermediary pillars between the piers of the two towers, and changed the design of the first bay of the center aisle as well as of the first two bays of the side aisles. He did, however, erect the tribune with very few modifications. Finally, he covered the various spaces mentioned above, including the first two bays of the nave. This campaign of work on the nave, probably carried out mostly during the tenure of Eudes de Sully, reached completion around 1210–15. By that time the interior of the building was finished, protected by a lead roof supported by a wooden frame. Only the vaults remained unbuilt.

In the course of this work the architect confronted many difficulties that left their mark on the building itself. It was during this period that the parvis was cleared, a process that entailed complete demolition of the western bays of the ancient cathedral. Its Portal of the Virgin was carefully dismantled and immediately reinstalled as the right portal of the new facade, which had been designed to accommodate it, with some crucial additions. Not all of the earlier ensemble was retained, however, as evidenced by the two archivolts now in the Louvre and other fragments discovered within the foundations of the southern pillar of the nave. This reuse makes it possible to assign similar dates to the demolition of the ancient cathedral to accommodate the parvis, the dismantling and reinstallation of the Portal of the Virgin, and the foundations of the second pillar of the nave.

Finally, the supports of the first two bays of the side aisles are misaligned, producing irregularities that are all the more striking in light of the careful alignment of those farther east. This is especially apparent to the south. To this first irregularity must be added a second, just as surprising: the heights of the bases in the northern and southern bays do not agree, whereas farther to the east they are perfectly consistent. This anomaly cannot be haphazard; it must have an explanation. There can only be one reason for it: obstructions that precluded the use of a level. By contrast with the north, in the south, construction of the supports had begun while a portion of the transverse walls of the fourth-century cathedral remained standing.

Construction of the facade and the first two bays of the nave advanced simultaneously, being mutually compatible. In 1220, the statues of the Gallery of Kings were installed. Work proceeded in horizontal increments across the entire width, as indicated by scaffolding holes disposed in horizontal rows. It continued in this manner as far as the openwork gallery, when the architect was obliged to focus independently on the two towers, erecting first the northern tower and then the southern one. A precise chronology for the work during this period eludes us, but we do know that it was completed around 1245, when a decision was reached not to erect steeples above the towers. This slowdown of a project previously carried out with such exceptional speed was due to the commencement of a new phase of the work, one entailing modification of the interior elevations as well as of the exterior massing. These changes were so significant that they effectively produced a new cathedral, consistent with a new aesthetic informing the design of the openwork gallery and the two towers. For the first time, the design formulated by Maurice de Sully was challenged.

Maurice de Sully was succeeded as bishop by Eudes de Sully, whose effigy appeared on his bronze tomb slab, formerly situated in the monks' choir. Of noble stock and possessed of an immense personal fortune, his profile could scarcely have differed more from that of Maurice, but he continued his predecessor's building plans. (Étienne de Boisses [?], drawing of tomb slab of Eudes de Sully, end of the seventeenth century. Bibliothèque Nationale, Cabinet des Estampes, Collection Gaignières.)

The Cathedral of
Maurice de Sully

M aurice de Sully must have chosen an architect whose capabilities were equal to his own ambitions. Doubtless there was much discussion between these two exceptional individuals during the planning stages of the project, which entailed recasting the eastern tip of the Île de la Cité. These work sessions would have occasioned the preparation of several visual documents meant to aid in the decision-making process: models, plans, and elevations, treating both the entire structure and its details. A design having been approved, the architect and his team would have then set about preparing the more technical specifications required to assure that the work was properly executed. Only with the help of such aids could the building's homogeneity have been assured, and their subsequent disappearance by no means implies that they never existed. How else are we to explain that the program devised in 1160 was respected, at least in broad outline, until the structure was complete? For such was the case, the changes introduced by successive twelfth- and thirteenth-century architects never having challenged the initial scheme in any fundamental way. Even the facade adhered to it, at least as high as the openwork gallery. Things proceeded differently, however, with the sculptural ensembles. These were completely rethought in the early thirteenth century to bring them into line with a new iconographic conception.

THE CONCEIVING ARCHITECT

The name of the first master is unknown to us, due to a paucity of documentation that has also generated many misconceptions about the building. Information is so scarce that we know nothing of his origins and training, just as we remain in the dark about the nature of his personality and earlier projects that presumably brought him to the attention of the bishop of Paris. We can only say that he must have taken part in the intense architectural activity that marked the Parisian region in his day. By default, our best source of information about him and his achievement is the building itself.

In response to the precise program that must have been provided him, he devised a gigantic plan consisting of a five-bay apse and choir unit for the main altar and the canons, an eight-bay nave for the congregation, and an imposing facade block supporting two massive towers. To properly assess this initial design, the viewer must imagine an envelope flush with the outer ambulatory supports and pierced, in all likelihood, by windows smaller than those visible today (see page 76). The transept arms did not extend beyond this same outer boundary, as indicated by evidence in the southeast corner of the southern arm: masonry stubs, use of different stone, variations in the foundation course heights and base designs. Within this strictly defined envelope devoid of

Opposite:
All the windows in the twelfth-century cathedral were of stained glass. Virtually all of them have disappeared, but a few fragments survive, having been reincorporated into the southern rose window in the thirteenth century.

excrescences, the architect divided the space into five aisles interrupted only by the transept arms and directly abutting the facade block: a center aisle roughly forty-one feet wide and two pairs of side aisles, each just short of twenty feet wide. The vaults of the latter rose to a height of almost twenty-six feet east of the transept and slightly more than twenty-seven feet along the nave, while the vault of the center aisle—towering above a four-level elevation consisting of large arcade, tribune, openings onto the eaves, and clerestory—attained a height of more than 108 feet. As was then standard practice, the nave vault was organized into roughly square units encompassing two bays each, resulting in a discordance between the quadripartite vaults of the side aisles and the sexpartite vaults of the nave. This approach also produced alternating spring configurations, reflected in the design of their supports (see page 70). To guarantee an effect of visual cohesion at the arcade level, the architect used columns both uniform in design and massive in size, each exceeding forty-three inches in diameter.

Similar columns of smaller diameter were used in both the ambulatory and the rectangular bays of the side aisles, where their deft placement obviated potential construction problems. In the curving portion of the ambulatory, for example, the architect used six columns in the arcade, eleven in the middle row, and fourteen to support the vault springs along the outer wall. This produced a network of perfectly aligned support spans defining triangular vault cells carried along the axis of the arcade by lancet arches and elsewhere by ribs. By and large, this design solved the problems posed by vaulting a curved space, but some awkwardness persisted in the initial vaults. This is most obvious in the first columns of the central row both north and south, whose diameters were reduced still further and whose capitals have square instead of chamfered corners and bases (see pages 68–69).

To underscore the distinction between the choir, reserved for the canons and their stalls, and the apse proper, the architect spanned the first area with two roughly square sexpartite vault units and the second with an octopartite vault radiating from a keystone situated immediately above the main altar (see page 70). He also took pains to downplay the alternation of the vault-spring

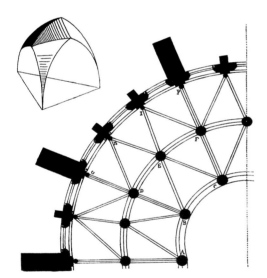

The Master of 1160 had to confront the same problem as the Master of Saint-Denis: how to vault a double ambulatory. His task was facilitated by the absence of radial chapels. The solution he devised was based largely on the use of aligned diagonal ribs. (Reconstructed plan by Eugène Viollet-le-Duc.)

Opposite:
The ambulatory had to surround the apse and the choir, which originally featured four-level elevations.

The Cathedral of Maurice de Sully

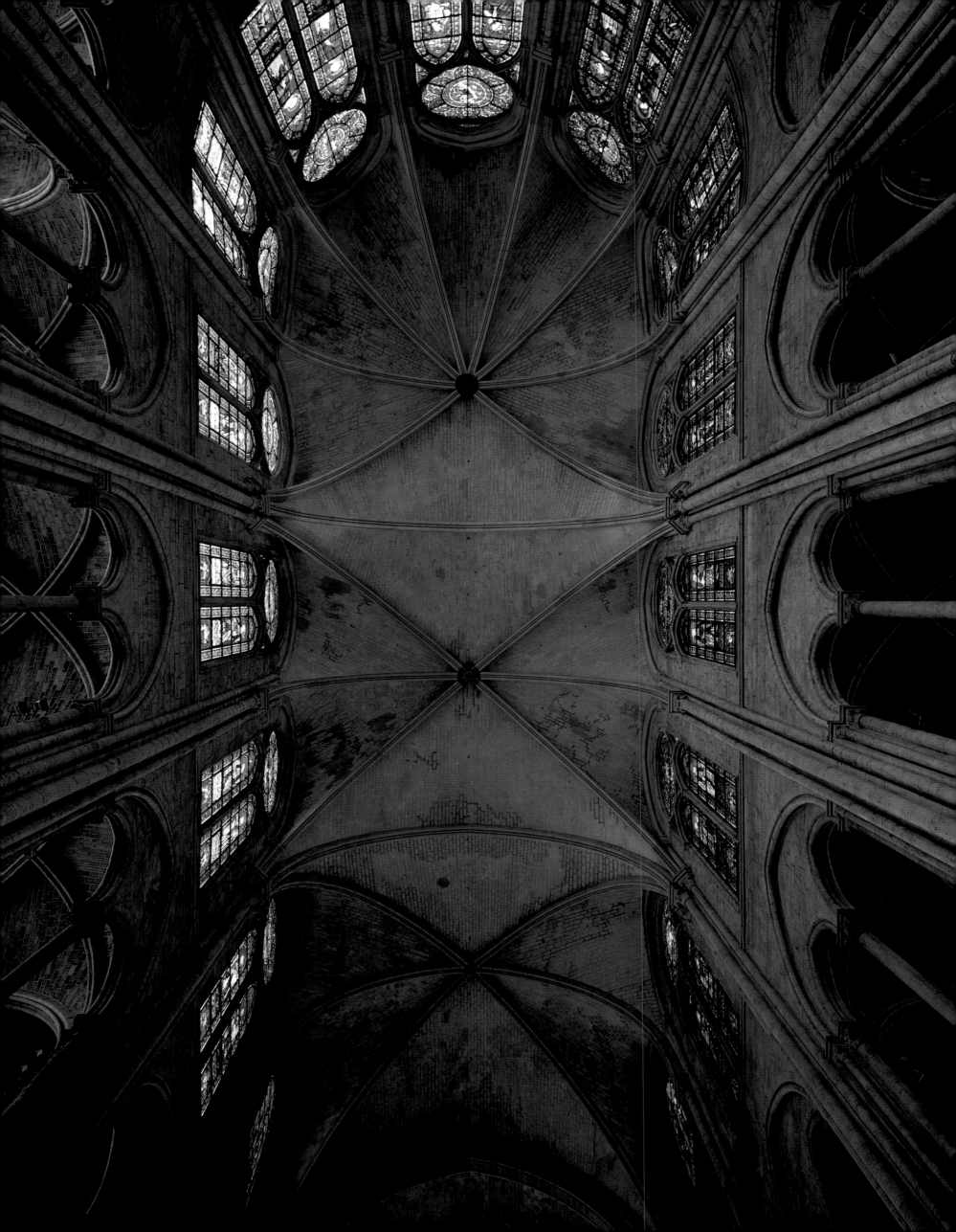

Pages 68–69:
It was essential to accentuate the turning dynamic of the ambulatory, as well as to set it apart from the apse.

Opposite:
The vaults of the apse and choir rise to a height of almost 107 feet, quite a technical feat at the time. It would be half a century before a height of 157 feet was attained.

Left:
In the thirteenth century, the original four-level elevation was changed to one with three levels, but in the nineteenth century the original design was restored in the first bay of the choir.

Technical virtuosity manifested itself
not only in the structural armature of
the chevet but also in lesser details, for
example, the use of slender colonnettes
en délit in the center of each double
arcade of the tribune.

configurations: from their bases just above the capitals of the arcade, their supports consist of
identical units of three attached colonnettes, with the central one projecting farther from the
wall than its companions in the cluster; only at the level of the springs does the use of alternation
finally manifest itself. In the complex springs, the single transverse rib and two diagonal ribs
each rise from a discreet capital, but the lateral ones do double duty, the adjacent wall arches
being provided with diminutive colonnettes that also rise from their abacuses; the intervening
springs, by contrast, need accommodate only a single transverse rib, so the lateral colonnettes of
each support cluster here rise unimpeded to the springs of the mural arches.

The architect treated the tribune of the choir with particular care, despite its relative inaccessibility (it could be reached only via two narrow spiral stairs). It is surprisingly spacious, being

The Cathedral of Maurice de Sully

more than nineteen feet wide and more than twenty-five feet high below the keystones of the vaults. Each bay overlooks the choir through a double arcade inscribed within a lancet arch; the latter are flanked by massive composite supports, with a colonnette *en délit* serving as the central support of each double arcade. The vault system is consistent with that used on the main level, featuring quadripartite units in the rectangular bays and trapezoidal ones in the curving bays of the apse. The initial form of the outer windows is more problematic, for those of the apse were recast around 1300 and those in the rectangular bays were abusively restored in the nineteenth century. Guidance is provided, however, by a drawing, dated April 18, 1849, that represents a window of small dimensions with unadorned jambs topped by a massive double keystone supported by intramural haunches; another drawing from the same period records traces left by the

The spaciousness of the tribune overlooking the choir and the apse prompts questions about its intended use, as well as about the extent to which its windows were enlarged at the beginning of the fourteenth century.

The tribune windows were initially shorter and narrower than they are today. Their openings were spanned by curious configurations of two stone slabs. In the thirteenth century, the eaves above the tribune vaults were lowered to accommodate longer clerestory windows, the original ones having been deemed too short. (Viollet-le-Duc and Jean-Baptiste Lassus, drawing of tribune window, dated April 1, 1849, and drawing of traces left by original sloped tribune roof, dated January 28, 1843. [C.N.M.H.S.])

Opposite:
The architect used the same elevations in the transepts as in the choir, replete with tribunes overlooking them from both their eastern and their western sides. These sides were initially linked by a passage—perhaps open, perhaps enclosed—that was removed when the transepts were extended.

original tribune roof: precious evidence, for its placement suggests that this was indeed the design of the twelfth-century windows. There is nothing remarkable about their small dimensions, but their double-keystone spans are surprising.

Restoration of the original third level of the elevation, suppressed in the first third of the thirteenth century, is equally delicate. We now know that Eugène Viollet-le-Duc's "restoration" of the original interior elevation in the bays next to the crossing is inaccurate. Recent examination of fragments discovered in the mid-nineteenth century indicates that both the design and the precise placement of the rose oculi were different. The network of tracery within these openings was denser and more substantial, presumably because wall piercings in this area could easily have compromised the structural integrity of the masonry.

Successive modifications to the chevet—effected first in the thirteenth century, then around 1300, and finally in the mid-nineteenth century—make it necessary to exercise special prudence here. The course of the original outer wall is easily determined, but its elevation requires close attention. The windows must have been relatively small, with the form of the engaged supports reflecting the configuration of the vault springs above and the size of the corresponding exterior buttresses. There must have been alternation, for, of necessity, the supports transversely aligned with the arcade supports would have been larger than those supporting the subsidiary vault springs. Reconstruction of the sloped roof protecting the outer aisle of the choir and the ambulatory is easy, thanks to the 1849 drawing; the course of the tribune roof is revealed by the surviving window, whose structural idiosyncrasies have already been noted. As for the roofing of the center aisle, its configuration remains unknown, its entire frame having been rebuilt in the thirteenth century with new wood, at the same time as the walls of the clerestory were reconfigured.

The most vexing question is that of the chevet's original buttressing system. Until recently, it was agreed that there were no flying buttresses in the original design. This view has now been challenged, along with analogous views concerning other contemporary buildings. For technical reasons, many specialists find it difficult to believe that such supports could have been absent from Gothic architecture's beginnings. But such generalizations are dangerous and should be avoided. The specifics of each building are different, and the use of flying buttresses during the style's early phase cannot be taken for granted. Judging from the precarious state of the Gothic monuments in the eighteenth and nineteenth centuries, their structural advantages are dubious at best.

With regard to Notre-Dame, no evidence pertaining to the twelfth-century buttressing system survives. The extant structure and the documents, both early ones and those dating from Viollet-le-Duc's restoration campaign, are alike mute on this point.

This leaves the field open for hypothesis. Conceivably, flying buttresses could have spanned the outer aisle and ambulatory and come to rest against the tribune wall, thereby providing reinforcement for the vault of the center aisle. But the absence of any trace of such structures is troubling; furthermore, the small size of the buttresses in the tribune and the center aisle—which date from the twelfth century—is inconsistent with such a theory. Designed to stabilize the wall masonry, they would have been insufficient to support such elements. More tellingly, we know that the eastern walls of the two transepts, intended from the beginning to receive sexpartite vaults, were never provided with flying buttresses, for their exterior buttresses begin to taper short of the clerestory gutter. This is a clear indication that the transept vaults, whose in fact minimal outward thrust equalled that of the nave vaults, required nothing exceptional in the way of exterior reinforcement. The same approach must have been used in the rectangular bays alongside the choir as well as in the chevet. It has been suggested that flying buttresses may have been incorporated into the eaves of the tribune in alignment with its supports, a solution discovered in the mid-nineteenth century to have been used at Laon. This hypothesis is seductive, but there is not a trace of concrete evidence to support it.

A final observation concerning the original appearance of the chevet is in order: overreliance on comparison with other monuments is likely to result in misunderstandings. Different buildings

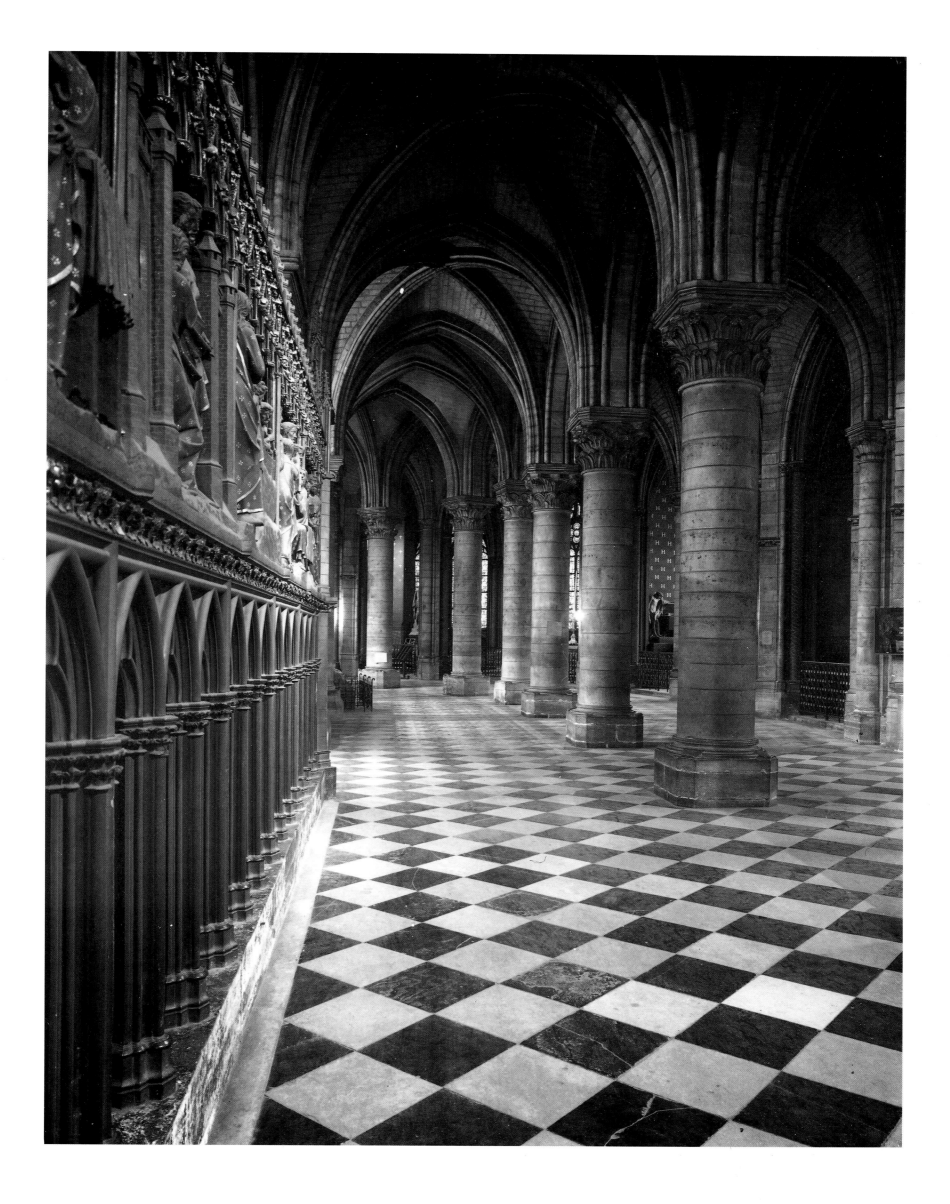

have different dimensions and structural peculiarities that necessitate the use of different building techniques. The walls at Sens, for example, are thick and heavy, while those in Paris are thin and exceptionally well crafted.

With this analysis behind us, we are better placed to assess the personality of the conceiving architect. It can be neatly summed up as follows: ambition, technical acumen, clarity, and serenity. Admittedly, the first of these qualities is not his alone, it having originated with the commissioning bishop, but our architect was happy to share in it. He had the audacity to devise and realize the largest and highest building yet erected within an urban framework. This structure had to be larger than the one it replaced. The widths of the two façades were comparable (131 feet versus 118 feet), but the length of the new building considerably exceeded that of the old (397 feet versus 263). The ancient cathedral's five-aisle plan inspired that of the new structure, but the latter's height of 108 feet placed it in a different class altogether from its predecessor and even set it apart from contemporary cathedrals at Sens (eighty feet), Noyon (seventy-one feet), Laon (eighty-five feet), and Poitiers (ninety-seven feet). Only a generation later, after some thirty years had passed, were higher vaults realized at Bourges (123 feet) and Chartres (121 feet).

His technical acumen, too, must be stressed, even if his immediate successor was still more remarkable in this regard. He knew stone: how to select it, how to choose the proper placement for it, and how best to build with it. He managed to surmount the difficulties entailed by constructing such an edifice on unstable or marshy ground. He made marvelous use of Gothic building techniques to minimize the structural armature. The table of figures pertaining to various monuments prepared by Antoine Rondelet in the early nineteenth century—designed to facilitate comparison of their respective wall areas, structural supports, and surface areas—is illuminating. Notre-Dame is revealed to have a most impressive ratio, with only 14 percent of its 59,000 square feet occupied by supports. It is surpassed in this regard only by the Constantinian basilicas, which, it must be remembered, were not vaulted but were covered by wood-frame roofs. The ratios for other famous structures are: Hagia Sophia, 22 percent of 103,000 square feet; the Pantheon, 15 percent of 60,000 square feet; dome of the Hôtel des Invalides, 27 percent of 29,000 square feet. Better ratios were to be obtained only after the advent of metal construction in the nineteenth century and of reinforced concrete in the twentieth. At no time in the previous history of architecture had voids triumphed so decisively over solids.

In formulating his design, the architect must have been doubly inspired: by the monument that he was in the process of destroying, but which he could still admire, and by the competitive Gothic dynamic to which he himself contributed. The buildings he sought to rival, and hopefully surpass, were, first and unavoidably, Saint-Denis such as Abbot Suger had left it at his death and before the alterations that began in 1231, then the Cathedral of Laon, which was contemporary with his own. Both architects used four-level elevations, a solution adopted previously, in 1145–50, by the Master of Noyon, where the third level is articulated by a purely decorative arcade intended to hide an otherwise bare stretch of wall. But in Paris the architect eschewed effects of the kind found in Noyon and Laon, for his use of very thin walls precluded narrow passages within the masonry and concomitant "baroque" gestures. Likewise, he did not manipulate the plane of the window wall by drawing it inward or expelling it outward, as was attempted in the transept at Noyon. He renounced the illusionistic devices that triumph there, as well as in Saint-Remi at Reims and in the southern transept at Soissons. In the design of the Master of Paris, the interior and exterior envelopes were one. The only liberty he permitted himself was the rose oculi piercing the wall at the level of the tribune eaves, whose role was purely aesthetic. Animating an area that otherwise would have been bare, they hinted at depths beyond, striking a note that would have been particularly welcome in so resolutely planar a design.

The architect of Notre-Dame strove to rival that of Saint-Denis in his liberation of interior volume. In both cases, the double ambulatories were conceived as integral spaces, with the disruptive effect of their intermediary supports being downplayed as much as possible. At Saint-

Page 76:
Reconstruction of the original outer wall makes it easier to grasp the design of the Master of 1160. He was clearly at pains to maximize the curving dynamic of the ambulatory.

Page 77:
The turn commences at the end of a sequence of rectangular bays parallel to the choir.

The Cathedral of Maurice de Sully

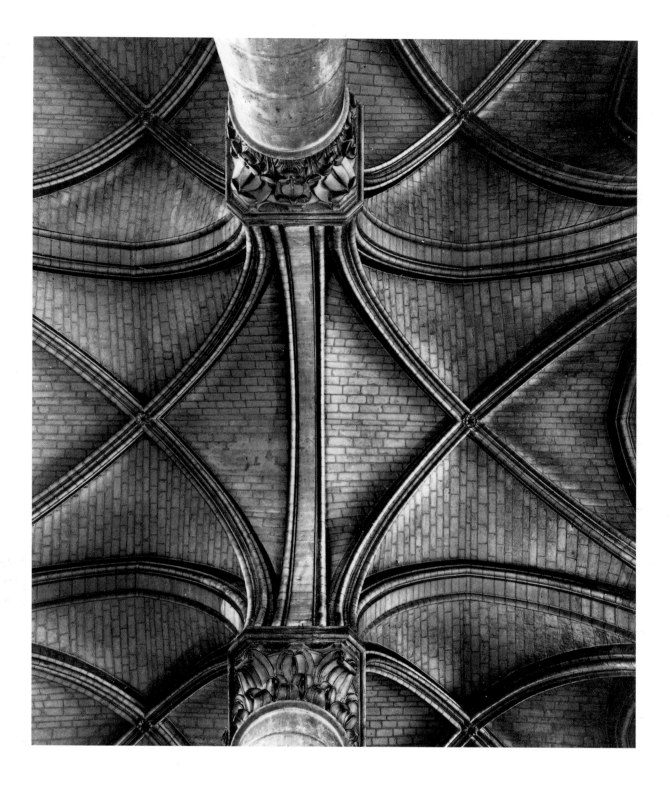

Denis, realization of this goal was facilitated by the use of slender columns *en délit,* but in Paris this solution was precluded by the weight of the tribune, which would have crushed such supports. Drum columns were used instead, but they are exceptionally elegant due to their superb proportions as well as to the designs of their bases and capitals. Vaults of identical height in the two aisles were deemed essential in both ambulatories. What most distinguished the two chevets was the presence of radial chapels at Saint-Denis as opposed to their absence in Paris, where the mural integrity of the outer envelope was uncompromised. An exercise of the imagination is required to grasp the beauty of the original volume, which was more brightly illuminated than at present, with light filtered through stained glass. The tribune repeats the curvature of the main floor but its volume is unimpeded, for it has only a single aisle. One cannot help but respond to the formal perfection of this space.

The Master of 1160 differed from his contemporaries in his decided preference for planar elevations. He minimized the relief projection of load-bearing trabeations. He thus produced a subtle shift in visual dynamics that favored verticals over horizontals, which were downplayed to such an extent as to become virtually invisible. The result has a serenity quite distinct from the

As in the ambulatory, the architect vaulted the two pairs of aisles flanking the choir at the same height.

The Cathedral of Maurice de Sully

In his design of the exterior of the chevet, the Master of 1160 sought to underscore the independence of the superimposed outer envelopes: they are distinct and successively stepped back.

Opposite:
As always in Gothic buildings, the vaults were the last elements to be built. Thus it was the second master who realized the vaults of the transept crossing, the choir, the transept, and the nave.

Page 82:
The second master's genius is most apparent in his liberation of the interior space. To this end, he abandoned his predecessor's design for the piers of the crossing, which relied on bundled colonnettes visible in the eastern pair, in favor of a more compact unit featuring pilasters, realized in the western pair.

Page 83:
This planar approach, with its singular use of pilasters, is also evident in the western elevations of the transept.

baroque exuberance of Laon, an impression reinforced by the relative heights of the various levels: in round numbers, thirty-nine feet for the arcade, twenty-six feet for the tribune, and thirty-nine feet again for the unit comprised by the two upper levels. This carefully gauged effect of equilibrium minimizes the building's gigantism.

Originally, the chevet must have produced an impression of serene calm. While the architect sought to integrate the interior spaces, he chose to individualize the exterior masses. The transept arms did not protrude, but the handling of their terminals and roofing gave them a strong presence. The three rounded envelopes, distinct and successively stepped back, abutted this transverse aisle. Here verticals were downplayed in favor of horizontals. The roofs reinforced this double movement, accompanying the turn, underscoring it, and establishing a link between the masses. The color of the roofing—it was lead—must have contrasted violently with the beautiful blond stone of the Île-de-France. The dark window piercings—relatively small for so large a building—added visual interest to this rigorous design, from which all decorative elements were banished. The one exception to this rule was the outer wall of the central aisle, where the windows and gutter level were adorned with geometric motifs meant to stress the presence of the apse immediately below.

Here again, the beauty of the chevet resulted from the harmonious proportions of its masses, not only their relative heights and setbacks but, above all, their superbly gauged curves. The light of the Île-de-France must have glided freely over the bare walls, punctuated at regular intervals by discreetly protruding buttresses. An arresting spectacle indeed for anyone who, around 1180, traveled down the Seine and suddenly came upon this powerful, proud mass standing out against an ever-moving sky.

The Second Master

Sometime during the 1170s, probably around 1177, the first master was succeeded by a new architect, likewise of unknown identity, who apparently continued the work without a break. For nothing suggests that there was a hiatus: construction seems to have continued at the pace established

over the previous twenty years. While adhering in broad outline to the design of the first architect, the second one proposed significant modifications that were accepted by Maurice de Sully. The initial plan was retained, as was the four-level elevation. His interventions manifested themselves in terms of construction technique, spatial conception, and style. They first appeared in the eastern tribune of the southern transept and continued in bays four through eight of the nave. He also realized the two sexpartite vaults of the choir, those of the transept, and the two eastern vaults of the nave.

It fell to him, then, to erect the transept terminals designed by his predecessor. The above-mentioned modifications to the southern tribune also appear in the western elevation, consistent with that of the nave. The original design of the northern and southern transept walls is unknown, for they were rebuilt in the thirteenth century. Doubtless they featured doors affording the bishop and the canons access to the building's interior; in the course of work on the foundations of the

The second master was exceptionally attentive to detail, as evidenced by the contrasting designs he adopted for supports of the main arcade and the side aisles.

Opposite:
The second master honored his predecessor's intention to employ uniform supports in the nave arcade, but he opted to abandon his use of alternation in the design of the vault-spring supports.

Pages 84–85:
The second master's use of pilasters made it possible for him to create a more spacious effect in the nave tribune, an impression accentuated by his introduction of triple arcades.

The Cathedral of Maurice de Sully

northern arm, Viollet-le-Duc even claimed to have discovered several carved fragments that, in his view, pointed to the existence of an early sculpted portal. The upper portions of these walls were probably pierced by rose windows, a practice increasingly widespread at the time. The presence in the current southern rose window of nine circular compositions treating the legend of Saint Matthew and datable to the period of the construction of the transept lends support to this theory. They are generally thought to have been reincorporated by the master glazier Brice in the eighteenth century, in the course of work initiated by Cardinal de Noailles, but they could just as well have been removed and reinstalled by Pierre de Montreuil in the mid-thirteenth century.

The first master sought to unify the interior volume by reducing the ground area occupied by supports, a project facilitated by the use of thin walls. His successor took this spatial experiment still further, reducing the size of the supports even more. He was able to do this thanks to his even more meticulous selection of stone. For the western piers of the transept, he used thick slabs of clicquart; for the columns of the center aisle, blocks of Bagneux stone. He gained floor space by making pervasive use of pilasters instead of engaged columns in the crossing and in the tribune arcade, as well as by minimizing the projection of the engaged supports along the outer walls. From a technical perspective, his treatment of the piers of the crossing is especially impressive. The design of the two eastern piers, with their projecting engaged columns, gave way in their western counterparts to one consisting of immense, bluntly profiled pilasters some seventy-nine feet high. He opted not to articulate the vault ribs below their springs, a decision that, in addition to producing a net gain in floor space, enlarged the openings of both the center aisle and the transept. In this way he maximized the thinness of the supports in relation to the load they carried to the maximum extent permitted by Gothic construction methods. At the same time, he modified the aesthetic profile of the building by using what was in effect a colossal order (see pages 81–83).

He extended the use of pilasters into the western walls of both transept arms, complementing them either with flanking colonnettes *en délit,* between the side aisles, or with engaged drum colonnettes, in the outer corners (see pages 160–61). He also used pilasters throughout the tribune arcade in the form of planar cruciform supports, articulating the vault springs only on their inner surfaces, with bundles of three engaged colonnettes *en délit*. This facilitated his replacement of the double arcade used in the choir with a triple one whose central opening is slightly higher than those flanking it (see pages 84–85). The liberation of space is just as apparent in the outer side aisle, where, to minimize relief projection, he aligned the colonnettes flush against the plane behind them and fused their bases and capitals, blurring their distinct identities.

Just as he generalized the use of pilasters, the second master made more pervasive use of *en délit* colonnettes. He had them carved out of soft limestone, in exceptionally long pieces, and used metal tenons to secure their superimposed, attenuated cylinders to the adjacent masonry. Examples of this technique are found on the western face of the transept arms; in the side aisles, along their outer walls as well as in their alternating central supports; below the springs of the tribune vaults; and below those of the center aisle. In the latter instance, they rise without interruption in groups of three from the abacuses of the main arcade to the vault springs; all are of like diameter, but each central colonnette projects slightly beyond its two companions, resting against a thin buttress hidden behind it. Despite the architect's continued use of sexpartite vaults, he chose to suppress all traces of the alternation still visible to the east (see pages 91–93).

By contrast, this principle is embraced in the center supports of the parallel quadripartite vaults of the side aisles, where simple drum columns alternate with other, thinner ones surrounded by twelve colonnettes of identical diameter and height. Here the alternation is purely aesthetic; it can have no structural justification, for *en délit* colonnettes collapse when made to bear more than minimal weight. The architect took particular care to avoid this possibility by reinforcing the bases and culminating elements of these units. To the same end, he also fused their capitals and abacuses and fixed them securely to the drum columns within.

Opposite:
The second master used assertive alternation in the side-aisle supports. This was a purely aesthetic decision, there being no structural justification for it. The effect is striking.

The Cathedral of Maurice de Sully

The second master's obligation to honor the broad outlines of the original scheme in the interest of homogeneity was especially binding in the central aisle. Thus he retained the four-level elevation, restored by Viollet-le-Duc in the final bay of the nave.

Pages 92–93:
Most important, the architect retained the rhythms of the large arcade.

As with the chevet, many questions about the nave have yet to find satisfying answers. The second master retained the four-level elevation, but he altered the design of the rose oculi, giving their tracery a more curvilinear pattern. The original form of the outer windows of the tribune remains problematic. The present ones were designed by Viollet-le-Duc, who had nothing to guide him. Documents predating the nineteenth-century restoration indicate a form rather close to that used in the chevet, while a more elaborate design would be expected from such an architect. Then there is the question of the original covering of the tribune. Viollet-le-Duc hypothesized that the outer portions of its vaults were originally elevated to accommodate higher windows and provide more light, a configuration that the architect did not hesitate to "restore" in the first bay. The result is scarcely convincing, the gain in illumination being insignificant. Furthermore, analysis of the masonry provides no indication as to the date of these sections of the vaults.

The flying buttresses pose another problem. Those that survive do not predate the thirteenth century and were substantially reworked in the nineteenth century. The surviving masonry provides no trace of the original flying buttresses. Pertinent documents, notably a precious drawing by Jean-Baptiste Lassus and Viollet-le-Duc dated January 28, 1843, make it possible to reconstruct the slope of the tribune eaves but offer no further guidance. Since Viollet-le-Duc, the existence of flying buttresses has generally been accepted, but none of the arguments advanced in support of this view carries conviction. Most prominent among them is the principle of alternation operative in the side-aisle supports, but, as already noted, this was the result of a purely aesthetic decision. Surely the architect's intention to adhere to the original interior design in the interest of consistency would have likewise influenced his handling of the exterior masses. The absence of flying buttresses in the chevet would preclude their having been used to support the nave.

Although he respected the original scheme, the second master introduced modifications that considerably refined it from an aesthetic perspective. They were made possible by a technical mastery mobilized to advance a unified vision. The result was a new approach to space, despite the fact that consistency with the chevet made improvement of the interior illumination to any substantial degree impossible. The new approach found its freest expression in the side aisles and the tribune, where the enhanced effect of spaciousness is striking. This is especially true in the nave tribune, as becomes clear when it is compared with that of the choir. Its ample volumes open onto the center aisle virtually unimpeded, offering views up and down the building's main axis of a kind impossible from the eastern tribune. The effect is subtler in the side aisles of the nave due to the alternating design of the central supports, absent in the side aisles of the choir. It is difficult to assess the impression originally produced by the resulting rhythms, for the subsequent construction of lateral chapels distanced the windows, thereby attenuating the light.

This new spatial conception is linked to the enhanced verticality produced by the use of pilasters and en délit stonework. As mentioned above, the former resulted in a kind of colossal order in the transept, but even in the tribune these elements produce a completely new dynamic, one further accentuated by the generalized use of the colonnettes. To be sure, these function as vertical counters to the regular horizontality of the drum columns and masonry courses. The results become clear when one compares the center aisle of the nave with that of the choir, an operation that reveals the degree to which the tension they introduce strengthens the coherence of the individual bays. The latter's integrity was still compromised by the use of two-bay, sexpartite vaults, which entailed discrepancies that the architect sought to temper.

The final contribution of the second master concerns the center aisle, whose design he profoundly modified by introducing triple instead of double arcade units on the second level of its elevation. This reduced the wall surfaces and added a new delicacy to their articulation. Moldings, bases, and capitals were all conceived with an eye to elegance, a quality clearly favored by this architect. While respecting the initial scheme, he strove to give the crossing and the nave a form more consistent with contemporary developments. Like his predecessor, he avoided illusionism and favored thin walls, but he took full advantage of the subtle effects made possible by

Above:
The fourth architect introduced an
important modification into the scheme
of 1160: he abandoned the previously
uniform design of the grand arcade
supports in favor of more complex ones.
But he took care to ease the transition,
using an intermediate design with only
one engaged column before introducing,
in the westernmost support, a design
with four engaged columns reminiscent
of a model used at Chartres.

en délit stonework. Even today, his adaptive intelligence continues to astound, revealing that such a gift need not be incompatible with creative genius of the first order.

THE THIRD ARCHITECT

The second architect must have died around 1200, when a decision was made to abandon momentarily construction of the nave in favor of commencing the facade block. The absence of documentation pertaining to this phase is virtually complete, making it difficult to establish a reliable chronology: the only evidence is provided by stylistic analysis, which is notoriously subjective. As was customary, the new architect would have begun by laying the foundations of the block's outer walls. Then he would have erected the supports, buttresses, and piers, completing the structure as high as the balustrade surmounting the Gallery of Kings. Thereafter, he set about linking the block with the nave, beginning with the exterior envelope. Here, however, he made a striking departure, abandoning the second master's pronounced taste for planar elevations in his treatment of the supports along the outer walls. He made the central colonnettes, still *en délit,* project slightly more than their two companions, and he made their respective bases and capitals more distinct from one another. This new approach, introduced in the bay abutting the facade block,

was continued through the two first bays of the nave. The new architect, too, favored *en délit* stonework, which figures prominently in the Portal of the Virgin. Its first level consists of an arcade of niches, whose rear planes are composed of thin stone slabs featuring engraved motifs of exceptional elegance (see page 111). This technique recurs in the Gallery of Kings, where the quality of the stonework is especially high.

Pages 96–97:
The modifications introduced by the fourth architect had no effect on the vaults. A sexpartite configuration was retained to assure the nave's homogeneity.

THE FOURTH ARCHITECT

The third architect must have died during construction of the facade (see pages 6, 156). His technique and style are recognizable as far as the Gallery of Kings. Thus it must have been around 1210–20 that a new architect was chosen and proceeded with the work. He built the intermediary supports below the towers, the chambers in these towers, and the level of the rose window. And he finally joined the facade block to the nave, which had been left incomplete many years earlier. He erected the two first supports, at least the three westernmost arcades, and four clerestory windows. The vaulting of these bays, however, was left to his successor.

The fourth architect also retained the four-level elevation, but he introduced modifications so substantial that, for the first time, there was a marked rupture with the scheme of 1160. First,

The Cathedral of Maurice de Sully

Pages 98–99:
The vaulting of the tower chambers presented special problems. The third architect managed the tour de force of giving the southern chamber a beautiful volume as well as ample illumination. This was made possible by his decision to shift most of the load-bearing masonry to the ground floor, entailing the use there of relatively massive walls.

Opposite and above:
By the nineteenth century, the western rose window—already glazed several times—was in such poor condition that most of it had to be either restored or replaced. Some of the surviving fragments dated from the beginning of the thirteenth century, for example, the month of February, represented by two fish (for the astrological sign Pisces), and this figure of a prophet, a rare example of a classicizing style also found in the cathedral's facade sculpture.

The Cathedral of Maurice de Sully

he abandoned one of Notre-Dame's most characteristic features, the uniform design of the grand arcade supports, in favor of a more complex design closer to the pattern established at Chartres, but he took care to ease the transition so that the change would not manifest itself with undue suddenness. He added a single engaged column to the interior face of the second support from the west, introducing a design featuring four engaged columns only in the first support. Second, he abandoned the use of *en délit* stonework: the three colonnettes rising from the abacus of the first support are coursed. This preference is manifest throughout his work, in the tower chambers as well as in the masonry level with the rose window. Doubtless he envisioned further modifications that were never realized. The first arcade support with its four engaged columns receives a subsidiary vault spring, launching only a transverse rib and the lancets of the clerestory wall, whereas its complexity leads one to expect a strong spring. As for the second arcade support, its engaged column and additional capital are in fact useless. Very likely the fourth architect, aware of recent developments exemplified by Chartres, had planned to cover the first two bays with rectangular quadripartite vaults. If so, his successor must have deemed this radical plan unduly compromising to the building's homogeneity and so renounced it.

The fourth architect's interventions in the facade block, where he was accorded greater freedom than in the nave, are more convincing. The upper chambers of the two towers are striking: their volumes and the plastic quality of their wall treatments create an effect of great beauty (see page 98). The most spectacular success here is the spiral stair that originally led to the eaves of the tribune, which is encased in an openwork masonry cage. The stonework at the level of the rose window, which also dates from his tenure, is of comparable quality. He must have introduced modifications into the original design that we can no longer judge. He rejected the initial scheme for the openwork gallery that surmounted the Gallery of Kings in favor of a more elegant design, removed by Viollet-le-Duc during his restoration, when one based on traces of the original balustrade remaining on the outer buttresses was substituted (for the fourth architect's design, see page 212). His conception of the wall is most readily apparent at the level of the rose window, where he boldly challenged its integrity by piercing the largest possible rose as well as pairs of lancet windows in the towers, decorating the spandrels above with shallow inset trilobes. In this way he created a subtle interplay of levels of depth without resorting to dramatic effects of the kind favored by the master of Laon. Even so, it must be said that he was the first architect of Notre-Dame to manifest such a strong interest in wall treatments.

If the fourth architect renounced *en délit* in favor of coursed masonry for aesthetic reasons, he nonetheless displayed considerable mastery in his handling of stonework. He made widespread use of upright slabs, with which he achieved remarkable effects. The rear planes of the six trilobes of the facade, for example, are composed of nine pie-slice slabs that come together in the center of each lobe. The original balustrade above the Gallery of Kings as well as the masonry cages of the spiral stairs in the two tower chambers were likewise composed of vertical slabs carved so as to create openwork screens. This is a purely decorative technique, for such stonework collapses when made to bear heavy loads, which explains its prevalence in balustrades, as well as the need to use coursed masonry in the rear plane of the blind rosettes between each pair of lancets flanking the rose window.

This same technical mastery is evident in the tracery of the rose window, which Viollet-le-Duc re-created in its original configuration. Thirty-one and a half feet in diameter, its rays radiate from a central oculus to define first twelve, then twenty-four compartments. It was carved from clicquart stone, an excellent material that made possible its extraordinary delicacy. Viollet-le-Duc even maintained that, with a solid-void ratio of 42 percent, it was the lightest window ever realized.

The fourth architect made exemplary use of vertically disposed stone slabs. The stair of the southern tower, with its delicately carved masonry cage, is a fine example.

The Cathedral of Maurice de Sully

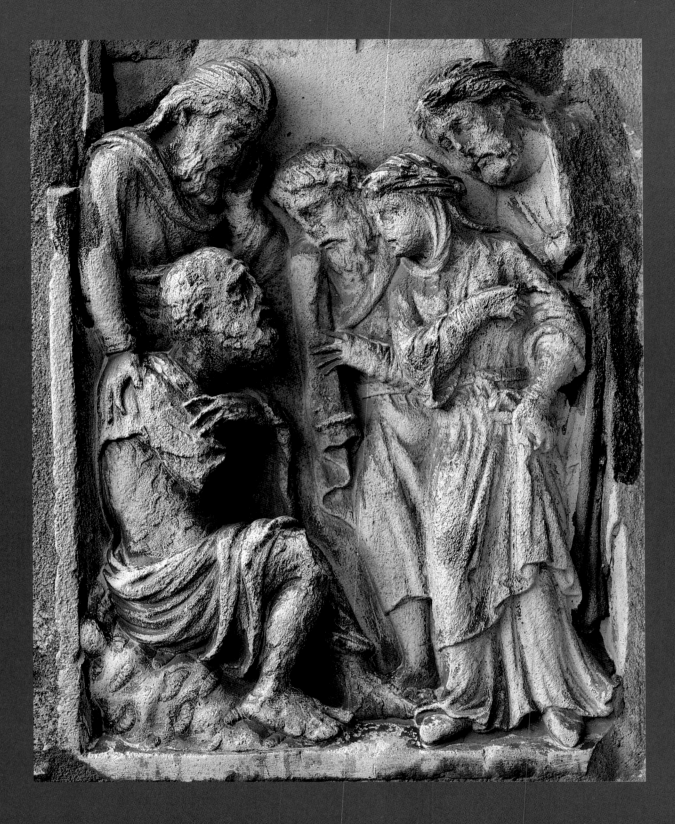

The Temple of the New Covenant

While formulating the architectural design of the Gothic cathedral that so unsettled the city's religious quarter, Bishop Maurice de Sully also elaborated a program for the sculpture to appear on the western facade. Knowing as we do the importance he attached to religious instruction, he must have taken great care with it. This program was intended to give the cathedral its larger significance. Unfortunately, it is impossible for us even to guess at the original conception, much less reconstruct it in full, so great were the changes wrought in western Christendom between 1160, when it was initially formulated, and 1200, when its realization began. Approaches to temples of the New Covenant had evolved. Along with parallel stylistic evolution, one of the major developments of this short period was a humanization of Christian iconography, which of necessity entailed a thematic recasting. At the moment when the facade of Notre-Dame was being built, a program conceived along lines similar to those used in the Royal Portal at Chartres in 1145–55 would no longer have been considered viable. The lateral portals at Chartres bear witness to the radical shifts that had taken place in the course of a mere half century. Hence the subjects treated on the western facade in Paris cannot belong to the program of 1160: the Last Judgment iconography cannot predate the early thirteenth century, the Coronation of the Virgin made its first appearance at Senlis roughly in the 1160s, and the cult of the mother of the Virgin, Saint Anne, became widespread only in the early thirteenth century. As for the gallery of the kings of Judah, the one in Paris was the earliest example. The program as realized was given its definitive form during the episcopacy of Eudes de Sully.

ICONOGRAPHY

As integrally recast, the program was something of a visual manifesto, and a grandiose one at that. It reiterated the building's prior dedication to the Virgin, but in altered terms. The reincorporation of one of the old portals—executed more than fifty years before—was consistent with this intention: although in large part retained, it was rededicated to Saint Anne. The northern portal, however, was devoted in its entirety to the Virgin, focusing on an image of her Coronation. She also figures in the Last Judgment of the central portal, where she intercedes with the Sovereign Judge. It is her ancestors who are depicted above, in the guise of the kings of the line of David. Finally, and perhaps most significantly, her central importance is conveyed by a group, reintroduced by Eugène Viollet-le-Duc and situated above this gallery, consisting of the Virgin and Child flanked by two angels. Facing the city on axis with the rue Neuve Notre-Dame, this figure both offers her protection to the faithful and invites them to enter the Temple of the New Covenant.

Opposite:
The original placement of this small relief representing Job on the Dung Heap is unknown. It is one of four, similar in style and format, set into the buttresses flanking the central portal at an undetermined date; this one is on the southern flank of the buttress to the portal's north. They are the earliest surviving sculpture in the cathedral.

Above:
The central portal of the western facade, devoted to the Last Judgment, was modified on two occasions, first around 1240 and then in the mid-nineteenth century. The composition is notable for its clarity of organization and its compelling rhythms. The iconography is easy to comprehend.

Right:
The tympanum depicts the Christ of the Second Coming. He displays the stigmata and is flanked by angels bearing the instruments of the Passion. The kneeling figures are the Virgin and Saint John, who intercede on behalf of humanity. The lower lintel is a nineteenth-century copy by Armand Toussaint.
Other nineteenth-century additions:
Trumeau: Christ by Adolphe-Victor Geoffroy-Dechaume.
Left jamb: Saint Peter by Louis-Joseph Daumas; Saint John by Louis-Eugène Bion; Saint Andrew by Taluet; Saint James the Less by Mirande; Saint Simeon by Alexis-Hippolite Fromanger; Saint Bartholomew by Geoffroy-Dechaume.
Right jamb: Saint Paul by Fromanger; Saint James the Major by Jean-Louis Chenillion; Saint Thomas by Prinsay; Saint Philip by Geoffroy-Dechaume; Saint Jude by Jacques-Eugène Caudron; Saint Matthew by Cavelier.

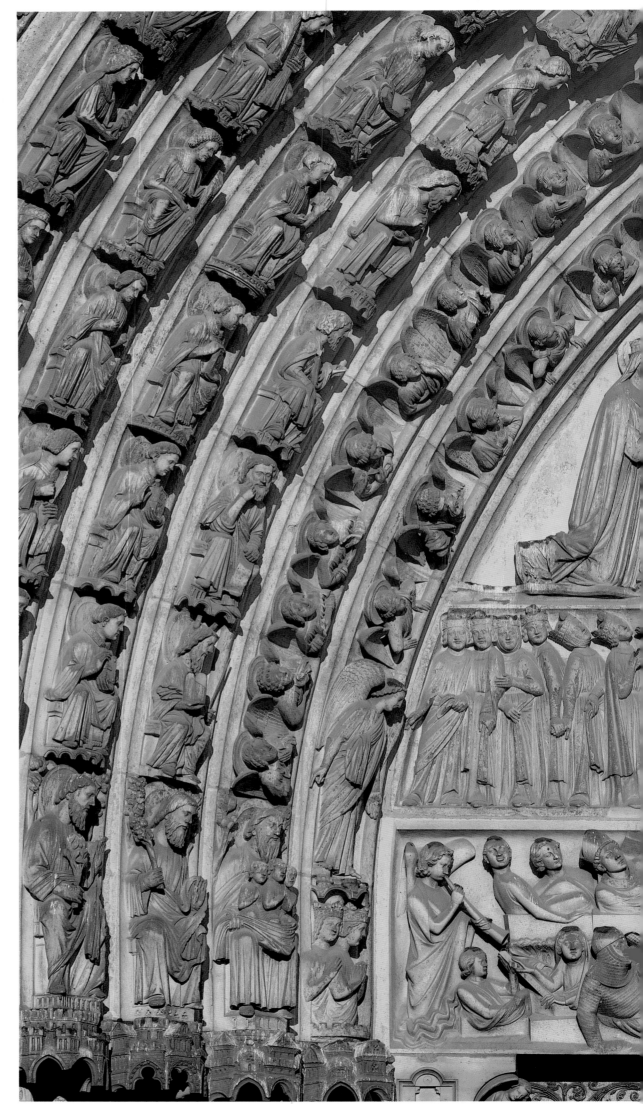

The Temple of the New Covenant

This immense ensemble took almost forty years to complete, but over that time span the conception remained unchanged. The iconographic program, then, must be analyzed as a whole, stylistic questions being reserved for subsequent discussion.

The iconography of the Last Judgment received what was long to remain its standard formulation in the southern portal at Chartres, but a refinement was introduced in Paris that guaranteed its success and was rapidly adopted elsewhere. It was determined primarily by the patrons' commitment to the principle of clarity. Anecdote was banished to facilitate immediate apprehension of the basic message. For some time, the announcement of the end of time and Christ's return to earth had been treated not as an apocalyptic vision but in more human terms inspired by the Gospel of Matthew. The preceding days of terror are evoked here only by the two horsemen of the Apocalypse in the archivolts (second and sixth archivolts, first row to the right). In the tympanum, Christ appears as the Redeemer displaying his wounds, flanked by two angels bearing the instruments of the Passion. The Virgin and Saint John intercede for humanity, in the name of his suffering. The lower lintel (replaced by a copy in the nineteenth century) represents the Resurrection of the Dead; above it is the Last Judgment proper (its central portion an approximate copy; see below) over which presides the Archangel Michael. The elect proceed to his right (our left) toward Abraham, depicted in the second archivolt, first row to the left; the damned to his left (our right), into the mouth of Hell. Bust-length angels observe the scene from the first two archivolts. They are succeeded in the third by seated patriarchs and prophets, including Moses and Aaron, while the outer archivolts are occupied by clerics holding books, martyrs carrying palms, and, finally, virgins. The central trumeau figure of Christ teaching is flanked by jamb figures of the apostles and, on the doorposts, smaller reliefs of the wise and foolish virgins. Below the apostles are personifications of Vices and Virtues. The latter, instead of being represented as warriors bearing lances to fend off the enemy, are now depicted as relatively calm seated figures (see also pages 116, 117, 119, 120, 145).

This Last Judgment, crisply focused on a clear opposition between Good and Evil, does not seek to frighten believers; its aims are legibility and tenderness. The Virgin and Saint John, seated on either side of the Redeemer at Chartres, here kneel humbly to further their cause. Apocalyptic imagery is reduced to the two archivolt groups, somewhat out of place among the adjacent ones evoking Hell. A humanizing intent is even more marked in the two rows of observing angel figures, which are individualized and whose placement violates celestial hierarchy. They all register undisguised amazement, leaning forward as if over a theater balcony to obtain a better view, their stupefaction manifesting itself in gestures and postures as various as they are expressive. The iconography of the Virtues and Vices is even more telling in this regard. Here the artists abandoned all hint of bellicose imagery, opting instead for readily identifiable scenes from everyday life. Despair is evoked by a suicide, Inconstancy by a monk tossing aside his frock. The Virtues are likewise readily identifiable, thanks to the symbols they bear: Faith carries a cross and Kindness the image of a lamb, while Fortitude wears a suit of armor.

Although certain subtleties remain elusive, the portal's basic import is easy to grasp. The goal was not so much to produce a striking effect as to convince. It carries conviction largely because of its accessibility. Its aspirations extend well beyond a bookish conception determined in its details by the New Testament and other texts to posit a subtler image-text relation taking fuller account of the power of the image. It is the latter that had the greatest impact on medieval man and woman, who lived in a world without the printing press. In that era, the language of images was both interpretively richer and easier to grasp than the written word. It could be understood on several levels, first on the most obvious one and then in terms of more erudite knowledge. Being subject to synthetic condensation, images were also richer insofar as they presented artists with opportunities to devise novel stylistic approaches to communication.

Basic compositional decisions clearly played an important role in the project to humanize the message. One need only compare this portal with those in Laon and Chartres, equally ambitious

The Temple of the New Covenant

Opposite:
In 1771, the trumeau, the central portions of both lintels, and the doorposts were removed to accommodate a larger, unimpeded doorway. This print after a drawing by Gilbert, published by Jean-Baptiste Lassus and Viollet-le-Duc as a frontispiece to their report on the cathedral (Musée Notre-Dame), gives some idea of the style of the Christ that, around the 1240s, replaced the original trumeau figure. The latter, nicknamed "the Faster," survived into the eighteenth century atop a fountain in the cathedral square (see pages 38, 41).

in their programs and close in date, to understand this point. Little would be gained by dwelling on that of Laon. The one in Chartres, despite its beauty, is much more confused than that in Paris. The latter is characterized by regular rhythms and an absence of anecdote that in no way compromises its monumentality. Such clarity cannot have been achieved easily; it must have been the result of prolonged study.

Nonetheless, the result lacks homogeneity, in technical as well as stylistic terms. The ensemble was modified sometime around the 1140s, but the extent of this campaign is difficult to determine in the wake of the mutilation effected by Jacques-Germain Soufflot in 1771, when the trumeau was removed along with most of the bottom lintel and the central portion of the upper one (see pages 210, 212). Close examination reveals that, in the tympanum, the nail-bearing angel and the Christ were added at a later date. This operation entailed modification of the Virgin and Saint John, which today tilt slightly forward, as well as of the cross-bearing angel, which had to be raised so that the horizontal bar of the cross would not hit the knee of Christ. In fact, this tympanum was completely dismantled and then ineptly remounted: the oblique figures were awkwardly installed and the resulting voids were filled with improvised blocks.

The lack of alignment between the jamb figures and the archivolts is also surprising. By the outermost archivolt, the discrepancy produced by this miscalculation attains almost a foot, which is considerable. When the spanner was remounted, it was necessary to recarve it and remove the canopies intended to protect the wise and foolish virgins; in effect, it had become indispensable to widen the span of the arch. The first row in the right archivolts has a special feature: archivolts three to six feature canopies carved from the same stone blocks, which entails superimposed canopies, for these features generally appear at the bottom of such blocks, where they serve to support the feet of the seated figures above. A similar error occurs on the left, in the fifth and sixth archivolts. Finally, the first archivolt to the right was recarved in its upper reaches because there was insufficient room to accommodate it. In the course of our stylistic analysis, we shall see that the right archivolts are in an idiom so different from the rest of the ensemble that they must be later in date.

Aside from the jamb figures, the Portal of the Coronation of the Virgin suffered little damage during the Revolution. (Engraving from Le Gentil de la Galaisière, "Mémoires sur l'origine du zodiaque . . .," *Mémoires de l'Académie des sciences,* 1785. Musée Notre-Dame.)

Porte de la Tour Septentrionale de l'Eglise de N.D. de Paris.
Dessinée pour indiquer la place (A.B.C.D) *ou se trouve le Zodiaque détaillé dans la Pl. Suivante*
Nᵃ *l'objet de cette Pl. étant de montrer le Zodiaque, on n'a point Dessiné les autres figures Scrupuleusement.*

Opposite:
The south portal of the western facade was conceived as a glorification of the Virgin, whose Coronation is represented in the tympanum. For the first time, saints of the diocese were included among the jamb figures.
Nineteenth-century additions:
Left jamb: Angel by Charles-Édouard Elmerich; Saint Denis by Geoffroy-Dechaume; Angel by Prinsay; Constantine by Chenillion.
Right jamb: Saint John the Baptist by Fromanger; Saint Stephen by Toussaint; Saint Genevieve by Michel Pascal; Saint Sylvester by Fromanger.

Evidence of a third kind provides further confirmation that the original portal was modified. An engraving of an eighteenth-century drawing predating Soufflot's 1771 modifications shows the Christ figure of the trumeau as well as the three prophets in relief below, seated in niches surmounted by crocketed gables and wearing robes with hooked folds; the latter differ so markedly from the corresponding Virtues below the jamb figures that there is also reason to suspect a partial recasting of the trumeau, now lost. By contrast, the rendering in this image of the two lower courses of the trumeau, featuring fleurs-de-lys inscribed within a diaper pattern and figure reliefs within circular medallions, is consistent with the original decor of the jambs. In fact, the early-thirteenth-century trumeau figure survived until 1748 in the cathedral square, where it was known as "the Faster" or "Mister Gray-Hair" ("le Jeûneur" or "Monsieur le Gris"). Abbot Lebeuf was not mistaken in this early identification, as is confirmed by other drawings (see pages 38, 41). This makes it easier to explain the stylistic difference between the two fragments of the lower lintel deposited with the Musée de Cluny during restoration work: like the other evidence, it lends support to the theory that this portal was reworked sometime around the 1240s.

Viollet-le-Duc (vol. 1, page 257) claims to have found in front of the portal "a certain number

of fragments from a central relief representing Christ in Glory on the Day of Judgment, like the one visible today. . . . This relief had been removed shortly after its completion and replaced by the present subject." These precious fragments have yet to be identified, but they would surely clarify what happened. Perhaps there was an accident during the mounting of the original portal, resulting in its having been left unfinished until a later date. Perhaps the initial installation was simply delayed, although it is difficult to imagine practical considerations that would have justified this. Finally, the changes might have resulted from a decision to update the iconography.

The Portal of the Coronation of the Virgin was as savagely mutilated as the two others in 1793–94, but the existence of ampler visual documentation has made it possible to restore it more convincingly. It marks an important step in the iconographic evolution of this scene. The tympanum is read from bottom to top. On the lower lintel, kings and prophets flank the Ark of the Covenant sheltered by a tabernacle, situated directly above the canopy protecting the trumeau figure of the Virgin. The upper lintel represents a Dormition-like Assumption of the Virgin. Two angels lift the Virgin from her tomb in the presence of her son, who blesses her, and all of the apostles, including Saints Peter, Paul, and John, who are sheltered by fig and olive trees. The tympanum proper depicts the Coronation: the Virgin, seated on a throne of glory at the right hand of her son, who blesses her, is crowned by an angel. The archivolts are occupied by kings and prophets (lowest row to either side), angels (first archivolt), patriarchs (second archivolt), kings (third archivolt), and prophets (fourth archivolt). A second innovation, just as significant, is the inclusion among the jamb figures of saints from the diocese: on the left jamb, Saint Denis flanked by angels and a king, as yet unidentified; on the right jamb, Saints John the Baptist, Stephen, and Genevieve as well as an unidentified prelate. The reliefs in the lower niches, badly damaged, depict episodes from the lives of the figures above. Finally, the doorposts and sides of the trumeau feature wonderfully concise scenes illustrating the signs of the zodiac, related rural labors, the seasons, and the stages of life (see also pages 126–27, 129, 132–33).

Meticulously dismantled and in large part reinstalled, the Portal of the Virgin (see page 25) was modified early in the thirteenth century with the intent of better taking into account the increasing popularity of the cult of the Virgin's parents, Anne and Joachim. A new lower lintel was added along with a new row of archivolt figures; the upper lintel was widened as well. Apocryphal scenes figure on the far right quarter of the new lintel and continue into the archivolts. Its left portion depicts the legend of the marriage of the Virgin, which continues as far as the center of its right half. This disorder has made interpretation of the program difficult.

The four buttresses of the western facade feature niches meant to contain statues; the originals disappeared in 1793–94 but were replaced by copies in the nineteenth century. Those on either side of the central portal were personifications of the Church and the Synagogue; that to the far right represented Saint Denis. The statue on the northernmost buttress has not been identified.

The long horizontal gallery that sweeps across the facade shelters twenty-eight statues of kings; the originals were smashed in 1793–94, but copies were substituted in the nineteenth century. Within decades of their completion there was already confusion about the identity of these figures. As early as 1284, a manuscript entitled *Les XII Manières de vilains* proposed that they depicted the kings of France, a notion that soon gained currency. In fact, this Gallery of Kings, a feature that made its first appearance in Paris and was widely diffused thereafter, was conceived as a visual gloss on the passage from Isaiah identifying the issue of the branch of David as the Virgin, and the flower blooming at the summit of this branch as Christ. On the basis of the genealogy in Matthew, this conceit was usually represented vertically, as the Tree of Jesse. In Paris, however, it unfolded as a horizontal sequence of twenty-eight figures. Not all of the individuals in the line were kings, which posed certain iconographic problems. These were addressed in the western gallery at Chartres by the addition of Jesse, the inaugural figure of the genealogical tree. In Paris, the gallery's meaning was clarified by the Virgin and Child figures surmounting it.

Opposite:
The Virgin and Child of the trumeau, now lost, was one of the most important works of its period; this eighteenth-century engraving gives some idea of the sculpture's elegance. Mary was shown effortlessly trampling the serpent. Also represented here are the reliefs on the doorposts and the sides of the trumeau, still in place, which depict the signs of the zodiac and associated images of rural labor. (Engraving from Le Gentil de la Galaisière, "Mémoires sur l'origine du zodiaque . . .," *Mémoires de l'Académie des sciences,* 1785. Musée Notre-Dame.)

The Temple of the New Covenant

THE SCULPTORS

Completion of so large an ensemble within a reasonable time frame entailed the collaboration of many sculptors, in this case all exceptionally accomplished artists. As opposed to what we will observe in the transept arms, here we find few if any weaknesses. From the start, this raises the difficult question of the organization of early-thirteenth-century sculpture workshops like this one, which had to execute a complex commission relatively quickly yet maintain a high level of quality. Was there specialization within each team, the master contenting himself with devising the model and executing the most important passages, notably the faces and hands? This seems likely, and we have proof that such a procedure was followed in the statues of the kings, whose bodies were carved by simple craftsmen but whose heads were reserved for the supervising sculptor. It should also be noted that with the passage of time the teams would have been reorganized, with the different sensibilities of their younger members gradually coming to the fore. This would have presented the project supervisor with the problem of maintaining a modicum of stylistic coherence among highly individual artists. We will never have access to the particulars of these human and professional relations, something that must be acknowledged if serious mistakes in scholarship are to be avoided. Even so, perhaps it would not be inappropriate to imagine arrangements conceived along lines similar to those devised by Charles Le Brun for the collaborative project of Versailles. In that case, surviving account books document attributions that we could never have hoped to ascertain solely on the basis of stylistic analysis.

THE PORTAL OF THE LAST JUDGMENT. Our ignorance of the precise chronology of the central portal as well as of the specifics of its reinstallation prompts a degree of prudence in undertaking a stylistic analysis. Formal variations now readily apparent to any practiced eye do not necessarily indicate different dates. We are sensitive to such differences today, but did the sculptors' contemporaries react in the same way? We cannot be sure. Even so, it seems safe to say that, in their view, iconography took precedence over form.

Analysis of the four reliefs set into the sides of the two central buttresses at an unknown date is particularly delicate. Their origins remain a mystery, and their subjects are also unclear due to damage and the absence of contextual guidance. But it is clear from both their technique and their style that they belonged to a single group. Of like dimensions, composition, and technique, they were clearly conceived as two pairs. Their frames are rectangular or arched to form an arcade. They are carved *en cuvette,* a technique that makes it possible to attain a degree of relief while still producing crisp, almost graphic outlines. Polychromy must have reinforced their illusionism, making the relief elements stand out against the rear plane. All four compositions are skillfully compact and turned in on themselves, such that each relief remains autonomous. The sculptor took pains to avoid showy effects. The relief whose iconographic significance has prompted the most discussion, Nimrod Battling the Sky, is especially revealing in this regard: despite a pervasive awkwardness, the sculptor here managed to concentrate the scene thanks to the device of the sun's rays. The most skillful of the four reliefs represents Job on a dung heap crawling with maggots; his figure is inscribed within a quadrant defined by his friends and his wife, an arrangement that focuses the viewer's attention on the prophet's tense, anguished face (see page 104). The third relief, which depicts a figure leaning on a staff, is dominated by a play of curves: the body bends forward in response to the arch above but is visually countered and stabilized by the opposite vertical of the gently swaying tree.

This compositional stability contrasts with the exceptionally supple handling of the bodies, hair, beards, and drapery. Each figure is frozen in mid-act, as if caught by a snapshot. Each of the scenes had to express a state of soul: affliction in the case of Job; firmness in that of the fourth relief, which features Abraham; effort in that of the hunter. The Nimrod relief aside, the artist's rendering of beards and hair is wonderfully pliant, notably in Abraham's cascading silken curls and

Job's frizzy locks. His genius is especially striking in his handling of textiles: they adhere to the bodies beneath and circle around the limbs, responding loosely, for example, to the movements of Job. The folds crisscross to create patterns that are in some instances deeply and in others shallowly carved. The wimple and scarf worn by Job's wife beneath her turban accentuates the roundness of her face.

This marvelous elegance, still apparent despite the reliefs' poor condition, suggests that a single artist carved all of them—excepting the Nimrod, whose quality is much inferior to that of the others. Clearly he was caught up in the broad stylistic current, affecting much of northern Europe in his day, explored so brilliantly in the exhibition *The Year 1200* mounted by the Metropolitan Museum of Art in New York in 1970. This trend was borne along by one of those waves of interest in antiquity that periodically flooded Europe, enriching it in the process. Fostering metaphysical reflection, it reinvigorated both literature and the visual arts. In this context, artists became newly responsive to ancient works long accessible to them as well as to others newly unearthed in the course of urban development. These four reliefs are best compared not with monumental sculpture but with small-scale pieces that aimed at similar effects. The composition, carving technique, and style of the Job scene, for example, bring to mind late antique ivories. But this comparison holds only within certain limits, for in the end our sculptor was a man very much

The four reliefs remounted on the buttresses flanking the central portal are among the earliest surviving examples of thirteenth-century Parisian sculpture. They inaugurated a style that remained dominant until about the 1230s. The subject of this composition (northern buttress, southern face), which represents a figure leaning on a staff, remains enigmatic.

Two sculptors with similar styles but distinct artistic personalities executed the Virtues and Vices below the jamb figures of the central portal. Their depiction as contrasting pairs—Virtues above, Vices below—instead of as personifications engaged in literal combat was an iconographic innovation. Both sculptors were influenced by the trend toward antique revival pervasive in the first decade of the thirteenth century.

Left jamb, right to left: Faith and Infidelity; Hope and Despair; Charity and Avarice; Purity and Injustice; Prudence and Folly; Humility and Pride.

Right jamb, left to right: Fortitude and Cowardice; Temperance and Wrath; Kindness and Cruelty; Peace and Discord; Obedience and Disobedience; Perseverance and Inconstancy.

The details show Faith and Infidelity, Hope and Despair, and Kindness.

The Temple of the New Covenant

This medallion from the right jamb of the central portal represents Cruelty, but its subject did not prevent the sculptor from visually linking its two figures. Their bodies are obscured by fluid draperies that create an impression of movement.

Opposite:
In the central portal, the architect framed the tympanum with six archivolts that effect a subtle transition between plane of the facade and that of the doors.

of his own time. We see this in his schematic manner of rendering trees, which resembles that used in contemporary manuscript illumination, for instance the Ingeburge Psalter.

The ensuing developments in Paris would have been impossible to predict. As yet, no further evidence has come to light suggesting the presence there of great artists capable of producing comparably arresting works of similarly high quality. Thus the realization of these four reliefs marks a turning point in contemporary sculptural production, announcing the impending emergence of Paris as one of the great creative centers in northern France, a development consolidated in the 1230s and 1240s with the formulation of an indigenous style. Thus it is worthwhile to speculate about the origins of this artist. In the 1190s, when the western facade of the Cathedral of Sens was being built, that city was an important creative center. Around 1200, work there would have been sufficiently advanced for one of the project's sculptors to respond to a summons issued by the bishop of Paris. In terms of style, parallels between the reliefs in Sens and Paris are easy to discern, yet the latter also mark a stylistic advance: they are more monumental, they eschew the use of "damp drapery," they feature less contorted figure postures, and their compositions are more amply distributed over their stone slabs. The arrival in Paris of the man responsible for these changes, at a time when sculptural commissions there were about to increase exponentially, proved determinant for future developments.

This vigorous new idiom, which appeared on the scene quite suddenly, was to undergo considerable evolution. The medallions depicting the Virtues and Vices provide the earliest illustrations. They are the work of two artists whose styles are quite similar but can be distinguished from one another after close examination. In conformity with the scheme devised by the architect, they carved two tiers of reliefs for each of the two central door splays, each Virtue in the upper tier

The Temple of the New Covenant

being coupled with a corresponding Vice in the lower tier. The Virtues appear within trilobate arcades supported by colonnettes, their postures inclining left or right to establish a steady paired rhythm. The Vices are placed within medallions that concentrate their compositions and are separated from one another by double grooves. One difference between left and right is readily apparent: the Virtues are separated by two colonnettes on the left, by three colonnettes on the right.

The configuration devised by the architect was awkward for the sculptors, who had to inscribe their representations of the Vices within compact circles yet place their Virtues within the more spacious niches of the arcade. Slightly different solutions were adopted on left and right. The master of the left displayed considerable ingenuity in exploiting the stipulated framework. He gave the Vices especially complex postures that resulted in their fully occupying their medallions. The prancing horse symbolizing Pride, for example, manifests a highly developed sense of composition. He also managed to suggest vigorous movement in ways that belie the spatial limitations, as in the personification of Folly. The master of the right splay, however, proved less adroit; he resorted to double figures to fill out the medallions, a solution that compromises the overall harmony of the design. Paradoxically, the violent gestures he favored seem less convincing than the extravagant but more fluent postures adopted in the left medallions.

In the case of the Virtues, both sculptors adopted the same approach, rendering them as single seated figures that occupy the allotted space differently, in ways that accord with their specific character. Here the greatest challenge was the relative breadth of the arcades. The second master addressed this problem by adding the third intermediate colonnettes. With the exception of Fortitude, the Virtues are rendered in partial profile, holding their symbolic attributes and sitting on long benches. The need to fill up the space influenced these decisions, prompting, for example, the lounging posture and disproportionately long right leg of Hope. Here again, the master of the left showed himself to be more inventive than his colleague on the right, despite the greater width of his arcades. Considerable imagination is apparent in his choice of bodily attitudes, which also manifest an acute sense of reality. His forms, too, are ampler and fuller, better suited to their roles than those found on the right, where the master preferred crisper forms that, while more arresting in graphic terms, are also stiffer.

The treatment of drapery is likewise revealing of their disparate sensibilities. The first master remained fond of damp folds that envelope the forms, accentuating a chest or clinging to a waist. He rendered them in shallow relief, as if seeking to create the illusion of metalwork. This approach increased the dynamism of the figures and consolidated the amplitude with which they occupy their wide trilobate arcades. The second master, too, remained faithful to damp drapery, but his handling of such passages has greater consistency. He did not so much chisel as carve them. The resulting forms are less apparent and more serene, creating a more monumental effect. At the same time, he achieved a greater sense of relief from the rear plane.

Within a conception that remains unified, then, two temperaments emerge. We do not know whether the two artists worked simultaneously or in succession. The difference already noted in the number of colonnettes—echoed in other details, for example, their bases and capitals—tends to favor the second hypothesis.

The rest of the portal dates from the second decade of the twelfth century: the jamb figures of the apostles, the Christ of the trumeau, the tympanum, and the archivolts. A headless statue (Musée Carnavalet), fragments discovered in 1839 and 1977, and the head of Saint Paul (Musée de Cluny) clearly indicate the presence of several sculptors. The Carnavalet figure, whose height is exaggerated, disappears completely beneath a mass of drapery from which only the hands emerge. The sculptor organized his work around emphatic verticals: a phylactery and folds interrupted at the hip. The robe is treated as a dense network of damp drapery folds, but the latter are deeply cut and rounded. Judging from what is admittedly a poor drawing, the first trumeau figure was conceived along similar lines. The sculptor of a second torso (Musée de Cluny), however, rejected this general softening. He, too, organized the composition of his figure around an emphatic vertical, in this case

A less fluid, more monumental antique style made its appearance in the central portal. Note the more rigid, less ample folds in the drapery worn by this figure, a prophet from the third archivolt on the right.

Opposite:
The two inner archivolts are occupied by bust-length angels that observe the central scene like an audience at the theater: they lean over the "balustrades," listening and watching with manifest amazement.

The Temple of the New Covenant

a section of the robe that falls from the left shoulder. But he then wound it around the hip, thereby condensing the robe's folds, which he carved very deeply to create a pronounced contrast between lights and darks. The same style recurs in several fragments discovered in 1977. This second master, a sculptor of great originality who may have played a dominant role in the execution of the apostles, effected a break with the style of 1200. He renounced the calligraphic approach inspired by metalwork in favor of a more monumental style, one probably influenced by the study of ancient sculpture. Despite its mutilated state, the head of Saint Paul has an analogous force and power. These works mark the emergence of a new generation of sculptors who, while remaining committed to the monumental tradition, struck out in a new direction. They were certainly contemporaries of the sculptors of the lateral portals at Chartres, but their sensibility was quite different, being characterized by a resolve to break with the classicizing *Muldenstil*. The relationship they established between column statues and the wall is telling in this regard. In the dialogue between statues and columns initiated on the facade at Saint-Denis in the 1140s, sculpture now took the upper hand, in the form of figures projecting well beyond the wall and fully occupying their own space. This was not necessarily an advance, but it certainly marked a radical change, one with decisive implications for the interaction of portal ensembles with their architectural frameworks.

The head of Saint Paul is the only one to survive from the jamb figures of the central portal. Despite its damaged state, the exceptional amplitude of its volume remains striking, as does the finesse with which the locks of its beard and hair were carved. It was presented to the Musée de Cluny in 1845 by Lassus.

Opposite:
This torso from one of the apostle figures of the central portal was discovered in 1839 in the rue de la Santé. Despite its damaged condition, it brings to mind the most beautiful examples of Romanesque sculpture, a resemblance especially apparent in the movement of the mantle as it wraps around the waist. (Musée de Cluny.)

The antique revival style remained current until late in the thirteenth century. In many respects, this angel sounding the last trump—perched atop the gable of the western facade—brings to mind some of the earlier apostle figures of the central portal directly below. (Photograph by Charles Nègre, before 1855. Musée Notre-Dame.)

Opposite:
Prophets and doctors from the third and fourth archivolts to the left of the central portal. The architect sought to achieve harmony between the sculpture and the architecture, such that the grand lines of the latter would never be compromised by the former.

Aside from the various elements dating from the 1240s, the tympanum and archivolts are so homogeneous that one hesitates to isolate different hands. Clearly a great sculptor with a powerful vision completely dominated the team of artists under his supervision, a circumstance sufficiently rare to merit emphasis. Similar features recur in each of the figures but never become tiresome: rounded faces devoid of expression; mouths, usually small, hinting at a smile; narrow almond eyes; forehead furrows that are carved instead of incised, as had previously been the norm. Beards and hair, often copious, sometimes feature regular, iron-curled locks but are often wavy. The figures are completely enveloped by their robes and mantles; vertical folds over the chest are intentionally flattened, as if ironed. Mantles often fall over a shoulder, an effect that animates the seated figures, such as Abraham, Moses, Isaiah, Aaron. In certain cases, as in the Moses, the sculptor did not hesitate to vary exaggerated rectilinear patterns with superbly gauged curves. Folds develop vertically without disruption or break delicately over the feet, as in the cross-bearing angel. The results are clarity, legibility, and serenity. Movement is eschewed in favor of postures that, while somewhat schematic, have a nobility that seems altogether appropriate here. In this context, the richly varied attitudes of the wondering angels in the first two archivolts strike an especially piquant note.

It remains to define the relation between this ensemble and the column statues. There are undeniable points of convergence, notably in the emphatic projection of the archivolt figures, but the stylistic departures made by the first master were attenuated by his successor. The heads of Jacob and the prophet in the third archivolt on the left are quite similar to that of Paul, but they lack the latter's expressive power and force of conviction. The upper ensemble is characterized by a calmer approach to drapery doubtless even more apparent prior to 1793. The handling is similar to that in the column statues, but the final effect is quite different in the latter, which bring to mind ancient sculpture. Nonetheless, it is the calmer, more serene style—likewise evident in the angel sounding the trumpet on the gable of the west facade, as well as in many other Parisian monuments—that seems to have prevailed at Notre-Dame.

THE PORTAL OF THE CORONATION OF THE VIRGIN. Émile Mâle stressed the remarkable quality of the Coronation portal, which he considered the greatest achievement of thirteenth-century French sculpture. His enthusiasm found additional support, if such be needed, in the wake of discoveries made in 1977. The head of an angel thought to come from the left jamb offers surprising, quite unexpected insight into the style and quality of the jamb figures. Since then, a second head, that of a prelate, has also been linked to the ensemble. The Portal of the Coronation of the Virgin is without question the great masterpiece of the cathedral, a status justified by its overall conception as well as by the details of its execution. Complicating factors like those clouding our judgment of the central portal—the nagging questions about its subsequent modification—do not exist here. The statues currently in place are nineteenth-century copies, but they are generally consistent with the style of the originals. The basic conception is instantly grasped. The different levels of the composition succeed one another without rupture, producing an impression of serene calm. At ground level, the splays are lightened by arcades that form niches; above these are the column statues, whose canopies are perfectly aligned with the archivolts. Everything is organized around the trumeau figure, surmounted by a canopy directing the eye to the Ark of the Covenant, itself surmounted by a tabernacle. This upward dynamic culminates in the proximate heads of the Son and the Mother in the tympanum. The result is a clear distribution between emphatic horizontals and a central vertical axis that links the various registers.

The tympanum is framed by four archivolts that focus the viewer's attention and set off its carefully studied composition. The lower lintel is conceived on a single plane, interrupted solely by the central tabernacle, which projects considerably. Things are different in the upper lintel, where the plane established below is broken three times, on each side as well as in the center, where the sarcophagus overhangs slightly. In the tympanum, there is again a slight overhang below

The Temple of the New Covenant

The tympanum of the Portal of the
Coronation of the Virgin is among
the most skillfully composed of the
period. The architect succeeded in
establishing a balance between horizontal
and diagonal axes. The archivolts were
charged with channeling and containing
these visual dynamics.

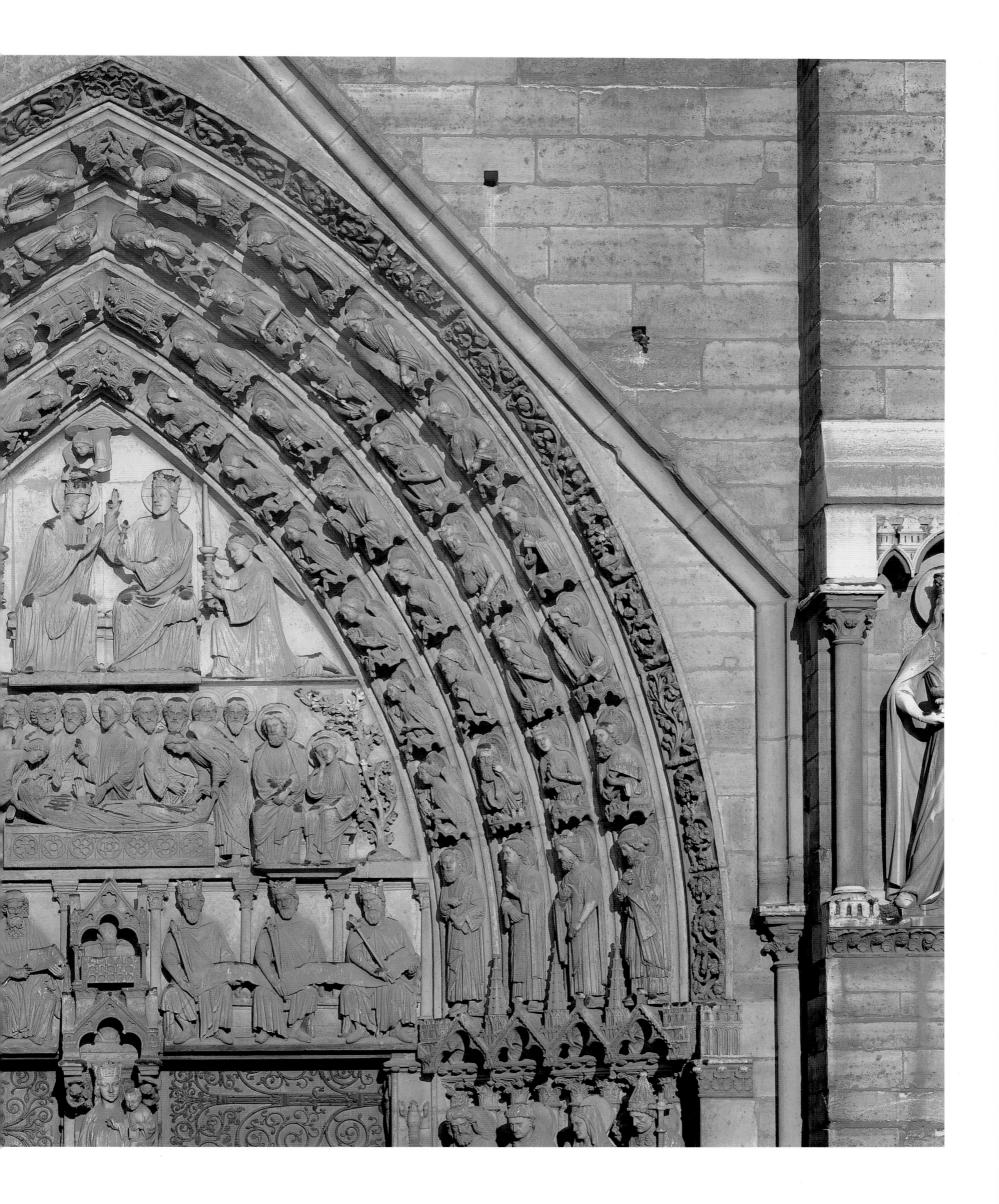

the central group. Additionally, a rhythm emerges based on differences between the temporal realm, represented by the upper lintel with its impressive number of figures, and eternity, represented by the tympanum and the lower lintel, where the sculptor opened up the scenes, leaving large areas of blank stone. Similarly studied oppositions operate within each register. The upper lintel is constructed around lateral and central curves that focus attention on the head of the Virgin. The lower lintel and the tympanum, by contrast, feature a sequence of verticals formed by the different figures and accentuated in the lintel by the engaged colonnettes that punctuate the rear slab. The sculptor took pains both to individualize the figures and to establish connections between them. The long phylacteries supported at left by the prophets and at right by the kings create a strong material link that passes in front of the engaged colonnettes. Connections are established more subtly in the tympanum, resulting from the reciprocal gazes of the Son and the Mother and the slight forward inclination of the latter. The presence of the gable above only this portal, recessed into the surface of the wall and articulated by a simple molding, makes sense: it sets the portal apart and concentrates it, thereby accentuating its force.

Stylistic analysis of the portal reveals, at least in its upper portions, a homogeneity so pronounced as to suggest that it was realized under the supervision of a master who succeeded in imposing both stylistic unity and rapidity of execution on his collaborators. There are a few lax passages, however: for example, the ten reliefs sheltered by the jamb niches. Here the sculptor was obliged to fill square fields, a challenge he addressed with varying degrees of success by using two or three figures. He sought to animate his compositions by means of vigorous action amplified by the drapery, as in the angel brandishing a sword. He did not hesitate, however, to repeat basic schemata with only minor changes, for example, the Martyrdoms of Saints Stephen and Denis, and Saint Michael and the Angel. He executed them in shallow relief, letting the niches generate strong effects of light and shadow that set off the sculpture. Furthermore, he accentuated the resemblance of his handling to repoussé by articulating the drapery folds on the surface. Like the author of the four reliefs of the central portal, he was not unsympathetic to the antique revival trend, although the dryness of his lines, his inability to convey the weight of fabric, and the awkwardness of his compositions set him somewhat apart from the other sculptor. Even so, some of his scenes carry conviction: for example the Stoning of Saint Stephen, where the executioner's twisted pose has a freedom that hints at things to come. But his renderings of vegetation are notably timid, especially by comparison with analogous passages in the reliefs on the sides of the trumeau.

The small reliefs devoted to the signs of the zodiac, related rural labors, the seasons, and the stages of life are clearly by another hand (see also pages 112, 132–33). Justly celebrated, they have acquired the status of emblems of the medieval period due to their evocative depictions of peasant life. They feature not the slightest trace of urban existence: whoever devised these compositions maintained close ties with agricultural laborers. The rightness of every gesture gives them a timeless quality comparable to that of the historiated initials in the *Moralia in Job* painted a century earlier in Cîteaux.

Rarely have the Middle Ages been so tellingly rendered. Both a sense of reality and this ability to capture the significant moment are manifest in the figurations of the zodiac. Surely the sculptor had never seen a lion, but he nonetheless instilled the model from which he worked with remarkable power. Just as he drew inspiration from a mode of everyday life with which he was familiar, he composed each of the scenes with consummate skill. These figures have an amplitude as well as a remarkable ease of movement and gesture that convinces the viewer they are about to move out of frame, but in fact they are rigorously contained within the limits of their visual fields. The sculptor did not hesitate to tilt them on a diagonal so as to more fully occupy the space. Faithful to the *en cuvette* technique, he placed his figures resolutely in the foremost plane in a way that accentuates the relief effect. In this respect he proceeded differently from the two sculptors of the Virtues and Vices, who made no attempt to evoke such powerful volumes. The results are remarkable, creating an impression of freedom as forceful as that of freestanding sculpture. Some traces

The Martyrdom of Saint Denis and the Struggle of the Angel with the Devil, two of the ten reliefs below the jamb figures of the Portal of the Coronation of the Virgin. While awkwardly carved, they manifest a new interest in depicting vegetation.

of the antique revival style remain, yet it is not continuity but rupture that is most striking here, as evidenced in the handling of the drapery. To accentuate the volumes and bodily movement, he renounced fluid, supple folds, then the rule, in favor of tubular ones that broaden as they fall from the shoulders or waist. Fabric is still sometimes stretched over the chest, but its folds are flattened in the way already seen in the central portal. He managed to make these figures come alive below their thick robes, and in some cases his interest in the human body prompted him to expose portions of it with a boldness rare in the period. The depictions of Adam in the central archivolt of the northern transept at Chartres, slightly later in date, are just as audacious but less convincing because of their gauntness. In Paris, the half-nude May and fully nude June feature full, rounded forms with taut but ample flesh. The modeling is smooth, such that light glides freely over it. The handling of the faces also manifests this new sensibility: full, serene, and alert, sometimes even smiling, they communicate the joy of life. This attentiveness to the exterior world also surfaces in the fondness for vegetation apparent throughout the Coronation portal, from the sides of the trumeau, where the plants are still somewhat dry, to the outer archivolt border by way of the upper lintel, where the branches are engorged with sap and the spring buds, if not already in bloom, are about to burst into flower. Here again, the sculptor carefully respected the field defined by the limits of the stone block, making the branches bend supply but luxuriantly to accommodate the border and frame the scene.

Two miraculously preserved heads, one of a prelate and one of an angel, give a lofty idea of the style of the column statues. The latter's relationship to the wall remains important but has been altered considerably: while still carved from the same blocks as the columns behind them, the figures now rest not on consoles but on bases that incline forward slightly. Furthermore, these

Pages 130–31:
Two heads from the jamb figures of the Coronation portal survive, those of the prelate (Musée de Cluny) and one of the angels (Musée de Cluny, Gift of the B.F.C.E.). The former was discovered in the rue de la Santé in 1839, the latter in 1977. Both are extraordinary, the prelate for its amplitude and the angel for its smile. The latter is the first smile in Gothic sculpture; this expression quickly spread, first to other sites in France, notably at Reims, then to the rest of Europe.

Coronation portal, reliefs
from the doorposts and
sides of the trumeau.
For these renderings of
the signs of the zodiac,
associated rural labors,
and the seasons, the
sculptor used a full,
vigorous style well suited
to the imagery.
Right: From the right
doorpost, clockwise
from upper left, Cancer,
Virgo (nineteenth cen-
tury), Libra, vintager,
and harvester.
Far right: From the left
doorpost, bottom to top,
Aries, Taurus, Gemini,
and Leo.
Opposite: From the left
side of the trumeau,
autumn and winter.

The Temple of the New Covenant

Above:
Detail of a prophet, fourth archivolt to the right.
With its inclined head lost in melancholy reflection, this figure is one of the master-pieces of the Coronation portal.

Right:
An interest in the natural world is apparent in the many depictions of animals and plants, all carefully studied and deftly rendered. This section is part of the outer border of the archivolts.

The Temple of the New Covenant

bases sit on a continuous slab supported by the niches below. The result is a liberation of the sculpture that anticipates things to come. As for the heads that now make stylistic judgment possible, they are clearly by the same artist, despite differences dictated by the iconography. Many features point to a single hand, notably identical triangular facial schemata, fluent modeling, eyes with slight bulges below the sockets, protruding chins, and precisely articulated locks of hair. The angel wears a hint of a smile whose tacit promise about the future was to be kept. The rare surviving images of the Virgin of the trumeau (see page 112) suggest it was a figure of extraordinary quality, featuring elegant carriage and fluent drapery, with part of her mantle being lifted by her left arm and ample folds falling gently over her feet. This is in fact a more monumental conception, one that takes us well beyond the style of 1200.

The tympanum and archivolts are admirably homogeneous: there are no weaknesses in this vast ensemble, which must have been conceived and executed with dispatch by a team working as one under the supervision of an exacting master. Analysis reveals stylistic nuances, but they are not sufficiently pronounced to support the identification of different hands. These sculptors apparently agreed to yield up their individuality in the interest of overall harmony. Such instances are sufficiently rare to merit emphasis. It is true that the artist responsible for the overall design seems to have been more at ease with individual figures than with interactive groups. The phylacteries

Coronation portal, left archivolts, third and fourth rows.
Above the full-length figures of the bottom row, the archivolts of this portal are populated by half-length figures. Some of them—for example, the prophet on the opposite page—display a rare combination of technical mastery, formal subtlety, and psychological penetration.

The Temple of the New Covenant

Lower lintel of the Portal of Saint Anne, detail of left side.
Added when the portal was reinstalled on the western facade in the early thirteenth century, this lintel represents episodes from the life of the Virgin. Its conception is anecdotal, as opposed to the monumentality characteristic of the Coronation portal. Depicted are, from left to right, the Arrival of Joseph; the Flowering Baton; and the Marriage of Joseph and the Virgin, with Saint Anne and Joachim looking on.

linking the kings and the prophets create a horizontal accent whose awkwardness outweighs its success as a connective device. In the upper lintel, the heads are aligned in a way that belies meaningful hierarchy, that of Christ being identifiable solely on the basis of its cruciform nimbus. In the tympanum, the link between Christ and his mother is established only by the tension of their gazes and not by gesture. One also senses that this artist was most comfortable when dealing with bust-length figures like those of the archivolts, as opposed to full-length seated figures.

This quest for individualization fostered the use of emphatically high relief. As in the column statues and the reliefs on the jambs, the figures project well beyond the stone blocks, from which they seem almost completely independent. Sculpture is thus privileged over the architecture, whose grand lines are obscured as a result. To grasp this point, one need only compare the archivolts here with those of the central portal.

The supervising sculptor's originality is also apparent in the handling of drapery, which is rendered in some instances with great pliancy and in others with pronounced rigor (see pages 126–27). The pliant approach is exemplified in the group of the Virgin and two angels on the upper lintel. Here the fabric reveals and accentuates the movement of the underlying bodies. Likewise, in the Saint John it envelopes the figure in a way that amplifies its melancholy expression. As for the more rigorous approach, it is epitomized by the Christ of the tympanum but in fact prevails throughout the latter's composition, where the sculptor used deep folds, which catch the light and give the robes weight and consistency. The figures of the bottom row of the archivolts are also striking examples of this new conception of the relation between drapery and the body.

Despite the differences discussed above, there are many similarities between the sculpture of this ensemble and that of the Last Judgment portal. This is a function of both teams having worked during the same decade. But the broad stylistic parallels coexist with manifestations of differing sensibilities. The Coronation portal is characterized by greater organizational rigor, the central portal by a heightened sense of monumentality; the former displays greater pliancy and refinement in its handling, the latter more vigor. Of the two, it was the Coronation portal that had the greatest impact on sculptors working on other Parisian projects, such as Saint-Germain-l'Auxerrois, Sainte-Geneviève, the tomb of Philippe Dagobert for Royaumont, and the portal at Longpont.

THE PORTAL OF SAINT ANNE. The additions made in the 1210s to the third portal on the western facade, the former Portal of the Virgin, reveal the same stylistic tendencies (see page 25). This becomes clear if one disregards the imitation twelfth-century passages—readily discernable as a result of their stiffness—to focus exclusively on the lower lintel and the first row of the archivolts. Judging from the lintel, the sculptor who carved them was not of the first rank. The figures are heavy-handed and awkward, disappearing beneath overcopious drapery, and their heads are disproportionately large. The deeply cut folds have straight edges and fall heavily, sometimes virtually crashing to the ground. The faces, however, are not without character: wrinkles appear below the eyes and the beards are treated with exceptional suppleness. A different hand reveals itself in the first row of the archivolts to the left. Probably one of the collaborators on the Coronation portal, he managed to instill life into these faces, whether round and clean-shaven or bearded with protruding cheeks.

THE GALLERY OF KINGS. The spectacular discovery in 1977 of 143 fragments of the statues of the kings of Judah cast welcome light on a vexing question. It also provided exceptional evidence of sculptural polychromy in this period. Finally, it prompted a new set of questions about the organization of sculpture workshops in the early thirteenth century. Regarding the last point, analysis of the fragments indicates a clear division of labor in the production of these figures. After the rough-hewn blocks had been prepared by stonecutters, journeymen carved the bodies in accordance with a model provided by their master, who reserved the carving of the heads for himself. The mantles are usually secured around the neck by a clasp; the robes have tubular folds and are clinched at the waist by a belt, stopping short of the feet. The carving is deep, the handling generalized. The great height at which these figures would be placed meant that broad effects would suffice: only summary execution was deemed necessary.

By contrast, the sculptor took great care with the heads, whose dimensions are impressive (roughly twenty-eight inches high). A single basic schema was used throughout the series. All the kings wear crowns and have long beards, except one who is clean-shaven (no. 7) and another whose beard is clipped (no. 9). The hair is generally long and disposed so as to frame the face. A lock of hair falls over one of the king's foreheads (no. 6), anticipating the future *dorelot*. The mouths are often slightly open, even fully so (no. 21), and the foreheads are carved with wrinkles of lesser or greater depth. The almond eyes are couched in fleshy sockets; in a few cases there are even small incised wrinkles below them (nos. 11, 12), as previously observed in some figures of the Last Judgment and Coronation portals. The Master of the Rounded Heads remained attached to the prevailing facial formula of the preceding decade (nos. 7, 9), while the other sculptors abandoned this in favor of a more elongated model. Two of these artists were especially gifted: the Master of the Fine Features (nos. 11, 12) and the Master of Head No. 6. The former rendered features with a rare subtlety, accentuating the cheekbones and introducing refinements into the shapes of the eyelids and lips. The latter gave his heads carriages of exceptional nobility. In this respect—insofar as we can judge, given the absence of the body—he broke with the generation of 1210 to introduce a new conception of sculpture.

Most of these heads retain only the slightest traces of their original polychromy. The pigments—yellow ochre, red ochre, and blue gray—were applied evenly over a white ground to isolate lips, nostrils, beards, and hair, with glazes being used to give a sheen to the faces and hands. Finally, the eyeballs were painted with black dots meant to stand out from the surrounding tones.

This ensemble, immense in both the number of its figures and their dimensions, was produced quickly in the 1220s by a team of sculptors manifesting a new sensibility. They broke completely with the style of 1200 in favor of a more monumental idiom meant to compete with the architecture on equal terms.

This page, opposite, and pages 140–41: Heads from the Gallery of Kings. Page 138: no. 9; page 139: no. 13; page 140: no. 10; page 141, clockwise from upper left: no. 20 (David); no. 12; no. 15; no. 19. (All Musée de Cluny, Gift of the B.F.C.E.) Discovered in 1977, these fragments offer unique documentation of stylistic developments in the 1220s. By and large, they were conceived along conservative lines, being more indebted to earlier work than anticipatory of future trends. A surprising amount of their original polychromy survives, making it easier for us to grasp the importance of the insistent horizontal rhythm they created across the width of the facade.

The Temple of the New Covenant

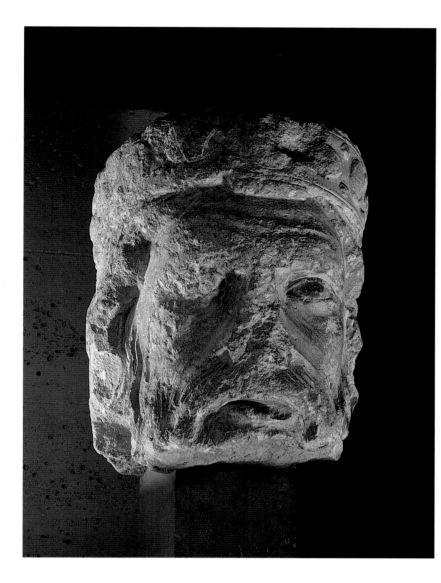

Pages 142–43:

Details of the nail-bearing angel and Christ from the tympanum of the Last Judgment portal.

In the course of the 1240s, the central portal was significantly modified. The nail-bearing angel, carved in the round, and the Christ Displaying His Wounds exemplify a new style whose mannerist accents signal a decisive break with work produced earlier in the century.

THE PORTAL OF THE LAST JUDGMENT. The additions to the central portal postdate the completion of the Gallery of Kings. The trumeau, the first row of the right archivolts, the left portion of the lower lintel, the Christ Displaying His Wounds, and the nail-bearing angel were all realized only in the 1240s. They mark the first appearance in Paris of what was to become a veritable stylistic revolution (see pages 136, 142–43, and 145), which manifested itself in several respects. The first is the renunciation of the ratio, used in early-thirteenth-century figural sculpture, of one-to-six for a new one of one-to-seven. Like the analogous development in Hellenistic sculpture, this change had radical effects, resulting in elongated bodies and disproportionately small heads. The new canon soon appeared in other Parisian projects and quickly spread well beyond the city limits.

The second major change concerns the way in which volume was rendered. Previously, a figure's volume had been determined by its clothing. Completely enveloping the body, leaving only the head and hands exposed, it generated both movement and mass. Suddenly this relationship was reversed: the body began to define volume, drapery being used as a means of accentuating it, accompanying it, and setting it off. Now movement began to be controlled by the body, with drapery being assigned the subsidiary task of conveying and amplifying the resulting tensions. In addition to introducing a new visual economy, this approach must have entailed new methods of work. One thinks of Rodin, who before producing the final version of his monument to Balzac with its voluminous dressing gown imagined the figure in the nude. There is no proof, of course, that any such procedures were used in the thirteenth century, but it seems reasonable to speculate along these lines, especially in light of the radical implications of this new departure. Furthermore, this period saw the production of a significant number of nudes. Reference has already been made to those in the Coronation portal and the north transept of Chartres cathedral. In the Last Judgment portal, the two horsemen of the Apocalypse in the right archivolts also speak to this point. They feature two nudes: an aged woman whose body is gaunt, even skeletal, and a younger man of more nubile form. The viewer senses the strain entailed by their effort to remain on their violently rearing horse: the muscles are tensed, the faces anxious. The Christ Displaying His Wounds could also be adduced in this connection, for part of his chest is exposed. This is certainly not the earliest such example, the formula having been introduced at Saint-Denis, but it is the first to reflect such close study of human anatomy. It does not necessarily follow from these cases that the sculptor worked from a living model, but it seems fair to say that he took pains to reproduce a reality of which he had become newly aware.

This rediscovery of the human body also entailed a new approach to the rendering of fabric. The extent of the transformation becomes apparent if one compares figures of varying dates within the tympanum. In the Christ, long, deeply cut folds break to form pronounced ridges. In the nail-bearing angel, the robe cascades downward, retaining all its weight and thickness. At the same time, clothing becomes looser to facilitate a fuller articulation of gesture. In a fragment from the lower lintel depicting one of the risen dead (Musée de Cluny), the cloth is so thin that the pliant body beneath is fully visible.

But it is the handling of the faces—not the monstrous ones of the archivolts but those in the lintel and the tympanum—that the new spirit is most readily apparent. The head of Christ is sublimely beautiful, projecting a serene calm that is altogether human. The hair, beard, and moustache are carved with exceptional suppleness, twisting onto themselves to create long locks that obscure the ears and fall gently onto the shoulders. The moustache has an especially vivacious form that was quickly imitated. More generally, in numerous figures the shapes of the skulls are discernible below the taut skin of the faces; the trajectory of eyebrows is stressed in a way that emphasizes the sockets, while the eyes themselves are shaped like distended almonds and have pockets below them; and one can almost sense the blood pulsing through the fleshy lips. This calm, which does not preclude austerity, gives way in the nail-bearing angel to a certain mannerism. The shape of the face, the tight lips, and the ringlets of hair reveal a more exacerbated sensi-

bility (see pages 142–43). The same mannered idiom is apparent in the fragment in the Musée de Cluny, where the heads are affected or have negroid features.

In fact, this stylistic revolution signaled a brutal rejection of the art of the first third of the thirteenth century, which had become exhausted in the course of the 1230s, when constant repetition of its formulas drained them of conviction. We must imagine a new generation of artists, drunk with freedom and fully aware of the possibilities opening up before them as a result of their audacity. They were not alone, for architects had already shown the way when one of them, in 1231, set out to recast the choir of the Abbey Church of Saint-Denis. This new style—known since the nineteenth century as Rayonnant—was to prevail in all media and all construction projects of the Île-de-France, whence it quickly spread to the rest of Europe.

Horseman of the Apocalypse flanked by two scenes from Hell. Central portal, first row of the right archivolts.
The sculpture in the first row of the right archivolts dates from the 1240s. Several important innovations are notable here: the intertwining of bodies, the bold use of nudes, the delight in deep shadows, and the tendency to liberate the figure groups from the archivolts behind them.

The Temple of the New Covenant

The Rayonnant
Cathedral

Maurice de Sully's initial project retained its authority through the first third of the thirteenth century, but before its completion there was a fundamental reorientation, one that seriously challenged some of the original plan's basic premises. Technical as well as aesthetic questions were raised, and the two modes of interrogation are so intricately connected that it is difficult to say which preceded the other. Technical concerns focused on illumination of the center aisle and on the drainage of water collected from the building's vast roofing system. In aesthetic terms, the central preoccupations—aside from completely new structural elements—pertained largely to the exterior: the clerestory elevations, the articulation of the different levels, and the design of the western facade. The decisions that followed gradually produced what was in effect a new building, one whose massing differed so greatly from that of its predecessor that the alterations must have been masterminded by a new architect. His identity remains problematic, but his sensibility clearly led him in a direction that broke with prevailing thirteenth-century notions traditionally associated with Chartres. A new generation of artists—sculptors and painters as well as architects—reconsidered basic formal questions, opening new perspectives in the process. In the domain of architecture, the master who, in 1231, designed the new choir of Saint-Denis cleared a path that would soon be taken by Jean de Chelles and Pierre de Montreuil in Paris, and by many others elsewhere. In the realm of sculpture, the artist who modified the cathedral's central portal was certainly affected by the trend, and he may even have been its initiator. In any event, the new style quickly spread to all contemporary building sites in the region, most notably the Sainte-Chapelle before 1248 and Saint-Denis in the 1240s.

The arts of color—stained glass, painting, illumination—also played a role in this transformation. Notre-Dame de Paris came to figure in the new current thanks to a new team of artists: its patrons accepted and perhaps even fostered the "modern" trend, sustaining it through their choice of younger artists—architects, above all—who guaranteed its continuing vitality.

From the beginning, the natural illumination of Notre-Dame had been deemed inadequate, and as the first third of the thirteenth century came to a close newer buildings began to make this flaw seem especially troubling. The large windows of more recent structures as well as the less saturated colors of their stained glass, some of which was even executed in grisaille, made for much brighter interiors. The darkness of Notre-Dame now became intolerable, for it made the great church seem positively archaic by comparison with the newer buildings. If it was to retain its preeminent architectural status, a way would have to be found to rectify this deficiency. Rebuilding from scratch was out of the question, so a decision was made to enlarge the clerestory windows. By eliminating the rose oculi on the elevation's third level, which opened onto the eaves above the tribune vaults, the architect made it possible to lengthen the windows directly above

them. The results were twofold: in addition to eliminating a level that provided absolutely no illumination, he managed to increase considerably the amount of natural light reaching the interior.

The architect proceeded with almost surgical precision, for he had to preserve the upper portions of the windows even as he pierced the wall below them. Traces of this operation are still visible on the exterior: the dentilated hood moldings, pointed arches, and supporting colonnettes survive from the original window articulations, frameworks for the new tracery having been installed within them. In fact, the architect devised what has been known since Eugène Viollet-le-Duc as the *fenêtre-châssis* (chassis-window), one in which the stone tracery—here two lancets topped by a circle—is structurally independent of the surrounding masonry. The use of mullions fixed to the adjacent stone by metal tenons gave the tracery an autonomy that accorded the architect greater freedom in designing it.

Downward extension of the clerestory windows entailed replacing the sloped roofs over the tribune with flat ones. For this purpose, the architect devised an ingenious system—known in French as terraced roofing (see glossary)—consisting of overlapping stone slabs supported by stone beams resting on transverse arches. This resulted in a crawl space above the tribune vaults accessible from below by stone trap doors. The new arrangement posed problems of water drainage that were especially pressing on the northern side. Previously, the slope of the tribune roofs generated enough momentum to propel rainwater through gargoyle spouts and well beyond the lower parts of the building. In the new design, the architect had sloped hollows carved into each slab that directed the water outward, thereby preventing troublesome accumulations. But this did not completely solve the problem. Of necessity, he also introduced an entirely new feature that remains in

Opposite and above:
Views of the flying buttresses and their gutters.
The headstones of the large flying buttresses connect with vertical drain pipes built over the twelfth-century buttresses. The system of gutters and drainpipes had finally been invented.

Page 150:
View from the terraced roof of the radial chapels.
Page 151:
View of a clerestory window and flying buttresses from the roof of the tribune. Downward extension of the clerestory windows necessitated the replacement of the sloped roofs of the tribune by flat, terraced roofs. To evacuate rainwater falling on the 592,000 square feet of the building's roofing system, the architect devised a system of flying buttresses spanning the tribune whose upper surfaces are grooved to serve as gutters.

The Rayonnant Cathedral

use today: a system of peripheral gutters that channel the water to vertical drainpipes emptying far from the foundations. Notre-Dame was the first building to employ such a drainage system. To assure that it functioned properly, the architect had to completely recast the upper portions of the structure, rebuilding the roof over the center aisle, reconstructing the upper portions of the outer wall that supported it, introducing gutters, and building flying buttresses over the tribunes.

The architect completely rebuilt the twelfth-century wood frame supporting the roof in accordance with a new design. As usual with such projects, work proceeded in stages: first the choir was completed, then the nave. The undertaking was complicated by the addition of a new element: the spire over the crossing. Admittedly, we cannot be sure that such a spire did not exist previously, but we do know the one that disappeared during the Revolution dated from this period. Another, equally vexing question arises in connection with the roof reconstruction: Did the new frame reproduce the previous roof slope, or did it introduce a steeper one? The latter hypothesis seems the more likely, for it would explain the fact that none of the wood from the original frame was reused. If the angle of the roof was indeed increased, then timber from the first roofing system would have been too short for the new design.

Reconstruction of the frame was preceded by a dismantling of the low twelfth-century support wall above the original denticulated moldings—triple in the choir, single along the nave— which were retained. The new roof rose from a masonry extension featuring a crocketed cornice topped by a diminutive arcade. Projecting from the plane of the wall to prevent drippage, this cornice was equipped with gutters designed to channel the water flowing off the roof toward regularly spaced drainage holes (see page 238). As a safeguard, the architect included gargoyle spouts on this level to accommodate overflows. But most of the water was evacuated through the above-mentioned drainage holes, via aligned vertical stone conduits situated between each bay, directly above the twelfth-century buttresses. These channeled the water downward as far as the top of the flying buttresses, which were equipped with stone gutters that in turn conveyed it over the side aisles toward the peripheral pinnacles, whence gargoyles expelled it far from the building. First adopted in the chevet, this system was subsequently introduced with minor alterations above the tribune and along the nave. The explanation for the curious structural weakness of the flying buttresses is to be found here: unlike most such constructions, they were designed less to counter outward thrust generated by the stone vaulting than to solve a drainage problem created by replacement of the sloped tribune roofs with terraced ones. Even so, the architect must have been aware of a certain structural vulnerability, for he also girdled the entire chevet with a series of metal tenons, embedded in the masonry behind the denticulated moldings and anchored in the eastern walls of the transept.

The Architect of the 1220s

There are no documents on which to base a chronology for the renovation campaign of the 1220s. Not a single contemporary reference to this vast undertaking survives, and stylistic analysis offers only approximate guidelines. Viollet-le-Duc dated its beginning to 1220, maintaining that it was occasioned by a large fire, evidence of which he claimed to have discovered. This remains hypothetical. It would be more prudent to postulate a date sometime in the 1220s, most likely in the second half of the decade. Work probably continued for several years. In addition to reconstructing the upper portions of the building, the architect introduced the tall gallery running across the western facade and spanning the gap between the two towers, thereby obscuring the gable of the center aisle. It is this feature that reveals his stylistic affinities, for it imparts an extreme elegance to the facade and effects a break with the pronounced murality of its lower portions. Not only did this architect make pervasive use of *en délit* stonework, he did so with exceptional virtuosity: the colonnettes in the gallery are less than eight inches thick but rise to a height of more than sixteen feet. He tripled them below the main vault springs, for obvious structural reasons. Decorative elements, hitherto used quite sparingly, now proliferate: for example, dosserets above the capitals, trilobes, and crockets. Abacuses flare outward and bases grow higher.

The architect's invention and technical virtuosity are likewise apparent in his modification of the clerestory windows, where, as previously noted, he introduced independent *châssis* tracery, eschewing more cumbersome, structurally integrated stone armatures. This technique, also used at Chartres early in the century, necessitated the incorporation of a metal armature: rabbeted sash-bars spanning the gaps between the simplified *en délit* stone tracery and the jambs. By comparison with the Rayonnant chapels at Reims, the architect in Paris displayed greater mastery of this technique, using an approach that, as noted, was also adopted in the clerestory windows there.

This architect's ingenuity with metal was not limited to the windows. He integrated it so completely into the structure itself that, by analogy with the modern term "reinforced concrete," we might well speak of "reinforced stone," a technique he pioneered here. The implications of this innovation would be developed fully only later, by the architects of the Sainte-Chapelle and Amiens, who completely girdled these buildings with metal belts. At Notre-Dame, metal tenons—punningly called *traits de Jupiter, trait* meaning both "bar" and "thunderbolt"—were embedded in the masonry to increase the cohesion of adjacent stone blocks (see page 239).

The genius of the Master of the 1220s is even more apparent in the design of the great flying buttresses that leap over the tribune, coming to rest against the upper wall. Both their extreme length and, especially, their amazing thinness are the result of exceptional technical prowess. In their reduction of structure to its skeletal armature they are the very image of Rayonnant architecture. Such audacity—the headstones are even pierced by trilobe oculi—was possible because, as previously noted, their primary function was not to counter the outward thrust of the vaulting but rather to support the water drainage system. As already observed in connection with the openwork gallery of the facade, this architect possessed a refined sense of design. In assessing his work, we must of course take later modifications into account, but surviving documents, notably daguerreotypes predating the nineteenth-century restoration campaign, suggest that his contributions remain largely intact.

Clearly the architect of the 1220s was one of the great geniuses of his generation. As so often with such figures from the period, his personality eludes us, but we can safely say that he was immersed in the most advanced tendencies of his time. He recast the design of the Master of 1160, both inside and out. Within, he modified the elevations by eliminating the dark oculi and extending the clerestory windows downward, but his interventions on the exterior had an even greater impact. He profoundly altered the relation between its lights—the blond stone—and its darks—the windows and the lead roof. He replaced the sloping roofs of the side aisles with terraced roofs, thereby accentuating the stepped profile of the building, but he also added successive batteries of flying buttresses, whose sweeping arcs minimized the discontinuities. The result, which presumably appealed to contemporaries, was an exterior full of visual incident and contrast. To imagine its original impact, we must block out the chapels subsequently erected between the buttresses of the nave and the apse, which again modified the building's exterior appearance.

Extension of the Transept Arms

No sooner had this campaign been completed than another was envisioned, one that was also to change the building's exterior appearance. The two projects are so close in time that they must have succeeded one another virtually without interruption. It seems clear, however, that the second had not been foreseen when the first was begun, for otherwise the new wood-frame roof would have been conceived somewhat differently. The second phase began before completion of the facade, and it seems likely that the decisions to renounce the steeples above the towers and to reconstruct the transept were reached at the same time.

It has often been suggested that the extension of each transept arm by half a bay was rendered

Above:
The northeast corner of the north tower.
Right:
Detail of the west facade, showing the
Gallery of Kings, the rose window, and
the high gallery.
Opposite:
View through the high gallery.
Prior to the first third of the thirteenth
century, the original design of the cathedral
had remained essentially unchallenged.
The design of the high gallery above the rose
window, however, represented a radical
departure. Its complete independence from
the masonry of the towers initiated a new
era of architectural experimentation.

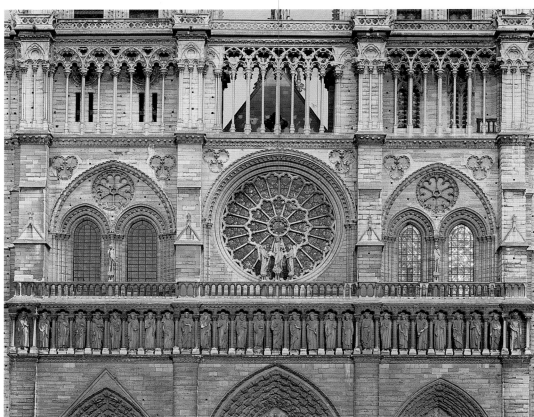

necessary by the construction of the outer chapels, which rose first between the buttresses of the nave, then between those of the chevet. The contention is that without such extensions the transepts would have stopped short of the new outer walls. There is some truth in this, but other considerations were involved as well. As is so often the case in medieval architecture, practical and material concerns were here paralleled by spiritual ones with emblematic overtones. The extensions amounted to only about thirteen feet at either end, but, perhaps more important, they occasioned the incorporation of new sculpted portals and rose windows, additions that greatly increased the magnificence of the transverse part of the building. Such projects were immensely troublesome and expensive, but the outlays they entailed would have found justification in the self-aggrandizing nature of human psychology. Canons and bishops liked to have grandiose entrances for use on feast days and other ceremonial occasions—entrances reserved exclusively for them, let it be emphasized; the regular congregation was allowed to enter the cathedral only through the western facade. Presumably, the results were shaped by programs of the officials' devising and thus reflect the extent of their ambition. The terminal of each arm was to be treated like a small, narrow facade since the transept in Paris—as opposed to that in Chartres—had no side aisles. The sculptural programs, too, correspond to the desires of their respective patrons: the southern portal, which faced the bishop's palace, was dedicated to Saint Stephen, like the ancient cathedral; the northern portal, which faced the canonial close, was dedicated to the Virgin, long the object of special devotion among the canons. Transformation of the transept was accompanied, in the choir and the apse, by construction of a new rood screen as well as a choir enclosure that took quite some time to complete.

We do not know when this phase of work began. Our only guideline is a famous inscription that runs along the foundation of the southern portal, which Pierre de Montreuil had carved in homage to his predecessor, Jean de Chelles, after the latter's death in 1258. Jean de Chelles, then, must have been the architect commissioned by the clergy to design the new transept. Apparently, he completed the extension of the northern arm and began work on the southern extension. After his death, work was continued by Pierre de Montreuil, who significantly modified the original design.

To preclude unnecessary disruption of worship, both architects erected the new terminals to their full height before razing the old ones. Only after the wooden roof had been extended to cover the new half-bays did the demolition proceed, so as to accommodate construction of the transitional transverse rib above new supports. The vault extensions would have been the last elements to be completed. Traces left by the construction are still visible in the masonry of the southern arm, especially its southeastern wall. There were few difficulties to the north, but things must have gone less smoothly to the south due to the instability of the soil. By the sixteenth century there were already alarming signs of movement in the foundations, shifts that adversely affected the rose window, which by the eighteenth century was on the verge of collapse. At the instigation of Cardinal de Noailles, the architect Germain Boffrand hired the master mason Claude Penel to repair it. This proved a formidable undertaking, requiring much time, from 1725 to 1727, and considerable expenditure, no less than 80,000 livres. Even so, the window remained in a precarious state in the nineteenth century. Viollet-le-Duc, judging the eighteenth-century restoration disastrous, dismantled the tracery, completely restored it, pivoted it fifteen degrees so that a mullion coincided with the vertical axis, and anchored it to the surrounding masonry with iron tenons. He also dismantled and consolidated the tracery of the northern rose window.

Left and above:

The southern transept extension.

The southern transept arm was begun by Jean de Chelles shortly before his death in 1258. His successor, Pierre de Montreuil, retained his basic design but modulated its transitions between the lower levels of the facade. He also dilated the portal and gave the rose window a more animated and elaborate design. On the interior wall, note the figures of a Last Judgment above the gables and within the spandrel to the left: Christ, two angels bearing the instruments of the Passion, and two angels sounding the last trump. The pinnacled niches originally held statues of Adam and Eve.

The superb carved inscription in the southern transept, restored by Viollet-le-Duc, finally provides us with an architect's name: Jean de Chelles. This is the only surviving reference to an individual who must have played an important role in the building's history, for otherwise he would not have been deemed worthy of so extraordinary a tribute. The implication, then, is that he must have overseen the project for several years prior to his death. Given the immensely prestigious nature of this commission, he must have worked at other important building sites before being entrusted with it. In any event, the task confronting him in Paris was formidable, for each of the two terminals was to be quite high as well as quite wide, and without side aisles. But he proved equal to the challenge. Although Pierre de Montreuil introduced significant modifications into the southern facade, he opted to retain his predecessor's basic design.

The exterior elevations are composed of three basic elements (see pages 244–45). On the lowest level is a deeply recessed, three-archivolt portal flanked by groups of three niches set into the wall. These various units are crowned by a sequence of successively smaller gables that unify the composition and establish a visual hierarchy: a high central gable over the portal proper, a lower one over each of the flanking niche units, and two still lower ones over blind lancets decorating the bottom of the buttresses. The second level is also tripartite in its organization, featuring on the first level a diminutive open arcade passing in front of the buttresses, on top of that a blind arcade set farther back, and above that a row of lancet windows. While Jean de Chelles stressed the horizontal boundaries between these superimposed elements, Pierre de Montreuil linked them by having the principal supports of the lancet windows pass in front of the intervening molding and descend into the blind arcade below. The third and uppermost level is occupied by an immense rose window, conceived along lines previously established in the transept at Saint-Denis. This entire portion of the wall is pierced and glazed, even the lower spandrels, the upper ones being left blind due to the presence of vaulting on the other side. The culminating gables are also pierced by rose windows, complemented on both north and south by smaller medallions.

Despite the almost identical configurations of the two facades, careful analysis of their detailing and mural articulations reveals the presence of two distinct artistic personalities. Pierre de Montreuil's wall treatments are extremely refined. He breaks down angles into smaller increments, avoids large unadorned areas, and uses engaged columns to set the wall vibrating. Niches are kept shallow to preclude violent shadows. Transitions are modulated, shapes carefully linked. The upward progression from the portal to the rose window is especially revelatory of his intentions: he accentuates the intervening horizontals and lowers the gable over the central portal, but he also manipulates the vertical dynamics in ways that tend to link the two areas. In this respect he is at odds with Jean de Chelles, who prefers cleaner, more assertive and abrupt definitions. The sculpture underscores the differences between their architectural sensibilities. We should remember, however, that they both had to take account of the very different exposures of the two facades as these bore on the question of illumination.

The rose windows of Notre-Dame de Paris are famous, and rightly so. They considerably brightened the interior, a result all the more striking given the pervasive darkness of the rest of the building, which the lengthening of the clerestory windows in fact changed very little. The color schemes of their stained glass were deliberately varied, so the effects they produce are quite distinct from one another. Their diameters, however, are identical: forty-two feet four inches, as opposed to thirty-eight feet at Saint-Denis. Viollet-le-Duc had the opportunity to study them during the restoration process and left a detailed account of their construction. Clearly the thirteenth-century architects calculated the statics as carefully as they could before drafting the final designs. The principal burdens were carried by the radiating bars of the tracery, which were consolidated and reinforced by metal elements, notably rabbeted sash-bars. Comparing the western rose window with the southern one, Viollet-le-Duc calculated that, proportionately, more stone was used in the latter.

The different conceptions of the two architects are still visible, despite changes effected in the southern rose window during its two successive restorations in the eighteenth and nineteenth centuries. Pierre de Montreuil complicated his predecessor's design by introducing trilobate arches on the periphery, between the outer circle and the primary radiating mullions. He divided the central rose into twelve major compartments, whereas the more prudent Jean de Chelles had opted for sixteen. In the interest of hierarchical clarity, he also took greater care to distinguish major and minor mullions from one another by varying their respective thicknesses.

Analysis of the interior elevations reveals parallel differences. To the north, Jean de Chelles superimposed the three levels without attempting to link them and set the blind lancets into the wall, minimizing projecting elements. To the south, the blind lancet units are gabled, project markedly, and also figure on the western wall. These changes could have been introduced by Jean de Chelles himself. Pierre de Montreuil's interventions are clearer in the upper elevations, where the wall treatments have a new subtlety. He established pinnacled niches between the gables and articulated the wall above them with attached colonnettes that rise into the supports between the lancet windows.

In the thirteenth century, then, two great masters succeeded one another at Notre-Dame. Both would have been famous in their day, and they must have known one another, for de Montreuil died just eleven years after de Chelles, in 1269. But nothing survives that might indicate the nature of their relations: for example, whether one was a student of the other or whether they were contemporary rivals. We know much more about Pierre de Montreuil than about his predecessor: he built the refectory and the Lady Chapel at Saint-Germain-des-Prés in 1239–44 and 1245, respectively, and documents likewise attest to his activity at Saint-Denis from at least 1247. Legend also attributes the Sainte-Chapelle in Paris and other buildings elsewhere to him. So striking was the genius of his designs that his fame all but obliterated the reputation of Jean de Chelles. Of the two, his was by far the greater technical mastery, and he also had a remarkable gift for lyrical formal invention.

THE SCULPTURAL PROGRAM

The extension of the transept arms occasioned the elaboration and execution of a vast sculptural program that significantly altered the meaning of the entire building. While its production was protracted, the iconographic program was conceived as a whole, encompassing both portals, the rood screen, and the choir enclosure. By contrast, the statues in the niches within the buttresses—since lost—are later in date, having been conceived after construction of the radial chapels of the apse.

Only by an exercise of the imagination can we hope to grasp the original meaning of this vast ensemble, which was almost certainly conceived in its entirety by Jean de Chelles, as we shall see. The rood screen was destroyed in the seventeenth century, and the hemicycle behind the main altar disappeared early in the eighteenth century, when the choir was redecorated to honor Louis XIII's famous vow of 1638.[1] The stained glass in the two rose windows, which greatly enriched the iconography, is now much altered. Finally, the jamb figures of the portals were removed in 1793 and 1794; fragments have since been recovered, but not all of them have been identified.

As already noted, the northern portal was consecrated to the Virgin and the southern portal to Saint Stephen, the cathedral's first dedicatee. The interior elements recounted the history of the Son of God, who descended to earth to redeem humanity and establish a new covenant. The basic iconographic scheme poses few problems, but there is much uncertainty about points of detail.

The identity of many of the jamb figures in the northern portal remains problematic. One jamb evoked the Epiphany, representing the three Magi bearing gifts to the infant Christ, carried by the Virgin of the trumeau (an arrangement also used in the Portal of the Mother of God in Amiens). The Magi were also depicted at the top of the northeastern buttress (a copy has since

1. *In 1630, suffering from a grave illness, Louis XIII vowed to dedicate himself personally to the Virgin should he recover; he did, and in 1638 he decided to make Notre-Dame the center of a national cult to the Virgin in satisfaction of his promise to her. Louis XIV resolved to realize his father's wish, despite serious fiscal impediments that were removed thanks to the generosity of Canon de La Porte. In 1708, Robert de Cotte (Hardouin-Mansart's successor as First Architect to the King) was placed in charge of the project, which was not completed until 1726. The Gothic choir— altar, stalls, rood screen, and hemicycle—were destroyed and replaced with a magnificent new ensemble consisting of a marble floor, decorative panels of marble and stucco, new wooden stalls enveloping the Gothic arcade, and an elaborate sculptural tableau disposed around a new altar in the chancel: a marble Lamentation group by Nicolas Coustou; kneeling figures of Louis XIII, by Guillaume Coustou, and Louis XIV, by Antoine Coysevox; and six bronze angels carrying the instruments of the Passion. On this ambitious project, see Maurice Vloberg, Notre-Dame de Paris et le voeu de Louis XIII (Paris, 1926).*

The northern portal, which faced the canonial close, was consecrated to the Virgin. The lintel represents episodes from the infancy of the life of Christ, while the two upper registers of the tympanum recount the story of the miracle of Theophilus, in which the Virgin's intervention is crucial.

replaced the original, now in the Musée de Cluny). According to Abbot Lebeuf, the opposite jamb featured three full-length Theological Virtues. As for the niches flanking the portal, now also empty, they may originally have held the personifications of Virtues and Vices said in the eighteenth century to have been in a ruinous state. Interpretation of the archivolts and the tympanum is less problematic. The lintel is carved with familiar scenes from the infancy of Christ. The upper levels represent the miracle of Theophilus, a priest in the bishopric of Adana, in Silesia; it was often evoked in sermons, notably on the feast of the Assumption. The depicted episodes capture the essence of the story, which stresses the Virgin's powers of intervention, demonstrated by her having successfully recovered from the devil a pact he had concluded with Theophilus in exchange for honors his bishop had refused him. In the tympanum, the bishop explains the miracle by showing the people, in the presence of the kneeling Theophilus, the charter and its seal. The archivolts are occupied by angels, virgins, and seated doctors. This ensemble was completed by four statues situated between the gables (removed by Varin and replaced by pinnacles) as well as by two angels within niches flanking the rose window. The canons' overall intention, then, was to honor the Virgin of Mercy: Our Lady of Affliction, who had given birth to Christ and was pursued by Herod's hatred but was honored by three kings from the wondrous East. She who was Faith, Hope, and Charity; who participated in the triumph of Virtue over Vice; who redeemed repentant sinners. Such was this portal's great lesson, rehearsed in condensed form for the canons' edification.

The program of the portal facing the bishop's palace was shaped by historical factors, the aim being to recall the cathedral's original dedication to Saint Stephen, doubtless largely forgotten by the mid-thirteenth century. The trumeau represented him dressed in his deacon's robes and carrying a book, and the entire tympanum was devoted to him. On the lower lintel, we see him expounding a sacred text to the Jews, preaching, and brought before the Sanhedrin. The upper lintel represents his stoning in the presence of Saul (far left), and Neodemus and Gamuliel placing his body in a sarcophagus. The tympanum proper represents Christ flanked by two angels. The niches in the buttresses contain statues of Moses and Aaron, whom the deacon had invoked. The archivolts are carved with angels, martyrs, and confessors. The jamb figures represented six apostles, while the flanking niches held figures of Saints Denis, Rustique, and Éleuthère to the left, Saint Martin and two other confessors to the right. The original statues were removed during the Revolution; those currently in place are approximate copies based on fragments unearthed in 1839 in the rue de la Santé. As in the northern portal, the original program featured four more statues situated between the gables, since replaced by pinnacles. The two upper niches in the buttresses now contain statues of Saints Stephen and Marcel, but they are known to have been empty in the eighteenth century. Finally, the gable above the rose window now supports a statue of Christ, but the original may have been a figure of Saint Marcel. This rather hodgepodge iconographic program was completed by reliefs set into the lower walls of the buttresses. It is often

The southern portal, which faced the bishop's palace, was dedicated to Saint Stephen, to whom the previous cathedral had been dedicated.

Page 166:
Reliefs from the buttress to the left of the southern portal.
The blind arcades on the buttresses of the southern portal are decorated with eight animated figural reliefs set within, and around, quadrilobe medallions. They are often said to represent student life, largely due to the casual nature of the sociability they depict, but their precise significance remains obscure.

The Rayonnant Cathedral

claimed that they depict student life, largely because of the casual atmosphere that pervades them. A few of the compositions could represent intellectual sociability of some kind, but others clearly do not, and the import of the series as a whole remains mysterious.

The extension of the transept arms led to changes east of the crossing as well. A new stone enclosure was built around the choir and chancel, probably to replace an earlier wooden one, the clergy having decided that a nobler material would be preferable. Such structures were becoming widespread in northern France, from Chartres to Strasbourg. Their sculpted decors were designed not for the clergy but for the lay congregation. The rood screen ran between the two eastern piers of the crossing and thus was visible to the faithful at all times. The choir enclosure was also accessible, at least when the gates of the ambulatory were open. Of this immense ensemble, produced over an extended period, all that survives are the northern and southern enclosure walls, a few statues high on the walls of the southern transept, and some fragments of stained glass, as well as a few fragments from the rood screen and the hemicycle discovered by Viollet-le-Duc during the restoration campaign. In all likelihood, the reliefs devoted to the Virgin now set into the exterior of the northern wall of the apse also came from this ensemble. Its destruction began in 1627, when Anne of Austria decided to rebuild the altar of the Virgin, situated against the southern portion of the rood screen; its final phase was initiated on April 29, 1699, when redecoration of the choir was begun in honor of Louis XIII's famous vow. Over the next several years the surviving portions of the Gothic rood screen as well as the curving hemicycle were removed, along with the main altar and much other ecclesiastical furniture, all to make way for an equally remarkable decor conceived by Robert de Cotte.

Reconstruction of the original iconography of the rood screen and choir enclosure poses a number of problems, even after surviving fragments and documents have been taken into account. The rood screen, which ran in front of the eastern piers of the crossing, was subdivided

Top:
Rood screen of Anne of Austria. (Drawing by Robert de Cotte, early eighteenth century. Bibliothèque Nationale, Cabinet des Estampes.)
Above:
Section of the cathedral with view of thirteenth-century rood screen. (Print from Jacques Cellerier, *Portraict et perspective du dedans de l'église Notre-Dame de Paris* [Paris, 1587]. Bibliothèque Nationale, Département des Manuscrits, Ms. fr. 9152.)
Despite the survival of a few fragments, our knowledge of the mid-thirteenth-century rood screen is limited. In the seventeenth century, construction of a new facade commissioned by Anne of Austria obscured all of it except the tip of the central gable, the crucifix, and the flanking figures of the Virgin and Saint John.

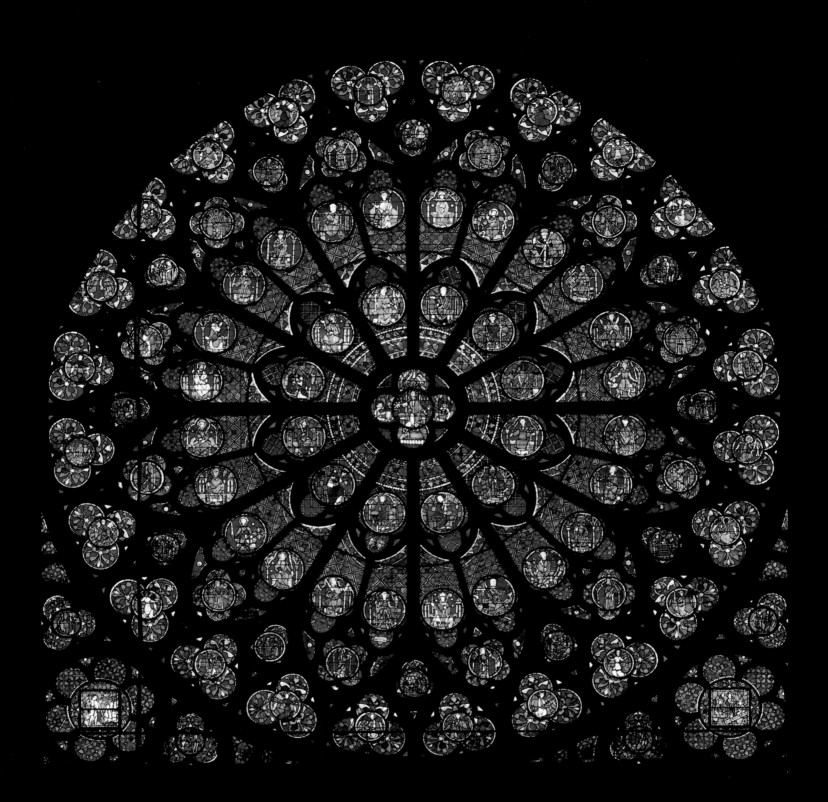

Page 168:
Northern rose window.
Page 169:
Southern rose window.
The Passion iconography of the rood screen was
extended by that of the two rose windows. The
northern rose was devoted to the Old Testament,
with a Virgin and Child group in the center.
The southern rose, depicting the Heavenly Host,
originally had at its center not the Christ of
the Apocalypse we see today but an image
of God the Father.

Above:
Crown-bearing angel from the southern rose window
(H-19).
Opposite:
Wise virgin from the southern rose window (B-12).
The stained glass of the transept rose windows were
executed in a somewhat less refined version of the
style found in the windows of the Sainte-Chapelle.
It is characterized by attenuated forms of a kind tradi-
tionally associated with Gothic mannerist art and by the
pervasive use of whites and lighter colors. Purples
and reds, for example, now become less saturated.

Opposite:
Holy knight from the southern
rose window (G-8).
Above:
Dream of Pharaoh from the
northern rose window (H-4).
Right:
Judgment of Solomon from the
southern rose window (J-2).
The new style evolved very quickly,
as evidenced by this comparison of
a detail from the northern window
with two details from the later
southern window.

into five bays; the central one contained a door, while a stair leading to an upper terrace was situated behind the two bays to the north. The sculpted scenes were placed within the blind arcades as well as in the spaces between their crowning gables. Their subjects, all relating to the Passion, included the Resurrection of Christ, the Resurrection of the Dead, several groups of the elect, and, finally, at the southeastern corner, a Descent into Limbo, now in the Louvre (see page 192). The whole was surmounted by a triumphal Crucifixion group with figures of the Virgin and Saint John. The delicate crucifix, some twenty-eight feet high, was especially admired, partly because it was mistakenly thought to be made of stone. A more precise reconstruction must remain hypothetical, although it seems likely that the elect, shown newly clothed, were to the north, and two half-medallions were set into the back wall.

The iconography of the rood screen was carefully coordinated with the decorative sculpture of the southern transept and the two rose windows. A few statues from a Last Judgment group survive. Figures of Christ and two angels bearing the instruments of the Passion remain in place above the gables on the southern wall; angels sounding the last trump are also still visible, at the same level, on the southwestern wall of the transept extension and the eastern wall of the original transept (see pages 160–61). They were originally joined by figures of Adam and Eve, placed in the now empty pinnacle niches flanking the central Christ; the Adam survives and is now in the Musée de Cluny. The program was completed by the rose windows, which were heavily restored in the nineteenth century. Of the two, the one to the north, devoted to the Old Testament, is the better preserved. In its center is a Virgin and Child enthroned; this is surrounded by eighty figures: prophets, judges, kings, and great preachers, all of whom turn or gesture toward the central medallion. This window features the largest known assemblage of Biblical figures in medieval iconography, but assessment of the composition is complicated by subsequent losses, modifications, and additions. The southern rose window, which depicts the Heavenly Host, has suffered even more. While the northern window has eighty-one compartments, the southern one has eighty-five. Its central medallion now represents the Christ of the Apocalypse, but it originally contained an image of God the Father. The first circle was reserved for the twelve apostles, the second for twenty-four martyrs and confessors. Beyond this point doubts arise. The original inclusion of virgin martyrs is a certainty, but that of the wise virgins remains problematic.

In fact, the iconography of the rood screen was part of a larger narrative sequence encompassing the northern and southern walls of the enclosure, which extended as far as the openings providing access to the choir. The entirety of their two relief cycles survives. To the north, the compositions unfold from east to west and narrate the life of Christ, treating the Visitation, the Annunciation to the Shepherds, the Nativity, the Adoration of the Magi, the Massacre of the Innocents, the Flight into Egypt, the Presentation in the Temple, Christ in the Temple, the Baptism, the Entry into Jerusalem, the Last Supper, and the Washing of the Feet. The southern cycle, which proceeds from west to east, is devoted to the Apparitions of Christ after his Resurrection: to Mary Magdalene, the holy women, Peter and John, the disciples of Emmaus, the apostles, Thomas, the apostles at the Sea of Galilee, the apostles in Galilee, and the apostles on Ascension Day.

Originally, the cycle continued on the hemicycle, which began after the break providing access to the choir. Unlike the surviving enclosure walls to the west, its upper portion was an openwork arcade, as was customary, so that the faithful could see the high altar. The narrative reliefs were thus situated on its lower portions, as opposed to the disposition of the balance of the enclosure, where they appear above a blind arcade. The reliefs were arranged in two superimposed rows. The first was composed of scenes from the story of Christ and the Virgin. Some of their subjects are recognizable from drawings commissioned in the late seventeenth century by Roger de Gaignières: the Entry into Jerusalem, the Christ Child among the Doctors, the Dormition, and the Assumption. The second series treated subjects drawn from the Old Testament; the very beautiful inscriptions identifying them are still extant. Finally, there were two kneeling

Opposite:
Saint Denis from the southern rose window (E-8).
This image of Saint Denis carrying his head is remarkable for the quality of the drawing of the almond-eyed face and for the effective use of reds and blues.

figures accompanied by long inscriptions: to the north, Jean Ravy; to the south, Pierre de Fayel. These also survive.

As in Strasbourg, the hemicycle also featured sculpture on its inner face: sculpture in high relief depicting stories from the Gospels and the Acts of the Apostles. A few fragments of these compositions survive, some at Notre-Dame itself and others at the Louvre. There were also some low reliefs illustrating scenes from Genesis.

In sum, this was one of the largest sculptural ensembles ever produced for a cathedral inte-rior. The analogous ensembles at Chartres and Reims—the latter no longer extant—are much later in date. Subsequent losses and damage make it difficult to assess the work in its totality, a task further complicated by the likelihood of the extended time-frame of its production having led to significant changes in the original conception.

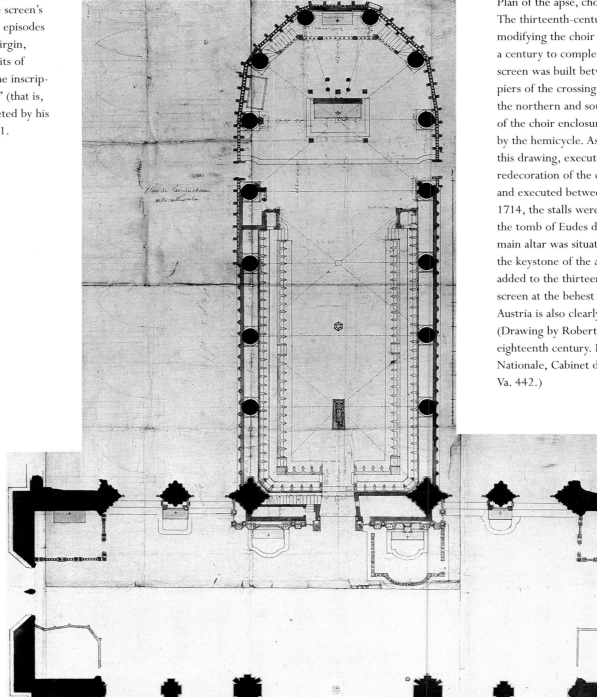

The Rayonnant Cathedral

STYLE

Each of these complementary ensembles evidenced changing attitudes toward both style and the relationship between sculpture and architecture. In fact, the two questions are so intricately connected in these projects as to suggest that it was the architect who had the lion's share of responsibility in their overall design. The transept portals are particularly revealing in this regard: their sculpture differs markedly in style, which suggests that Jean de Chelles and Pierre de Montreuil assembled different teams of sculptors to realize their diverse aims.

Opposite:
North portal of the western facade, trumeau and portion of the lintel.
The Virgin and Child of the north trumeau is one of very few statues to remain in place after the Revolution, when it was deemed sufficient to remove the florets of her crown. It was much imitated in the years immediately following its execution, in ivory as well as in stone.

In the northern transept, Jean de Chelles reconceived the relationship between the sculptural elements and their architectural framework. Despite subsequent damage, it is clear that the jamb statues were completely independent of their niches. Such an approach could have resulted in a total disjunction between sculpture and architecture, but this was avoided thanks to the assertive design of the architect, who doubtless also influenced the style of the figures themselves through his choice of sculptors. The jamb niches are deeply recessed and resemble tabernacles, featuring canopies supported by engaged colonnettes separated by larger colonnettes with elaborate capitals; the bases, which tilt forward, are supported by elegant blind arcades that establish a clear distinction between the upper and lower portions of the jambs. This design tends to produce strong contrasts between light and shadow, but they are attenuated to some degree by the soft northern light. These novel framing elements (now empty), rigorously designed yet supple in the effects they produce, must have given the statues an entirely new dimension. They were also placed higher on the wall: Jean de Chelles raised them some eight feet, which considerably altered

Above:
North portal, details from the lintel.
On the left, Mary, Joseph, and the infant Christ from the Flight into Egypt. On the right, Herod Ordering the Massacre of the Innocents.
The master who carved the lintel of the north portal combined a monumental approach to form with a feeling for narrative. The handling of the drapery is ample, with many tubular folds; the treatment of the faces, by contrast, has a mannerist preciosity.

The Rayonnant Cathedral

Above:
Head of one of the Magi figures from the left jamb of the north portal. (Musée de Cluny, Gift of the B.F.C.E.)
Opposite:
Head of a Theological Virtue (?) from the right jamb of the north portal. (Musée de Cluny, Gift of the B.F.C.E.)
Both pieces were discovered in 1977. The crown worn by the Magi figure evidences the widespread taste in this period for goldsmith work. Its curving locks have a wonderful finesse that is echoed in many other meticulously rendered details, for example, the incised wrinkles of the brow and the crow's feet at the corners of the almond eyes. The handling of the other head, which probably represents a Theological Virtue, is quite close to that of the king. Although the lower part of the face is plumper, it features the same carefully incised crow's feet.

the viewer's angle of vision. As a result, it became necessary to lengthen the figures and give them heads that, when seen from a certain distance, seem disproportionately small—just short of a foot high, on figures of almost six feet. The basic effect can still be judged from the Virgin of the trumeau, which remains in place (see also pages 164, 244).

Examination of the Virgin of the trumeau and the surviving fragments of the jamb statues reveals a preference for ample, simplified volumes. These pieces have an assertive plastic presence, an effect produced by a deliberate reduction in the forward masses and a retention of much of each block's rear mass. This approach was carefully gauged to maximize the play of light and shadow within the niches. The handling of drapery reveals parallel concerns, as evidenced by the Virgin and Child, which, aside from the loss of the Christ figure, is extremely well preserved. She supports the infant in her crooked right arm, a gesture that prompts a delicate bending of her left knee. This double movement, necessary to maintain her balance, creates hooked folds in her mantle that catch the light. Both the weight and the consistency of the fabric are admirably conveyed by the sculptor. The relief depicting the Magi—now headless—also represents a departure, this time in its successful evocation of three figures of unusual volumetric presence in a single block of stone.

These characteristics suggest an approach that favored monumentality, but the heads of the jamb figures have a remarkable delicacy suggestive of metalwork. Here the sculptors clearly sought to achieve effects of considerable refinement. The overall designs are rather schematic, but the details are meticulously rendered: bags beneath the eyes; incised creases at the sockets; projecting cheeks that enrich the modeling of the face; high, knitted brows; silky hair and beards whose locks form sensuous S-curves. One of the Magi wears a crown in which each jewel is carefully rendered in stone, additional testimony—if such be needed—of the prevailing taste for the luxury arts.

In our discussion of the western portals we were at pains to stress their uniformly high quality, but by the mid-thirteenth century such consistency would seem to have become a thing of the past. In both transept portals, the jamb figures are of exceptional quality while the tympani are much less distinguished and the archivolts frankly mediocre. A hierarchy in sculptural production seems to have emerged over the first half of the thirteenth century that was now largely taken for granted. There are many possible explanations for this, the most likely being quite straightforward: economy.

Another sculptor, then, was responsible for the lintel reliefs depicting scenes from the infancy of Christ in the north portal (see page 164). His originality is apparent in both the overall design and the handling of specific passages. While retaining a conventional frieze composition, he refined it by more carefully integrating the figures of each scene. Several of the figures in the Presentation are virtually crammed together, but the Massacre of the Innocents is more successful, thanks to the sense of movement that pervades the scene and to the use of higher relief. The handling of the drapery is often rendered monotonous by repetition. The Virgin of the Flight into Egypt, where light-catching details are in short supply, is especially dull. Nonetheless, there are a few passages of great beauty: the head of Joseph in the Flight and the head of Herod, for example, have a delicacy of touch comparable to that of the jamb statues.

The two upper registers of the tympanum are the works of a sculptor whose originality is most evident in the overall conception. He broke with the conventional frieze disposition, most obviously by having the niche housing the votive image of the Virgin project so markedly from the stone slab. He was also much more accomplished than his predecessor in group composition, although he often achieves cohesion through subterfuge: for example, the use of emphatic gestures and hand motions to establish connections between the various figures. His personality also surfaces in the handling of the faces. Generally rounded, they tend to lack expression, and their mouths, chins, and eyes have an affected air. He also favors drapery that adheres to the bodies beneath, an approach that results in heavy, sometimes inelegant effects, as in the Virgin.

In the southern transept, Pierre de Montreuil's refinement of his predecessor's design exceeded exclusively architectural concerns to affect both the sculpture and its relation to the

Right:
A niche statue in the blind arcade to the
left of the south portal, possibly depicting
a saint. (Musée de Cluny.)
Opposite:
Apostle, jamb statue from the south portal.
(Musée de Cluny.)
Pierre de Montreuil assembled a new
team of sculptors to execute the south
portal. These statues from the ensemble
feature drapery folds whose complex
patterns animate the figures, but despite
the occasional deep recess, light tends
to glide smoothly over their surfaces.
Both were discovered in 1839 in the
rue de la Santé.

Above:
Saint Stephen, fragment of the southern
trumeau figure. (Musée de Cluny.)
Despite serious damage, the axial stasis
of the Saint Stephen remains powerful.
The vertical folds, stabilized by the
horizontals of the arms supporting
the book, grow wider as they fall.
The figure was discovered in 1839.

Opposite and pages 186–87:
Details from the tympanum of the
southern transept portal.
Opposite: Saint Stephen before the
Sanhedrin.
Pages 186–87: Top left, the Stoning of
Saint Stephen; bottom left, Saint Stephen
Conversing with the Doctors; right,
Saint Stephen Preaching to the People.
A taste for rich, complex effects is appar-
ent in the scenes of the tympanum, which
the sculptor animated with pervasive
curves and countercurves. The drapery
patterns generate visual rhythms that
bind the figures together.

surrounding architecture. A telling indicator of the distinctness of his approach is the absence
from the southern portal of work by any of the sculptors who had contributed to the northern
portal, with the exception of secondary works—statues of Moses and Aaron, and reliefs of Saint
Martin and the soul of Saint Denis.

Pierre de Montreuil's innovations are most apparent in the architectural framework: quite
assertive to the north, here it is toned down. Two features exemplify the new approach: the supports below the jamb niches are more restrained, featuring less elaborate relief work; and the
lateral niches have no canopies, their height having been reduced to expose bare wall above them.
The result is a certain inconsistency with the jamb niches.

In Jean de Chelles's design, the jamb statues project outward with great force from distinctive tabernacle-niches. Pierre de Montreuil preferred to increase the breadth of the niche statues.
Some of them spread their arms, requiring their sculptors to treat their drapery with greater
amplitude. One seems to turn, a movement that animates the folds, but the effect is less dramatic
now than it would have been when the figure was within its niche. Furthermore, iconographic
considerations suggest that the more energized figures were in the jambs, while the more static
ones were placed in the lateral niches. The sculptors seem to have turned this stylistic disjunction
to advantage: in the trumeau, the vestments of Saint Stephen fall in emphatic vertical folds consistent with its axial position. Differences between the old and the new team of sculptors also surface in their respective handling of drapery: here the folds are not deeply cut, with some scarcely
being articulated; the garments adhere to the bodies beneath, amplifying their forms and movements. The resulting patterns are sometimes complex, and they must have been especially arresting
under the bright sunlight of the southern exposure. At least three distinct hands are discernable
in these statues, all pursuing goals at odds with the monumental tradition of the 1250s. They mark
the emergence of a new mannerist current in Gothic sculpture that was to triumph some thirty
years later.

The same audacity of conception is apparent in the tympanum (see page 165). The sculptor
retained superimposed registers but broke with precedent in his handling of the frieze format. He
created homogeneous groups through a subtle play of gesture, movement, and interlocking gazes.
The number of groups in each register is an important feature of the composition, passing from
three on the lower lintel to one at the top. This exceptional organizational scheme made it possible
for him to cover each slab completely and generate a lateral dynamic previously unknown. Its success is reinforced by the sculptor's equally original approach to the composition of each distinct
group, some being open, such as Saint Stephen Preaching, and others closed in on themselves, for
example, the Entombment of Saint Stephen.

The gestures interlock, generating an emphatic lateral movement in such scenes as Saint
Stephen before the Sanhedrin. This same sidewise momentum is apparent in the Stoning of
Saint Stephen, but here the rhythms are choppier and more violent, as befits the subject. The
figure of Stephen is especially audacious: having fallen to the ground, he twists awkwardly and
raises one hand in a fruitless attempt to protect himself from his executioners, who completely
surround him. The result is one of the most original and compelling of all Gothic compositions. To animate the scenes and make them more accessible, the sculptor also incorporated
anecdotal and picturesque elements: a woman nursing, a Jew pulling his beard and hair, faces
with negroid features.

He also managed to integrate bodily motion and draperies. The latter are thin and pliant,
bending with the limbs and amplifying their movement. The stylistic coherence of this tympanum
is so striking that it must have been executed under the close supervision of a single sculptor,
although he doubtless worked with assistants.

Unlike the large portal of the northern transept, the Red Door was meant for everyday use
by the canons, whose enclosure it faced. Located in the third bay east of the north portal, it
afforded them ready access to their choir. In the 1260s, when chapels were built between the but-

tresses of the northern wall of the choir, it was decided to decorate the doorway with a sculptural program. A Coronation of the Virgin in the tympanum was complemented by scenes from the legend of Saint Marcel. Two statues in the jamb niches were also envisioned, but these may never have been executed; in any event, they had disappeared by the eighteenth century. Many questions about the iconography of this ensemble remain unanswered. In the tympanum, the kneeling king and queen on either side of the central group have traditionally been identified as Louis IX and his wife, Marguerite, but if that is indeed who they are, then this is a unique instance in the period of contemporary lay figures having been incorporated into such a sacred composition. The juxtaposition of the legend of Saint Marcel and the Coronation is also surprising. In the mid-twelfth-century Portal of the Virgin he was depicted on the trumeau (see page 27), but here his legend was more amply developed in six archivolt reliefs evoking the dragon living in the coffin of the adulterous woman (now a nineteenth-century copy) as well as Marcel baptizing, celebrating mass,

Left:
View from the high altar down the choir toward the crossing.
This drawing represents the choir as it appeared prior to the redecoration campaign begun in 1699 to honor the vow of Louis XIII. The towering Crucifixion group from the thirteenth-century rood screen is still in place, as are the thirteenth-century stalls. (Drawing by Israël Sylvestre. Musée du Louvre, Cabinet des Dessins, Inv. 33009.)

instructing clerics, fighting the dragon, and healing a possessed man. Doubtless the canons had their reasons for selecting these themes, but the program's underlying rationale now eludes us.

It seems likely that the sculptor responsible for this ensemble also worked on the northern transept portal. One finds here the same handling reminiscent of repoussé as well as the same approach to figure composition, facial features, and drapery.

Returning to the cathedral's interior, stylistic analysis of architectural and sculptural fragments from the rood screen suggests a dating in the 1260s and an attribution of the overall design to Pierre de Montreuil. A paucity of images as well as the small number of surviving fragments makes reconstruction difficult. Despite their poor condition, these remains are sufficient to indicate that the ensemble was not executed by the same team as the Saint Stephen portal. The manifest similarities between the Adam from the southern transept extension (Musée de Cluny) and

Opposite:
Top: The Red Door, end of the eighteenth century. (Drawing by Charles Percier. Bibliothèque de l'Institut, Ms. 1013, plate 18.)
Bottom: The Red Door, view of tympanum and archivolt.
The tympanum of the Red Door is decorated with a high relief of the Coronation of the Virgin. The two jamb niches may originally have contained statues, but if so they had disappeared by the eighteenth century. The door was also flanked by high, blind lancets that once held statues, as indicated by this drawing.

Above and opposite:
Adam (detail and full view), formerly in
one of the interior pinnacled niches of
the southern transept extension. (Musée
de Cluny.)
The iconography of the rood screen was
further developed by statues placed in
both of the transept arms. The statue of
Adam, originally in the southern arm,
is one of the most beautiful surviving
nudes of the Middle Ages. The same
subtle, sensuous modeling of human flesh
is found in the fragment of a Descent
into Limbo now in the Louvre (see
page 192), originally on the southwest
corner of the rood screen. The two
works are probably by the same sculptor.

the Descent into Limbo fragment (Musée du Louvre) strongly suggest that these two works are from the same hand. Both pieces are striking for their audacious depiction of the nude figure. The Adam has a supple pose that would only be possible in freestanding sculpture. The modeling is full of subtle transitions that are rendered even more seductive by a skillful use of curves and countercurves. The Descent into Limbo is even more daring: here the sculptor delighted in describing svelte female forms with narrow waists and clearly articulated busts. This sensual approach to the human body was not altogether unprecedented in the Middle Ages: slightly earlier, in the 1250s, the sculptor at Bourges had produced comparable nudes in his Descent into Limbo and Leviathan compositions, and his Eve is the most beautiful female nude of the medieval period, or at least the most suggestive. The Adam of Notre-Dame produces a completely different effect, in part because of the polychromy that, thanks to a recent cleaning, is still discernable: the entire figure was painted a fleshy beige tint complemented by delicate pink highlights. When new, this coloring must have greatly intensified the sweet melancholy of the face, whose lips seem poised to address us.

The two surviving portions of the choir enclosure must be numbered among the major surviving ensembles of Gothic sculpture. In both cases, assessment is made difficult by polychromy that, while present on the reliefs from the beginning, was poorly restored in the nineteenth century and obscures details of the faces and drapery folds. The result, especially to the north, is a gummy quality that the sculptor cannot have intended. This problem also complicates the determination of a precise, as opposed to a relative, chronology. The northern cycle was exe-

cuted first; it dates from the first third of the thirteenth century, immediately after completion of the rood screen. The southern cycle probably dates from the early fourteenth century, a period from which few analogous productions survive. All that remains of the great projects produced under Philip the Fair, in the Palais de la Cité and the Priory of Saint-Louis at Poissy, are a few odds and ends. So comparative elements are cruelly lacking.

To the north, the scenes unfold in a continuous frieze, an effect emphasized by the thin strip of foreground vegetation that runs from one end to the other, virtually without interruption. As a counterpart to this element, the designer used baldachins to vary the visual rhythms and isolate certain groups—the Visitation, the Presentation, the Wedding at Cana, and the Last Supper. He also employed another means of visual punctuation to parse this long band: figures rising to the full height of the slab. In terms of style, too, the most striking characteristic is the deliberate elongation of the figures. Some are so tall that their heads interrupt the upper border of the visual field, their verticality being further accentuated by the fall of their drapery. But supple drapery sometimes softens their stiff postures. Long tubular folds, straight and deeply cut in the best mid-thirteenth-century tradition, prevail in some scenes, whereas others are characterized by curving, harmonious drapery that signals an intent to recast the style, as in the Adoration of the Magi, the Presentation, and Christ Entering Jerusalem.

To the south, a radical transformation has taken place (see pages 77, 198–99). The stiffness of the first cycle has given way to great pliancy and freedom. It is as though the new sculptors had realized that it would be impossible to resolve the tensions inherent in the earlier style and so decided to reject it completely. The break manifested itself in two ways. First, the designer abandoned the goal of a continuous narrative, introducing canopies supported by colonnettes that isolate the various scenes from one another. Second, he opted for high instead of low relief. Many parts of the figures are completely undercut, and instead of being fully integrated into the scenes, as in the northern cycle, the gilded backgrounds isolate and set off the figures, which are given considerably more breathing room than in the northern cycle. This is not the first time such an approach was used; it is also employed in the Portal of the Gilded Virgin at Amiens, which dates from the mid-thirteenth century, but there it found no imitators. Here it resurfaces with exceptional mastery. The canopied frames with their pendants create little theaters for the play of light and shadow, suggesting that the sculptor consciously set out to exploit the crisp southern light. He also had an acute sense of drama: these scenes have a vitality that belies their being frozen in stone. Within each composition, the figures are linked by gestures of an immediacy and affective power never before seen in medieval sculpture. This quality finds its fullest expression in the Apparition of Christ to the Holy Women (see pages 200–201), whose composition is based on a subtle interplay of gestures: Christ leans affectionately to his right; the three women manifest their wonder in various ways, but coherence is assured by their all joining their hands in prayer. The similarity of these compositions to contemporary illumination is striking, especially to the group of works associated with Master Honoré: one finds here the same corporeal grace, elegance of posture, and skillful depiction of drapery. Furthermore, the gold grounds play a similar role, creating an abstract framework that pushes the figures into the foreground. The faces, too, have a delicate beauty typical of Gothic mannerist art at its most accomplished.

The stained glass of the northern rose window is in a style that was current in the Île-de-France from the 1240s to the 1260s. Some of its master glaziers must also have worked at the Sainte-Chapelle, which was completed in 1248. One finds here the same elegance of design and color, but the traditional contrast between blue and red is tempered by a pervasive use of white. This softens the color scheme and gives it a violet cast, with results that Viollet-le-Duc found remarkable and that prompted Émile Mâle to write of "a beautiful flower of mourning."

Things evolved considerably in the southern rose window, despite the likelihood that it, too, was produced by master glaziers who had worked at the Sainte-Chapelle. A certain schematism is in evidence here, although it is countered by an increase in refinement. Mannerism is apparent

Opposite:
Fragment of a Descent into Limbo from the southwest corner of the rood screen. (Musée du Louvre, Département des Sculptures.)

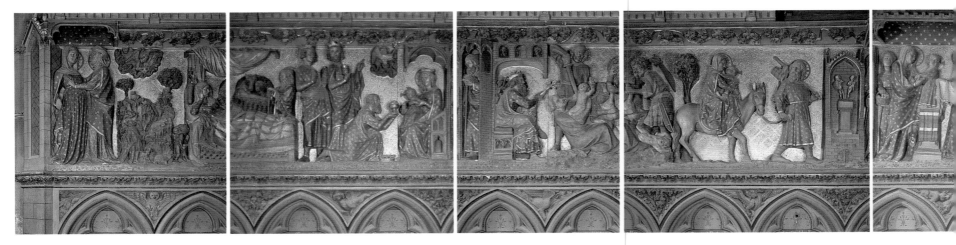

Above right, and pages 196–97:
Reliefs on the northern wall of the choir enclosure.
The reliefs on the northern wall of the enclosure, facing the side aisles, depict twelve episodes from the lives of the Virgin and Christ: The Visitation, the Adoration of the Magi, the Massacre of the Innocents, the Flight into Egypt, the Presentation in the Temple, Christ among the Doctors, the Baptism of Christ, the Wedding at Cana, Christ's Entry into Jerusalem, the Last Supper, the Washing of the Feet, and Christ on the Mount of Olives.
Right:
The Presentation in the Temple, Christ among the Doctors, the Baptism of Christ.
Pages 196–97: The Adoration of the Magi.

Above, right, and pages 200–201:
Reliefs on the southern wall of the
enclosure.
The reliefs on the southern wall of
the enclosure represent Christ's nine
apparitions after his Resurrection.
From left to right: Apparitions to Mary
Magdalene, to the Three Holy Women,
to Peter and John, to the Disciples, the
Supper at Emmaus, Apparitions in the
Upper Room, to Thomas, on the Shore
of the Sea of Galilee, the Last Supper.
Right:
The Apparition of Christ to Mary
Magdalene.
Pages 200–201:
The Apparition of Christ to the
Holy Women.

Christus resurgens apparet Marie Magdalene

Chriſtus apparet ſancti

ing spaces were covered with ribbed vaults. The consequences were significant, both inside and outside. Articulation of the interior space became much less clear with the disappearance of the original outer wall, whose importance in this regard has already been stressed. The additions also darkened the interior by distancing the light sources. The exterior appearance was affected to an even greater extent, for the building now became more solidly rooted in the ground. Running between the outer supports of the flying buttresses, the new wall did away with the emphatic projections that had punctuated the exterior elevation. The result was a unified envelope that began at the west end of the cathedral, continued without interruption through the new transept facades, and wrapped around the chevet.

The chapels were associated with newly established chaplaincies. Initially, the altars associated with these clerical posts were placed perpendicular to the original outer wall or, in the case of the turning ambulatory, against it, but this arrangement proved so cumbersome that it was decided to build chapels to house them. Thus the establishment of the chaplaincies does not necessarily correspond to the construction of the chapels. The erroneous assumption that the two dates do tally has resulted in many incorrect early datings. Their defenders have pointed to the archaic structural features of some of them to support their views, but these features are evidence only of

Above:
The first chapels along the northern side of the nave.
Beginning in the mid-thirteenth century, chapels were erected along the nave. The building's original outer envelope was demolished and new exterior walls, pierced by large windows, were erected flush with the outer faces of the buttresses, which were left essentially unaltered to their full height.

The Rayonnant Cathedral

mediocre construction. The question is further complicated by the fact that several of them were considerably altered between the seventeenth and nineteenth centuries. According to the documents, the oldest of these chapels (no. 2), to the north, in the nave, was dedicated to Saints George and Blaise slightly before 1252 (see page 249). The first built to the south (no. 45), dedicated to Saint Anne, appears to be contemporary with it. The last ones built along the north side of the nave (nos. 5, 6, and 7) are in the style of Pierre de Montreuil and thus cannot be earlier than 1258, the year he succeeded Jean de Chelles.

Luckily, the history of the chapels in the ambulatory is better documented. The oldest were built shortly before the transept extensions. Archeological evidence suggests that the four to the north (nos. 15, 16, 17, and 18) were the product of a single campaign. The Saint Agnes chapel in this series (no. 15) provides us with an important chronological benchmark, for we know that it existed prior to the death of Alphonse of Poitiers in 1271. Thus it seems reasonable to situate the beginning of this campaign in the 1260s, the same decade that saw construction of the Red Door ensemble. It came to a close shortly after 1288, with the chapel dedicated to Saint John the Baptist and Mary Magdalene (no. 18). At his death in that year, Canon Gilbert of Soana bequeathed 100 "livres tournois" for its construction.

Three of the chapels directly opposite to the south (nos. 37, 36, and 35) are contemporary. Work then proceeded along the axis of the building with construction of the axial chapels (nos. 25, 26, and 27), continued with the six flanking chapels (nos. 24, 23, 22; 28, 29, 30), and reached completion with three each to the north (nos. 21, 20, and 19) and to the south (nos. 31, 32, and 33). We are rather well informed about this campaign, which, although conceived as a whole, took more than three decades to complete. Initiated in 1296 by Mattifas de Buci, bishop of Paris from 1289 until 1304, it began, as noted, with the three axial chapels; Mattifas's marble tomb and the painting above it were placed against the south wall of the southernmost of them. A full-length statue of him was placed on a column at its entrance. It is still in place, and its inscription states that he contributed 600 "livres parisis" toward the construction of these three chapels. He also contributed 200 "livres tournois" toward the construction of other chapels. It is he, then, who was responsible for having initiated the radical alteration of the exterior of the chevet, an operation that continued well beyond his death. The Chapel of Saints Peter and Stephen (no. 31) and the Chapel of Saint Rémi (no. 32), financed by Canon Eudes de Corbeil, were all but complete in 1316. Likewise the Saint Foy chapel to the north (no. 22), destined to house the tomb of Eudes de Corbeil. The remaining chapels to the north (nos. 19, 20, and 21) were completed on July 9, 1320; indeed, we know that no. 20 was finished as early as 1318.

While construction of the extensions along the straight portions of the ambulatory did not present major complications, the chapels abutting the bays of its curving portion did pose problems. This phase of the work was informed by ambition of a higher order: Mattifas de Buci clearly set out to achieve something remarkable here, for considerable expenditure and complex technical operations were involved (compare the plans on pages 58 and 241). The only twelfth- and thirteenth-century elements to be retained were the large buttresses. After construction of the chapel extensions, the walls of the old envelope were demolished and rebuilt as open arcades; the intermediate supports that had hitherto been engaged were now freestanding, no perpendicular walls having been erected to link them to the new envelope. This produced open units consisting of several bays, and the resulting effect, accentuated by the immense new windows, was one of great spatial amplitude. On the exterior, the new lower envelope now linked the outermost faces of the flying buttresses, thereby muting the strong rhythms initially established by their projection beyond the foundations. In addition, two new subsidiary flying buttresses were sprung from the axial support of the tribune. To harmonize the overall design of the chevet, the windows of the tribune were enlarged and provided with crocketed gables similar to those used in the chapel window treatments. This construction campaign proceeded incrementally: it began with the axial unit, proceeded along identical lines in the flanking units, also consisting of three chapels each,

Opposite, top:
View of the tribune overlooking the chancel.
Opposite, bottom:
View of the chevet.
Construction of the radial ambulatory chapels occasioned substantial work. The envelope was shifted outward to become flush with the outer buttress supports. To harmonize the resulting elevations, the tribune windows were enlarged and provided with crocketed gables similar to those in the treatments of the new chapel windows below.

Top:
Late-seventeenth-century drawing of
the marble tomb of Mattifas de Buci.
(Bibliothèque Nationale, Cabinet des
Dessins, Gaignières Collection.)
Above:
Late-seventeenth-century drawing of
the stone statue of Mattifas de Buci.
(Bibliothèque Nationale, Cabinet des
Dessins, Gaignières Collection.)
Construction of the radial chapels of the
ambulatory was initiated by Mattifas de
Buci, who was depicted in a full-length
statue on a column outside the chapel
that houses his tomb.

and reached completion in the two-chapel units, which are accessed through double rather than triple arcades. There has been much speculation about the identity of the architect responsible for this transformation of the chevet. A document of 1316 relating to Chartres cathedral identifies one Pierre de Chelles as the *maître-d'oeuvre* of the Cathedral of Paris. Did he occupy this post in 1298, when Mattifas de Buci launched his construction campaign? The possibility merits consideration, for his name also appears in 1298 in connection with the installation of the tomb of Philip the Bold at Saint-Denis. In any event, he must have died shortly after 1316, for around 1318 Jean Ravy assumed his post, which he was to retain for some twenty-five years.

If Pierre de Chelles was indeed the supervising architect, then he must be considered one of the great creative figures of the early fourteenth century, for this design is quite remarkable. While basically consistent with Parisian Rayonnant architecture of the thirteenth century, it refines the idiom in very subtle ways—as did the Priory of Saint-Louis at Poissy, built at exactly the same time. It articulated the volume of the radial chapels and maximized their openings onto the ambulatory; it gave to the exterior envelope a rounded movement of exceptional elegance, downplaying emphatic projections; and it established a new rhythmic relationship between the stepped masses, one that integrated them to serene effect.

The seven reliefs set into the exterior northern wall of the apse have long attracted attention. Their subjects pose no problems, being readily identifiable as episodes drawn from the life and legend of the Virgin. However, vexing questions persist about their original placement. Examination of the masonry that now surrounds them indicates they were set into it later, despite the fact that their dimensions make for a nice fit. The attached pinnacles that frame them were shortened when they were moved, but we know neither when the transfer took place nor where the reliefs were originally placed. The pervasiveness of delicate passages reminiscent of metalwork suggests that they must have been intended for the building's interior, and gaps in the narrative sequence indicate that only a part of the cycle has survived. They may have been carved for the mariological cycle decorating the outer face of the hemicycle, which was destroyed when the choir was redecorated between 1699 and 1714. This theory is supported by the similarity of both their quatrefoil frames and their compositions to the reliefs visible in two drawings from the Gaignières Collection representing the kneeling effigies of Pierre de Fayel and Jean Ravy (see page 177). Additional support is provided by a relief fragment, in the Louvre since 1894, depicting Joseph being beaten in the presence of Potiphar. Its style is very close to that of the mariological reliefs: the handling of the mantle covering the shoulders of Pharaoh's officer, for example, is similar to that of the cloaks worn by the apostles carrying the coffin of the Virgin. If such is indeed their origin, then these reliefs offer a rare glimpse of stylistic tendencies current in early-fourteenth-century sculpture, and in particular of the style of Jean Ravy and his nephew Jean Lebouteiller, who completed the cycle of the chancel screen in 1351. The idiom in question is somewhat over-refined, and a certain awkwardness is apparent in the compositions. We might well say that these works exemplify the final phase of Gothic mannerism.

The Rayonnant Cathedral

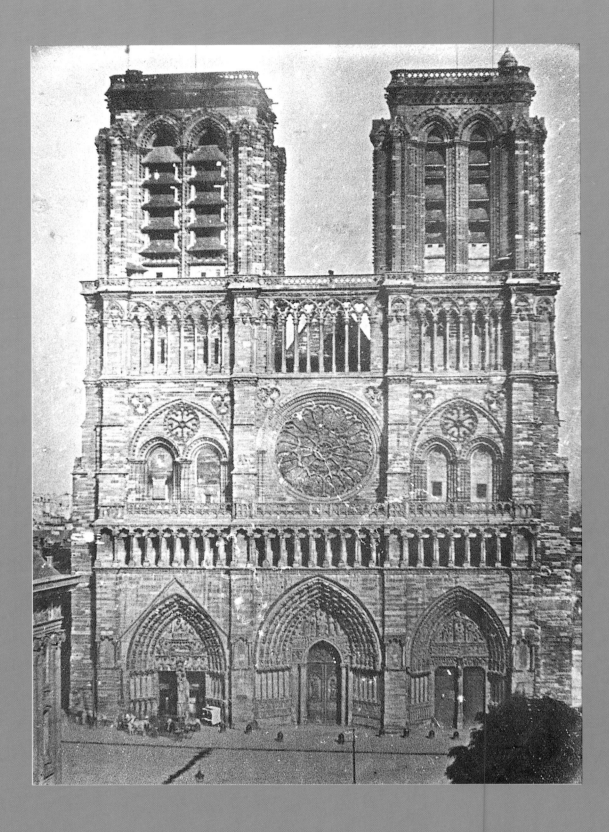

The Cathedral Rediscovered

Between the sixteenth century and the Revolution the cathedral was very poorly maintained. Only when the situation became serious did Cardinal de Noailles intervene, initiating restoration work in the southern transept, especially its rose window. Admittedly, the decision made in 1698 to redecorate the chancel and choir around a new sculptural group honoring the vow of Louis XIII was one of the great commissions of Louis XIV's reign; the fiscal difficulties that almost postponed it are well known. But the basic structure of the building was left intact during this extended period, save for Jacques-Germain Soufflot's redesign of the central portal. By 1843, however, it was in a pitiable state, as evidenced by the condition reports prepared at the time. Contemporary daguerreotypes are cruelly revealing on this point. Its structure had been weakened, its sculptural decor had been mutilated, and many of its movable furnishings had disappeared. Much of the masonry was in serious disrepair, while florets, gables, and pinnacles were essentially in ruin. The crossing had lost its spire. The monumental sculpture was first compromised in 1793 by the removal of everything suspected of relating to monarchical imagery, then in 1793–94 by the removal of the jamb statues. Only a few full-length figures remained in place: the Saint Marcel, on the trumeau of the Portal of the Virgin, the Virgin of the north portal, and the three kings at the top of the northeast buttress, all of them damaged. The only figures to escape mutilation—those high on the transept arms and atop the gable of the nave—did so because of their inaccessibility. The interior had suffered much less, although many works of art had been removed, some of them finding their way into the famous Musée des Monuments Français established by Alexandre Lenoir. The choir decor conceived by Robert de Cotte was now bereft of its sculptural tableau around the altar. The building's environs had also been affected. The bishop's palace was violently attacked on two occasions, during the Trois Glorieuses, in 1830, and again on February 14, 1831. In the end, it was demolished and replaced with a public promenade.

The state of the building soon became a focus of public concern. In 1831, the publication of Victor Hugo's novel *Notre-Dame de Paris* sparked a renewal of interest in the cathedral, for the author's powerful imagination had made it seem once more vital and approachable. To be sure, the book would not have had much effect without that larger movement, Romanticism, which defined a new relationship between the individual and the world. By calling rationalism into question, it had cleared the way for a more subjective approach to history, thereby prompting a sudden rediscovery of the past that expanded people's horizons. In this new context, Notre-Dame de Paris emerged as the privileged site of convergence of different currents of thought and sensibility: a Catholic movement seeking to reinvigorate a great religious tradition; a monarchical project to reclaim a past that, while recent, nonetheless seemed remote in the minds of many; and a growing secular concern with humanitarian issues. Despite this renewed interest, the cathedral of Paris

Opposite:
The façade before 1841.
By the 1840s, the cathedral was in a disastrous state. The central portal had been mutilated in 1771. The trumeau figures, jamb statues, and kings of Judah were all missing, as was the group featuring the Virgin above the Gallery of Kings. Much of the masonry was loose, and the spire had vanished. (Daguerreotype by Vincent Chevalier. Private collection.)

did not become as prominent a cultural emblem as that of Cologne, which after the devastation of the Napoleonic Wars served as a rallying point for all of Germany, the project for its belated completion becoming the focus of an emergent nationalist movement. First Joseph Goerres, then Goethe managed to find words that channeled a people's energy toward it for almost half a century (a "new cornerstone" was laid in 1842, and the building was completed in 1880). In France, the early stages of this mobilization campaign cannot have failed to make an impression on the public authorities.

In 1841, a committee was established in Paris to address the question; it circulated a letter to a number of important figures requesting support for its program. Times had changed: architects were no longer the masters of their building sites; now they had to negotiate public opinion. Étienne-Hippolyte Godde, the architect in charge of the cathedral, was severely criticized by the members of a new generation. More sensitive than he to the beauty of Gothic monuments, and more demanding in the matter of restoration techniques, they judged his work unacceptable.

Faced with this movement, the Ministry of Justice and Religion decided to undertake a restoration campaign of vast scope. Godde was replaced by Jean-Jacques Arveuf, the only architect initially asked to submit plans. In response to mounting public pressure, projects were also solicited from Jean-Baptiste Lassus and Eugène Viollet-le-Duc, who on the recommendation of Félix Duban had been given a free hand at the Sainte-Chapelle. These architects were soon joined

and announced that, indeed, there could be no question of removing the decorative ensemble conceived by de Cotte. Finally, they claimed to have located, through soundings, the thirteen steps traditionally thought to have existed in front of the facade. Here again, there are many blatant errors and approximations, but haste was unavoidable: they had to win over public opinion, and quickly.

Close contact with the building itself prompted them to modify these overly systematic views, resulting in numerous hesitations and revisions that are still visible in the monument. A preliminary study would have made it possible to avoid many of these missteps, but none was prepared. The *Journal des travaux,* which scrupulously recorded all stages of the work, makes it possible for us to follow every problem, hesitation, and error that had to be dealt with along the way. As the project advanced, invention became bolder due both to increasing familiarity with the building and to the growing national stature of Viollet-le-Duc. He was becoming a ubiquitous presence at the great historical sites, and in 1854 he began to publish his *Dictionnaire raisonné de l'architecture française,* which immediately became famous. It is worth stressing the care with which the work advanced. The architects did not always make do with consolidation of the existing masonry: they often outright replaced it, on both the interior and the exterior. The extent of their intervention is often difficult to determine, requiring close analysis of the stone; generally speaking, it was much more extensive than might be expected. As always in such restoration projects, attempts were made after the fact to minimize the archaeological traces that might have made it easier to follow the footsteps of Lassus and Viollet-le-Duc.

View of the cathedral from the south, 1847. Notre-Dame was covered with scaffolding almost as soon as the restoration campaign began. (Daguerreotype. Private collection.)

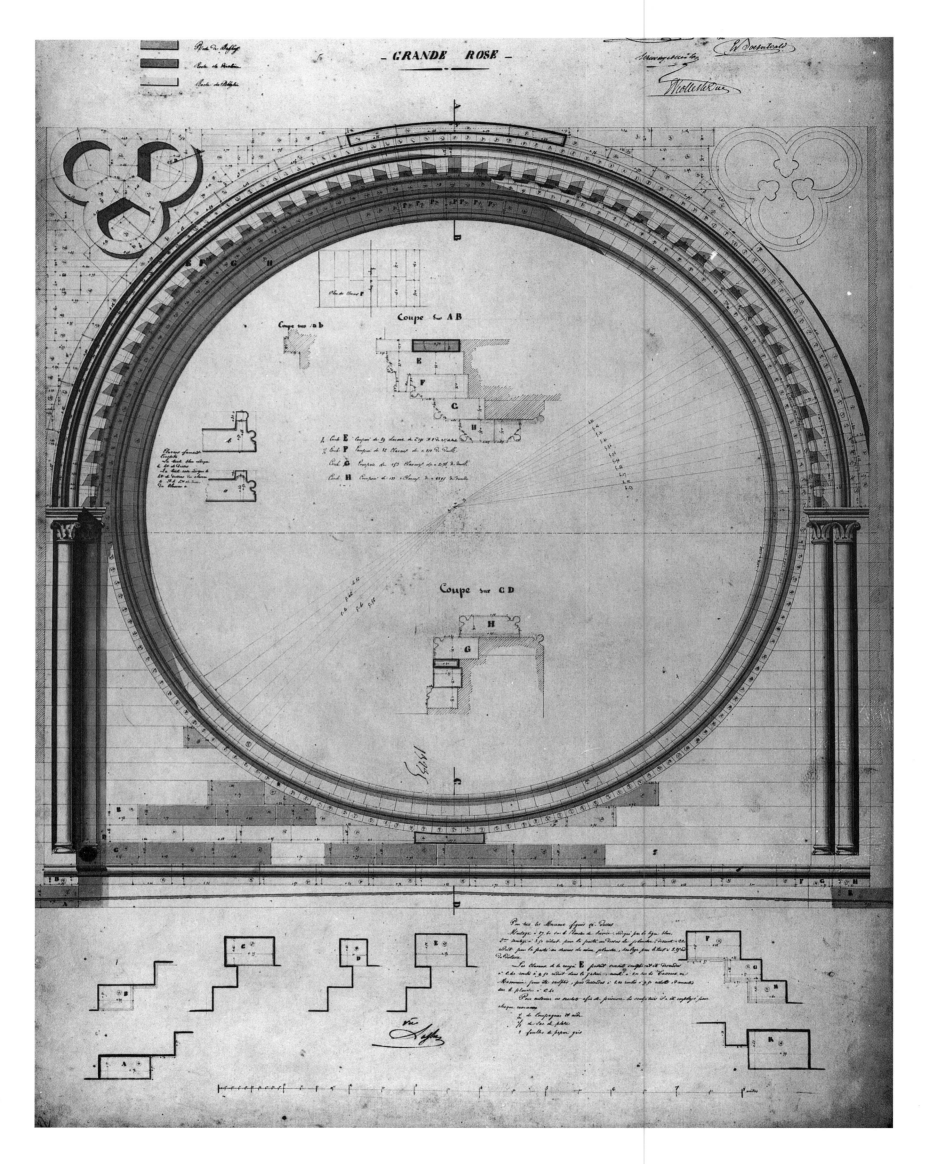

- GRANDE ROSE -

Many changes were introduced. Worn bases were recarved with profiles that might differ from the original ones. The southern rose window was completely dismantled, then reinstalled with wider radiating mullions. The western rose window, although found to be in good condition, was reconstructed in 1847 with new stonework. It must be admitted that copious documentation makes it easy to reconstruct the work done on the building's exterior, but this is much more difficult on the interior, due to dust covering the walls and worn masonry as well as to a relative paucity of documentation.

It is the window piercings that pose the greatest problem: those in the tribune of the choir and the nave as well as on the clerestory level. We now know that the shapes used there are mis-

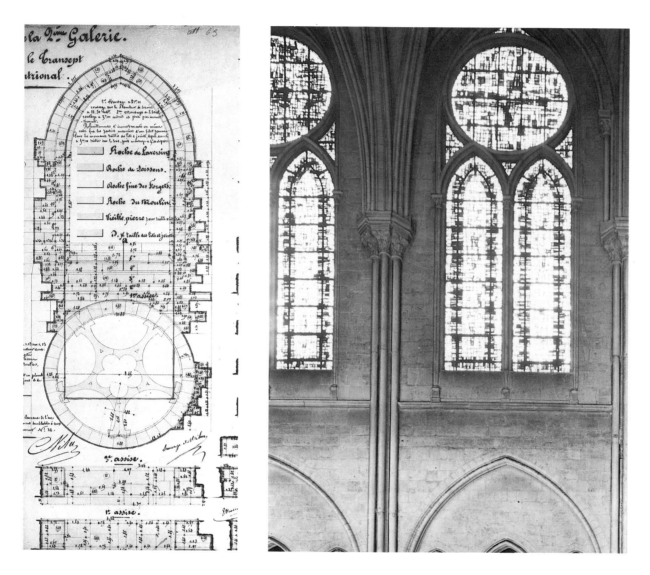

Far left:
Study of the proposed reconstruction of the original upper elevation, eastern window, and oculus of the north transept arm. (Archives Direction du Patrimoine.)

Left:
Photograph of one of the thirteenth-century clerestory windows.
The architects set out to reconstruct the original interior elevations of the cathedral. The discovery of stone tracery fragments led them to attempt a reconstruction of the rose oculi. This detailed study of masonry indicates how the stonemasons made the necessary adjustments.

Opposite:
Sauvage and Milon, Entrepreneurs, study of the western rose window, pencil and watercolor, 1847. (C.N.M.H.S.)
This study of the masonry surrounding the western rose window indicates that much of the facing stone was replaced during the restoration work, which is substantiated by visual analysis of the present masonry.

taken. The Conseil des Bâtiments Civils rejected the plan to employ a uniform treatment consisting of two lancets and a rose in all the tribune windows, insisting that the existing treatments be retained. But the discovery in March 1849, in the eaves of the southern tribune of the choir, of fragments that could be assembled in a rose configuration, prompted them to propose such a design. After receiving the enthusiastic support of the writer Prosper Mérimée (who was appointed inspector general of historical remains in France in 1833), it was approved, and four rose windows were duly pierced in the tribune of the choir, two to the north and two to the south. This treatment was then abandoned in favor of twin lancets inscribed within a relieving arch, and in the end the windows of 1300 were retained. But the discovery in July 1856, in the southern wall of the second bay of the nave, of fragments of another network of rose tracery, some of them still in place, made it clear that originally they were inscribed within oculi in the tribune eaves. Thus was recovered the basic disposition of the original elevation, previously known to have consisted of four instead of three levels. The architects now modified their design of 1843, proposing to

Pages 222–23:
Left: Viollet-le-Duc, design for the spire, pencil and watercolor, October 29, 1857. (Documentation C.N.M.H.S., cat. 85.)
Center and right: Photographs of the spire. Reconstruction of the spire above the crossing was one of the priorities of the restoration campaign. Viollet-le-Duc and Lassus found it difficult to settle upon a design. This project by Viollet-le-Duc, virtually identical to the one that was built, takes liberties with the thirteenth-century spire but is nonetheless a spectacular success. The copper statuary, all by Adolphe-Victor Geoffroy-Dechaume, contributes greatly to the overall effect.

The Cathedral Rediscovered

NOTRE DAME   DE PARIS

CATHEDRALE DE PARIS.

RESTAURATION DE LA FACE NORD
UNE TRAVEE,

A L'ECHELLE DE DEUX CENTIMETRES POUR METRE.

COUPE SUR A.B.

COUPE SUR LE MILIEU DE LA TRAVEE.

restore this elevation throughout the interior. Their intention was realized in part, first in the final bay of the nave and on the western wall of the southern transept (August–September 1856), then on the western wall of the northern transept (June–September 1857), and finally in the first bay of the choir and on the eastern walls of the transept (February–July 1858). These delicate interventions entailed extensive reconstruction of the adjacent masonry, which was carried out with exceptional care, as evidenced by related drawings (see page 221). But they were problematic in other ways as well: the precise placement of the oculi is far from certain, the tracery configuration is inaccurate, and, most important, these piercings now functioned very differently in the elevations than they did originally, due to the subsequent replacement of the sloped tribune roofs with terraced ones. In the twelfth century, these oculi opened onto dark voids; penetrating the entire thickness of the wall, they effectively expanded the interior space. As reconstructed in the nineteenth century, they functioned variously, but almost always in a manner at odds with the initial intent. Something like the original effect is still achieved in the outer bays of the western wall of the transept arms (see page 83). But in the inner bays of these transept elevations as well as in the nave, light penetrates the space behind them through recessed grisaille windows, and on the eastern transept walls and in the first bay of the choir, the oculi have been glazed with brightly colored stained glass (see page 71). What were originally wells of darkness are now brilliant sources of light. This transformation reinforces the planarity of the elevations, while the twelfth-century oculi tended to complicate and nuance this quality.

Identical problems arose in connection with the windows of the nave tribune. The architects had proposed a new design—clearly inspired by what they had seen and studied at the Sainte-Chapelle—consisting of independent rose windows inscribed within lancet triangles. Mérimée's enthusiastic support for this solution proved decisive, and it was finally approved and implemented. As a result, forms dating from a much later period were woven into the fabric of the building's interior.

Lassus and Viollet-le-Duc knew that the facade had initially been conceived with steeples above the towers. Viollet-le-Duc went so far as to re-create them in a drawing that, until quite recently, was a favorite target of critics (see page 215). Very likely the design is mistaken in its details, but the basic idea is not. In any event, all intent of building such steeples was abandoned when it was decided to erect a spire above the crossing. Here the architects relied on the 1780 drawing by Garneray and on the surviving base. In their 1843 design, also based on the eighteenth-century drawing, they had nonetheless chosen to reduce its two levels to one and to lower its height. Viollet-le-Duc's design of October 29, 1857, is very different, returning to a two-level base but otherwise taking many liberties with the thirteenth-century design (see pages 222–23). He made the first level quite elaborate, piercing it with wide double lancets supporting quatrefoils. The second level features trilobate lancets surmounted by high gables pierced by quatrefoils. He also envisioned four sequences of four statues—apostles and evangelists—along the descending diagonal rafters. He oversaw the realization of his design with particular care, confiding the carpentry to Bellu, who had also constructed the spire of the Sainte-Chapelle. As for the statues, in copper repoussé, they are the work of Adolphe-Victor Geoffroy-Dechaume. The overall result is spectacular, in terms of its detailing and harmonization with the building. Working with fewer constraints than elsewhere in the building, the architect as well as the sculptor here managed to recover the underlying inspiration of the thirteenth century. The beauty of the volumes is in perfect step with the handling of the draperies, and some of the figures have a freedom of movement that is quite remarkable, especially the Saint Thomas.

Restoration of the sculptural program occasioned the two architects' most convincing work. Less invested in this domain than in that of architecture, here they proved more objective. Notre-Dame de Paris is exceptional in this respect. No other restoration project of the nineteenth century involved sculpture to the same extent, and none of them addressed the problem at such a high qualitative level, with the exception of Pierrefonds, which was different in key respects.

Top:
Rose oculus, northern elevation of the last bay of the nave.
Above:
Rose window, southern tribune of the choir. Fragments of stone tracery discovered within the thirteenth-century masonry prompted an attempt at reconstruction, but their original placement was unknown. The architects began to incorporate them into the outer walls of the tribune of the choir before discovering that they came from the nave.

Opposite:
Lassus and Viollet-le-Duc, exterior elevation of a northern bay of the nave, with section of chapel and side aisles, pencil and watercolor, 1850. (C.N.M.H.S.)
Another crucial decision concerned the form to be given the tribune windows, a matter that caused the two architects much trouble. They finally settled on the chassis-window treatment seen here, whose design is anachronistic, having been inspired by a later idiom. At this point, they also envisioned the addition of a crocketed gable above the outer window of each chapel of the nave.

Above:
Viollet-le-Duc, drawings of decorative
sculpture, 1849.
Opposite:
Ghoul.
The inventive genius of Viollet-le-Duc
flourished in his designs for gargoyles and
other monstrous animals for the building's
upper reaches. The winged ghoul is
perhaps the most famous of them.

In the view of Lassus and Viollet-le-Duc, if the building were to become comprehensible again, it would have to recover its finery. The agendas of the two men were not identical, being primarily religious for one and primarily aesthetic for the other. Even so, from the beginning, in 1843, both of their designs featured sculpted decor. The report is eloquent on this point, expressing their unequivocal opposition to the use of any second-rate materials, notably cement, and their preference for new stonework in the form of copies after contemporaneous works from Chartres, Reims, and Amiens. These attitudes determined the organization of the sculpture workshops. The two architects assembled a large team of sculptors under the direction of Geoffroy-Dechaume to execute seventy-one works for the exterior. They were not great creative figures of the period but rather skilled craftsmen sufficiently modest to yield to the building's own laws. Excessive independence would have resulted in stylistic discrepancies incompatible with the desired homogeneity. The sculptors were already bound to one another by solid ties. Many came from the studio of David d'Angers: Geoffroy-Dechaume, Jean-Louis Chenillion, Jacques-Eugène Caudron, Michel Pascal, and Armand Toussaint. They were all virtually the same age, having been born in the 1820s. Several

The Cathedral Rediscovered

Above:
Viollet-le-Duc, design for the main altar.
(C.N.M.H.S., cat. 439.)
Opposite: Viollet-le-Duc, design for
lectern, March 1868. (C.N.M.H.S.,
cat. 436.)
The restoration campaign occasioned the
production of new ecclesiastical furniture.
In designing these elements, Viollet-le-Duc
chose to work in a twelfth-century instead
of a thirteenth-century style.

with assessing the central portal, dated June 24, 1849, focused on details, posture, and the handling of drapery; it said not a word about style, which suggests that consensus on this point had been reached.

The ambitious sculptural restoration campaign began on June 3, 1847, with the central portal. Reconstruction of the two lintels posed few difficulties, clear guidelines being provided by surviving fragments and Gilbert's drawing. Such was not the case with the jamb figures, of which no trustworthy depictions survived. For the consoles beneath the apostles, the sculptors looked to prints of the south portal at Chartres; for the statues themselves, to prints of the jamb figures at Bordeaux. But criticism of the results was so severe that these proposals were abandoned. The final sculptures, based primarily on Gilbert's drawing of the central portal, are equally dubious. Both architects and sculptors, convinced that the original must have been stylistically homogeneous, attempted to emulate the style of the trumeau in the jamb figures. This resulted in a pronounced stylistic discrepancy between the jamb figures and the other sculpture, some of which dates from the mid-thirteenth century. But it is hard to imagine how they could have proceeded otherwise: how could they have determined, solely on the basis of the drawing, that the portal of the first decade of the thirteenth century had been significantly recast some thirty years later? Clearly the design team took all possible care. In the Saint Anne portal, for example, a plaster completion of the surviving trumeau served as a model for the copy carved by Geoffroy-Dechaume. After it was finished, the original was sent to the Musée de Cluny. Only recently, when the plaster additions were finally removed, did the full beauty of the twelfth-century original become apparent (see page 27).

As we said earlier, outright mistakes are rare. One of them has yet to be fully explained, and it is a particularly unfortunate one, for it muddles the iconography of the western facade. Above the Gallery of Kings, on a level with the angels flanking the central Virgin and Child group, figures

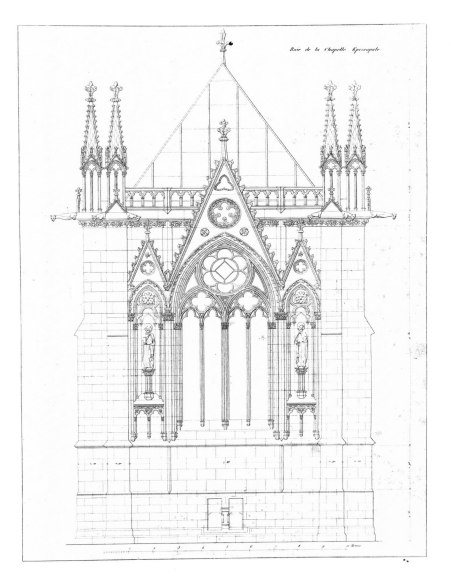

of Adam and Eve were placed in front of the double lancets. Frail and melancholy of aspect, carved by Chenillion, they were a miscalculation, for prior to the nineteenth century there was no sculpture here.

Final assessment of this massive undertaking must proceed on two different registers. On the architectural level, both the western facade and the southern transept portal reacquired their original grace thanks to the restoration of their statuary. Blank areas were again filled, banishing an exaggerated contrast between light and shadow that had disturbed the carefully gauged, serene visual rhythms of these compositions. As becomes clear from the comparison of before and after photographs, restoration of the figures in the Gallery of Kings had an especially beneficial effect, reestablishing the harmony of a facade over which light was meant to glide smoothly rather than proceed by fits and starts. The failure to restore the jamb figures to the north, however, deprived this scheme of its original meaning, resulting as well in overdramatic light-versus-dark contrasts inconsistent with the original intent of Jean de Chelles.

The second level of assessment pertains to the quality of the individual sculptures. Here a certain poverty of imagination and lack of character is apparent. Many of the faces are inexpressive and the execution of the drapery often seems mechanical. Given the archaeological nature of the enterprise, however, could it have been otherwise? By contrast, considerable invention is in evidence in the gargoyles and other monstrous creatures. The ghoul has since become an emblem of the cathedral, and many other animals dating from the restoration campaign also seem to breathe the air of authentic medieval fantasy.

Beyond the monumental sculpture, the cathedral furnishings also fell under the aegis of the two architects. Their first project encompassed only the rood screen and the hemicycle, leaving stained glass, painting, and other ecclesiastical furniture aside. As the work progressed, however, they came to appreciate the importance of these items. Their initial neglect of stained glass is surprising, given their previous experience at the Sainte-Chapelle. Their proposed solution to this problem, formulated in close collaboration with the archaeologist François de Guilhermy, was demanding. Thanks to the intervention, from 1756, of the Le Vieil brothers, who had introduced many grisaille windows with colored borders, there was now no shortage of natural light. The architects' increasing interest in colored glass may have resulted from their experience in building the new sacristy. Initially, it had been envisioned with white windows, but Mérimée intervened in 1847, convincing them of the preferability of painted glass. Only in 1867, however, were images of the bishops of Paris installed in the principal room. The work of Maréchal de Metz, their colors were harsh and their designs rather crude. Another team was engaged to realize the windows of the galleries: Louis Steinhil produced the cartoons and Alfred Gérente executed them. Here the color scheme is less intense, even pale, but the drawing of the figure of Saint Genevieve is of exceptional delicacy. In the cathedral, the restoration of the rose windows in 1855 must have heightened everyone's awareness of the importance of this question. Lassus having died by that point, Viollet-le-Duc himself solicited the collaboration of the preeminent master glaziers of the day: Gérente, Steinhil, Antoine Lusson, Adolphe Didron, and Charles-Laurent Maréchal. Didron's advocacy of what he called "archaeological stained-glass" proved decisive. The parallel historicism of Viollet-le-Duc was reflected in the painted decors executed in some of the chapels, notably the spectacular one realized for the baptism of the Prince Impérial. The same approach

Above:
Viollet-le-Duc, southern elevation of the sacristy. (Musée Notre-Dame.) Construction of a new sacristy, part of the initial competition program, posed a number of problems. The architects chose to design it in a thirteenth-century style to assure its harmonization with the nearby chevet.

Opposite:
Adolphe Didron, stained-glass window representing the genealogy of the Virgin, in the sixth nave chapel to the south, 1860. The two architect-restorers eventually devoted much attention to the role of color in the building's interior. Large mural paintings were executed, many of which survive in the chapels of the ambulatory. They also supervised the execution of numerous stained-glass windows for both the sacristy and the cathedral, of which this is among the most successful.

Early daguerreotype showing the eastern end of the Île de la Cité during construction of the new Hôtel-Dieu. (Musée Notre-Dame.)

As in the thirteenth century, work on the cathedral was accompanied by a complete restructuring of the urban fabric of the eastern end of the island. Many new buildings were erected, including the new Hôtel-Dieu, which rose on the site it had occupied prior to 1160 to the north of the square. Several designs were also prepared for a new bishop's palace, but they were never realized.

shaped the new ecclesiastical furniture, as evidenced by designs for the main altar, lectern, and pascal candelabrum as well as for metalwork: a reliquary for the crown of thorns and another for the holy nail, both realized by great contemporary goldsmiths.

Lassus and Viollet-le-Duc had hoped to transform the immediate environs of the cathedral as well, but they finally had to make do with erecting a few subsidiary buildings. Demolition of the ruined bishop's palace in 1831 necessitated its replacement. In 1841 and 1842, the architects presented two successive projects, both calling for the reuse of stone from the hôtel Legendre, then known as the hôtel La Trémoille, in a building to be situated on the island's eastern tip. In 1853, they proposed a third design, more ambitious as well as more original in conception, but none of these schemes was realized. The need for a new sacristy was more pressing. All that survived of the one built by Soufflot in 1760 was a block abutting the cathedral. Lassus and Viollet-le-Duc devised several preliminary schemes before proposing the one that was built. From the beginning, they chose the same site as the previous building—its advantages in terms of access were obvious—and opted for a style in harmony with that of the nearby chevet. The third new building they envisioned was one for the staff, which was constructed according to their plans some twenty years later. While not a large building, its volumetric conception is rather ambitious: unlike the adjacent structures, it emphasizes the planes of the walls, with window piercings kept to a minimum.

The immediate environs had been somewhat affected by external circumstances, but now the surrounding urban fabric was altered more radically, as part of a considered plan. First, Claude-Philippe-Barthelot Rambuteau, prefect of the Seine under the July Monarchy, launched a campaign of work that resulted, in 1837, in the piercing of the rue d'Arcole, consolidated from several existing streets, and of the rue de Constantine from the rue de Lutèce. The goal was to ease congestion and, above all, to improve hygiene in a quarter deemed foul even by contemporaries. During the Second Empire, growing concern in official quarters about the displacement of the capital toward the northwest led to the adoption of drastic measures on the Île de la Cité. Baron Haussmann, determined to reclaim some of the quarter's historical significance, set out to improve sanitary conditions there and to reenergize it by erecting emblematic public buildings. The speed with which these various projects were undertaken is an index of his resolve: 1860, Tribunal de Commerce; 1865, Caserne de la Cité (now the headquarters of the Paris police); 1869, Hôtel-Dieu. Other buildings in the vicinity were enlarged. The former palace of the kings of France, now the Palais de Justice, was extended westward to the edge of the Place Dauphine, whose eastern segment was finally demolished. The Marché aux Fleurs grew larger, and the square in front of Notre-Dame, now some 657 feet by 493 feet, became a parade ground for soldiers stationed in

The Cathedral Rediscovered

the caserne. In this new urban symphony, the cathedral continued to play a principal theme, thanks to its considerable mass, height, and stone construction. Nonetheless, the new administrative complex gradually displaced the religious one, whose population was reduced, between 1856 and 1900, from 15,000 to 5,000.

This secularization altered the meaning of the cathedral, which now became a national symbol. Amid the unfolding dramas that successively engulfed the country, it stood firm, always present as a source of solace and strength. The vow sworn by Louis XIII and given physical form at the behest of Louis XIV had finally been realized. In moments of sorrow as well as of jubilation, those in power came to the cathedral accompanied by anonymous crowds whose members had always remained attached to it. The leaders from the entire world converged upon it for the 1970 funeral mass honoring General de Gaulle, transcending divisions of race and religion to render him unambiguous homage.

At the close of the twentieth century, the history of Notre-Dame is far from finished. In recent years, work on the building has been limited to renovation of the square, which once more presents a welcoming face to visitors. The former barracks is now headquarters of the Paris police. The charity hospice continues to provide care to the disadvantaged. As for the cathedral itself, its ties to the nation remain strong; it is still a privileged site of collective expression, whether of grief or of joy. Great national events take on a special resonance beneath these vaults, which have echoed with victory Te Deums as well as with funeral chants. Crowds continue to flood through its portals. Some seek a place to reflect; others come to see one of the world's most famous monuments. All are affected by the peaceful aura of the building, conveyed both by its ample volumes and by its sculpture. Even those unable to decipher its iconography are touched by the Christ above the central portal, whose serene demeanor invites the pilgrim to enter. The ceremonies presented within this rich framework evidence the continuing power of the Christian faith. Addressing themselves not only to the inhabitants of a depopulated island or even to those of the diocese of Paris, they resonate well beyond, encompassing the whole of humanity.

Page 236:
The ritual of Ordination has lost none of its solemnity.

Glossary

The illustrations here are from Viollet-le-Duc's *Dictionnaire raisonné de l'architecture française*, 10. vols. (Paris, 1854—68).

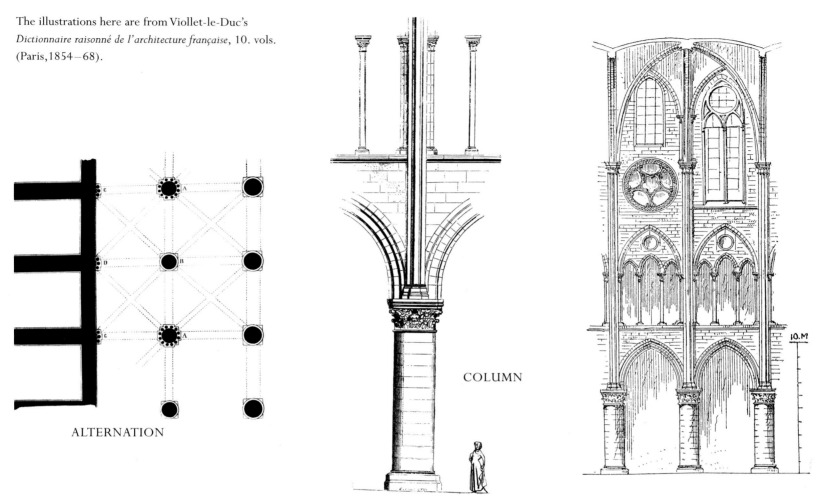

ALTERNATION

COLUMN

ELEVATION

Alternation. In architecture, the deliberate alternation of vertical supports—columns or colonnettes—of different diameter and design. The alternation of supports in the center aisle of Gothic churches is generally associated with the use of a sexpartite vault. The architects of Notre-Dame de Paris opted for identical supports in the main arcade (except for the first two bays) but used alternation in the intermediate supports of the side aisles of the nave.

Column. An upright support, in Gothic architecture usually tubular in form. Sometimes, as in the ambulatory at Saint-Denis, columns are *en délit,* but usually they are coursed, or composed of superimposed masonry drums. Drum columns can bear far more weight than *en-délit* columns.

Column statue. Full-length columnar statues carved from a single block of stone and usually situated in the jambs of a portal or as arcade supports; they evolved from the columns previously found in these locations. Invented in the mid-twelfth century, such figures became widespread in northern France after completion of the west facade of Saint-Denis in 1140 (see pages 26—27, 34).

Elevation. The first master of the cathedral of Paris designed four-level interior elevations consisting of a large arcade, a tribune arcade, rose oculi opening onto the tribune eaves, and clerestory windows (illustration, left). In the thirteenth century, the number of levels was reduced to three by eliminating the oculi and increasing the size of the clerestory windows (illustration, right), a modification made possible by replacing the pitched roofs over the tribune with flat, terraced roofs.

En délit. French term—literally, "off-bed"— designating pieces of stone deployed perpendicularly in relation to their original orientation in the stone bed of the quarry. In anticipation of such use, very long and narrow pieces can be cut from the living stone, but they are more delicate than blocks whose natural orientation is maintained, and they cannot bear much weight. Hence their primary use is as decorative, non-load-bearing elements, such as colonnettes and mural facings.

Flying buttress. A support structure transmitting much of the outward thrust generated by a heavy stone vault through arches to coursed, wall-like supports that stand perpendicular to the building. Its assumption of support functions previously carried by masonry walls made possible the attenuation of the structural armature, and the attendant increase in window size, characteristic of Gothic architecture. At Notre-Dame de Paris, however, the primary function of the flying buttresses was to channel rainwater and propel it, via projecting gargoyles, far from the foundations (see pages 152—53).

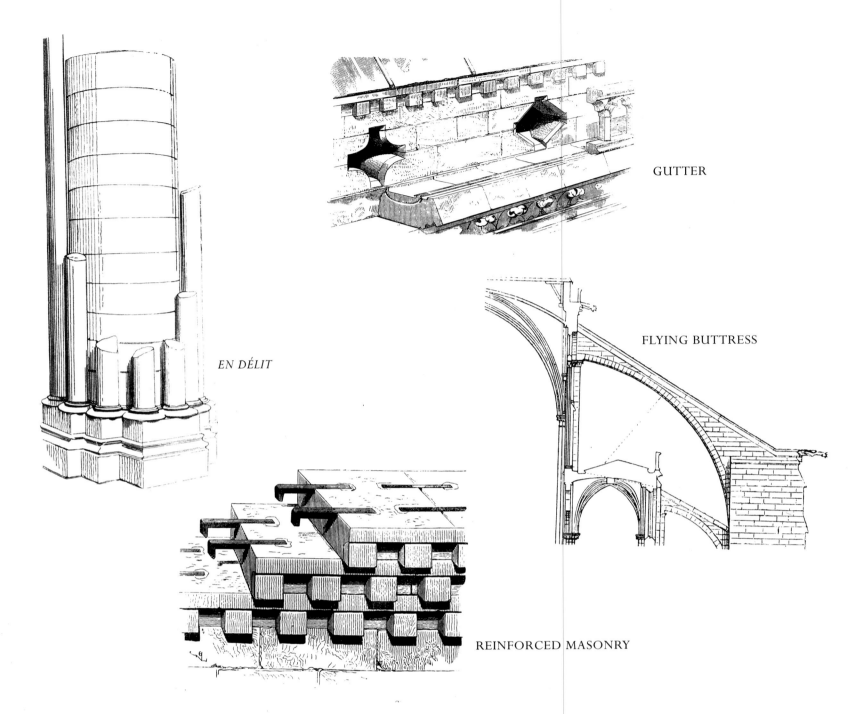

EN DÉLIT

GUTTER

FLYING BUTTRESS

REINFORCED MASONRY

Gutter. Due to the immense size of Gothic cathedrals, evacuation of the rainwater collected by their roofs presented architects with special problems. On the west facade of Notre-Dame de Paris, the architect devised a gutter at the base of the balustrade and equipped it at regular intervals with drains. In the choir and the nave, drains conduct water through vertical stone gutters to channels atop the flying buttresses, which expel it far from the foundations through projecting gargoyle spouts.

Pilaster. A shallow attached rectangular column. Since they project less than attached round columns, their use tends to maximize free floor space. At Notre-Dame de Paris, they were used by the architect of the nave in the western piers of the crossing and the western transept elevations (see page 82), in the responds of the tribune arcade (see page 84), and in the responds of the outer wall of the side aisles (see pages 83, 161).

Reinforced masonry. To facilitate the use of thinner walls, larger windows, and pervasive *en-délit* masonry, thirteenth-century architects developed a construction technique known as *"pierre armée,"* or reinforced masonry. Used tentatively at first, it soon became more pervasive, reaching its fullest development in the Sainte-Chapelle, which is completely girdled by metal bands. At Notre-Dame, metal tenons already figure in the clerestory masonry of the chevet, the chassis-windows are reinforced by rabbeted sash-bars set into the masonry, and some *en-délit* colonnettes are anchored to the walls with metal clasps.

Rood screen. The enclosure running between the eastern piers of the crossing to separate the choir, reserved for monks or nuns, from the nave, intended for the lay congregation. At Notre-Dame de Paris, there is also a *clôture,* or enclosure, separating the choir from the adjacent side aisles. In addition, between the early fourteenth and the early eighteenth centuries there was an openwork arcade, or hemicycle, separating the chancel from the ambulatory.

Beginning in the early thirteenth century, many rood screens and/or choir enclosures were rebuilt with elaborate sculptural programs (Chartres, Bourges, Paris, Strasbourg). Integral reconstruction of the ensemble in Paris is difficult (see page 167).

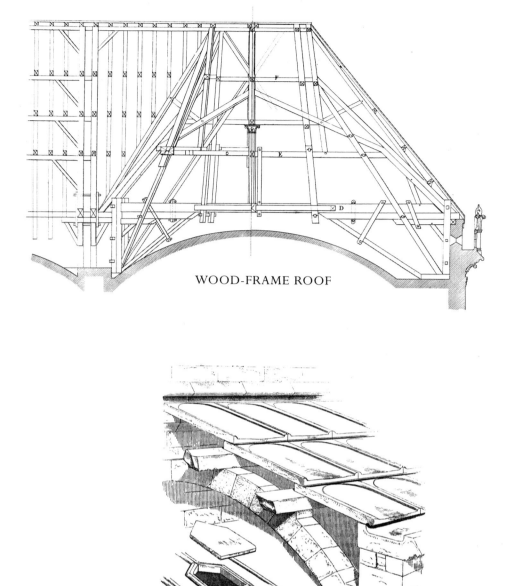

WOOD-FRAME ROOF

WINDOW

TERRACING

Terracing. A roofing system composed of large stone slabs—slightly inclined and hollowed to facilitate the drainage of rainwater—supported by lateral stone beams that are in turn supported by transverse arches. Trapdoors provide access to the crawl spaces beneath them.

Thin wall, thick wall. Norman architects invented "thick" masonry walls into which passages and illusionistic recesses could be incorporated. Thin walls consist solely of two layers of masonry separated by infill.

Vault. At Notre-Dame de Paris, the vaults of the nave and choir are sexpartite. Each unit is virtually square in plan and features six cells separated by two diagonal ribs and a central transverse rib. Of minimal convexity, they generate little lateral thrust (see pages 70, 81, 96–97).

Window. There are three kinds of windows in Romanesque and Gothic architecture: 1. the free window, without any internal subdivisions; 2. the constructed window, whose large size necessitated the introduction of a central coursed mullion set into the surrounding masonry; 3. the chassis-window, in which coursed mullions give way to *en-délit* mullions and stone tracery secured to, but independent of, the surrounding masonry.

Wood-frame roof. In Gothic architecture, the exterior roofing system, above the stone vaults, supported by a network of wooden beams. At Notre-Dame de Paris, the roof above the center aisle and transept was completely rebuilt in the thirteenth century during reconstruction of the clerestory level. The design devised at that time is a king-post roof reinforced with a network of struts and collar beams.

Bibliography

The bibliography relating to the cathedral of Paris is quite large, dealing with the various periods of its history and its construction. Regarding its history, an annotated bibliography can be found in Marcel Aubert, *La Cathédrale Notre-Dame de Paris: Notice historique et archéologique* (Paris: Firmin-Didot, new ed. 1950). Complementary bibliographies may be consulted in Pierre-Marie Auzas, *Les Grandes Heures de Notre-Dame de Paris* (Paris: Édit. Tel, 1951); M.-C.-P.-G. Guillot de Montjoye, *Description historique des curiosités de l'église de Paris* (Paris, 1763); and Pierre Du Colombier, *Notre-Dame de Paris* (Mémorial de la France; Paris: Plon, 1966). Regarding the subject of the present book, we must first cite sources predating the Revolution: Abbé Lebeuf, *Histoire de la ville et de tout le diocèse de Paris* (Paris, 1883), vol. 1; François-Philippe Charpentier, *Description historique et chronologique de l'église métropolitaine de Paris* (Paris, 1767). Post-Revolutionary period: A.-P.-M.-G. Gilbert, *Description historique de la basilique métropolitaine de Paris* (Paris, 1821); F. de Guilhermy and E. Viollet-le-Duc, *Description de Notre-Dame, cathédrale de Paris* (Paris, 1856). Images of the cathedral: André Marty, *L'Histoire de Notre-Dame de Paris, d'après les estampes, dessins, miniatures, tableaux exécutés aux XVe-XIXe siècles* (Paris, 1907).

Chapter 1. Origins of Paris: Félix de Pachtère, *Paris à l'époque gallo-romaine* (Paris, 1912); Paul-Marie Duval, *Paris antique, des origines au IIIe siècle* (Paris, 1961).

The wall: Silvie Legaret, "L'Interprétation des dessins de Vacquer. Essai de méthode," *Cahiers de la Rotonde,* no. 2, 1970.

Discovery of the Pillar of the Nautae: Moreau de Mautour, *Observations sur des monuments d'antiquité trouvez dans l'église cathédrale de Paris*; Baudelot, *Description des bas-reliefs anciens trouvez depuis peu dans l'église cathédrale de Paris* (Paris, 1711).

The origins of Christianity in Paris: Dom Jacques Dubois, "L'Organisation primitive de l'église de Paris du IIIe au Ve siècle," *Cahiers de la Rotonde,* no. 11, 1988.

Discovery of the ancient cathedral: Albert Lenoir, *Statistique monumentale de Paris* (Paris, 1867), an account of the excavations supervised by Vacquer; Michel Fleury, *La Cathédrale mérovingienne Saint-Étienne de Paris* (Mélanges Franz Pétri, 1970), with a large bibliography; Francis Salet, "Notre-Dame de Paris. État présent de la recherche," *La Sauvegarde de l'art français,* no. 2, 1982, 89–113, an excellent update.

The canons, from the eighth century to 1160: Robert de Lasteyrie, *Cartulaire général de Paris* (Paris, 1887); M. Guérard, *Cartulaire de Notre-Dame de Paris,* Collection des cartulaires de France, 4 vols. (Paris, 1850); Victor Mortet, *Étude historique et archéologique sur la cathédrale et le palais épiscopal de Paris du VIe au XIIe siècle* (Paris, 1888); Étienne de Garlande and P. Bournazel, *Le Gouvernement capétien au XIIe siècle (1108–1180)* (Paris, 1978).

Chapel of Saint-Aignan: Charles Sellier, *Procès-verbaux de la Commission du Vieux Paris* (Paris, 1908); Michel Fleury, ibid., 1980.

Portal of the Virgin: J. Thirion, "Les Plus Anciennes Sculptures de Notre-Dame de Paris," *Comtes-rendus de l'Académie des Inscriptions et Belles-Lettres,* 1970; W. Clark and F. M. Ludden, "Notes on the Archivolts of the Sainte-Anne Portal of Notre-Dame de Paris," *Gesta,* vol. 25, 1986, 109–18.

Removal of the statuary during the Revolutionary period: Alain Erlande-Brandenburg and D. Kimpel, "La Statuaire de Notre-Dame de Paris avant les destructions révolutionnaires," *Bulletin monumental,* 1978.

Sculptural fragments discovered in the nineteenth century and in 1977: François Giscard D'Estaing, Michael Fleury, and Alain Erlande-Brandenburg, *Les Rois retrouvés* (Paris: Cuénot, 1977); Alain Erlande-Brandenburg and Dominique Thibaudat, *Les Sculptures de Notre-Dame de Paris au musée de Cluny* (Paris: Réunion des Musées Nationaux, 1982), with bibliography.

Chapter 2. Maurice de Sully: V. Mortet, "Maurice de Sully, évêque de Paris (1160–1196). Étude sur l'administration épiscopale pendant la seconde moitié du XIIe siècle," *Mémoires de la Société de l'Histoire de Paris et de l'Île-de-France,* vol. 16, 1889.

Hôtel-Dieu: E. Coyecque, *L'Hôtel-Dieu de Paris au Moyen Age. Histoire et documents,* 2 vols. (Paris: Champion, 1891).

Bishop's palace: T. Crépin-Leblond, "Recherches sur les palais épiscopaux de France au Moyen Age (XIIe–XIIIe siècle)," *Positions de thèses . . .* (Paris: École Nationale des Chartes, 1987).

Canonial close: J. Meuret, "Le Cloître de Notre-Dame," *La Cité,* vol. 7, 1912.

Related urban development in the parish: Abbé Friedman, *Paris. Ses rues, ses paroisses* (Paris: Plon, 1959).

Construction history: M. Aubert, *Notre-Dame de Paris: Sa Place dans l'histoire de l'architecture du XIIe au XIVe siècle* (Paris: Laurens, 1920; new ed. 1929); F. Salet, ibid.

Chapter 3. Issues of chronology: C. Bruzelius, "The Construction of Notre-Dame in Paris," *Art Bulletin,* 1987.

Flying buttresses: W. Clark and R. Mark, "The First Flying Buttresses: A New Reconstruction of the Nave of Notre-Dame de Paris," *Art Bulletin,* vol. 66, 1964.

Rose oculi of the four-level interior elevation: C. Hardy, "Les Roses dans l'élévation de Notre-Dame de Paris," *Bulletin monumental,* 1991.

Chapter 4. Western facade: Wolfgang Sauerländer, "Die Kunstgeschichtliche Stellung der Westportale von Notre-Dame in Paris," *Marburger Jahrbuch für Kunstwissenschaft,* vol. 17, 1959, 1–56; *La Sculpture gothique en France, 1140–1270* (Paris: Flammarion, 1972).

Central portal: Alain Erlande-Brandenburg, "Les Remaniements du portail central de Notre-Dame de Paris," *Bulletin monumental,* 1971 and 1974.

Portal of the Coronation of the Virgin: Alain Erlande-Brandenburg, "Une Tête de prélat provenant du portail du couronnement de la Vierge à Notre-Dame de Paris," *Revue du Louvre et des Musées de France,* 1986.

Chapter 5. Architecture: Robert Branner, *Saint Louis and the Court Style in Gothic Architecture* (London: Zwemmer, 1965).

Sculpture: Dieter Kimpel, *Die Querhausarme von Notre-Dame zu Paris und ihre Skulpturen* (Bonn, 1971).

Portal of the Virgin: Alain Erlande-Brandenburg, "Une Tête inédite provenant du bras nord du Notre-Dame de Paris," *Mélanges Michel de Boüard,* 1982.

Rood screen and choir enclosure: Alain Erlande-Brandenburg, "Le Jubé de Notre-Dame de Paris," *Bulletin de la société nationale des antiquaires de France* (Paris, 1975); D. Gillerman, *The Clôture of Notre-Dame and Its Role in the Fourteenth Century Choir Program* (New York and London: Garland, 1977); Cesare Gnudi, "I relievi esterni del coro di Notre-Dame e la Vergina Annunciata del Metropolitan Museum," *Mélanges Sterling* (Paris, 1975).

Stained glass: Jean Lafond, "Les Vitraux de Notre-Dame de Paris," *Corpus vitrearum dedii aevi,* France, vol. 1 (Paris, 1959); Louis Grodecki, C. Brissac, and J. Le Chevalier, *Les Vitraux de Notre-Dame de Paris* (Paris: Nouvelle édition latine); H. Krauss, "New Documents for Notre-Dame's Early Chapels," *Gazette des Beaux-Arts,* vol. 74, 1969, 121–34, and vol. 76, 1970, 271.

Chapter 6. The basic structure of the cathedral was little altered between the sixteenth and eighteenth centuries. From the accession of Henry IV to the throne, privileged ties were established between the monarchy and the building, which gave the latter a special status. These developments climaxed in the "Vow of Louis XIII" and its realization in the early eighteenth century under the direction of Robert de Cotte. On this ambitious project, see Maurice Vloberg, *Notre-Dame de Paris et le voeu de Louis XIII* (Paris, 1926); see also page 163 of this volume.

Chapter 7. Documentation preceding the restoration campaign: Daguerreotypes: *Paris et le daguerreotype* (Paris: Musée Carnavalet, 1989), where the reproductions are reversed; Émile Leconte, *Notre-Dame de Paris, 1841–1843* (Paris, 1843).

Documentation: Archives des Monuments Historiques, which publishes a *Journal*; Centre de Recherches du Palais de Chaillot; the model.

Studies: D. R. Reiff, "Viollet-le-Duc and Historic Restoration: The West Portals of Notre-Dame," *Journal of the Society of Architectural Historians,* vol. 30, 1971; J.-M. Leniaud, *Jean-Baptiste Lassus (1807–1857) ou le temps retrouvé des cathédrales* (Paris and Geneva, 1980); Alain Erlande-Brandenburg, in *Viollet-le-Duc* (Paris: Galeries Nationales du Grand Palais, 1980).

Plans and Elevations

In the years leading up to 1843, Émile Leconte took remarkably accurate measurements of the cathedral, the only existing set that predates the restoration. The plans and elevations he produced from them reflect the state of the building prior to the interventions begun in 1845, and they were published as *Notre-Dame de Paris, 1841–1843* (Paris, 1843). Nine of the most important of them are reproduced here.

Plan of the arcade level.

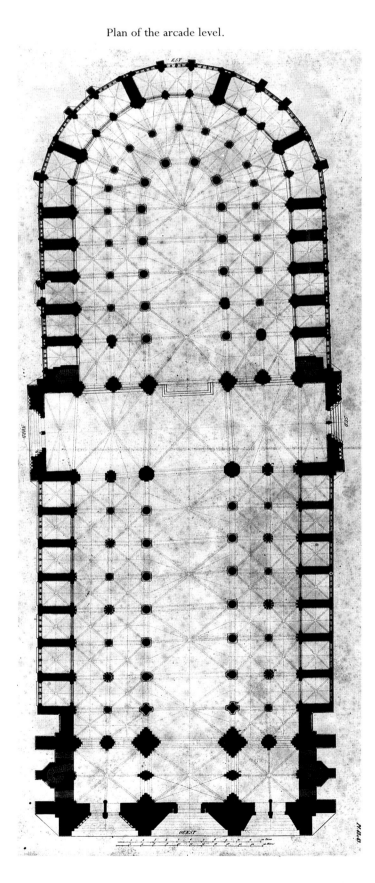

Plan of the tribune level.

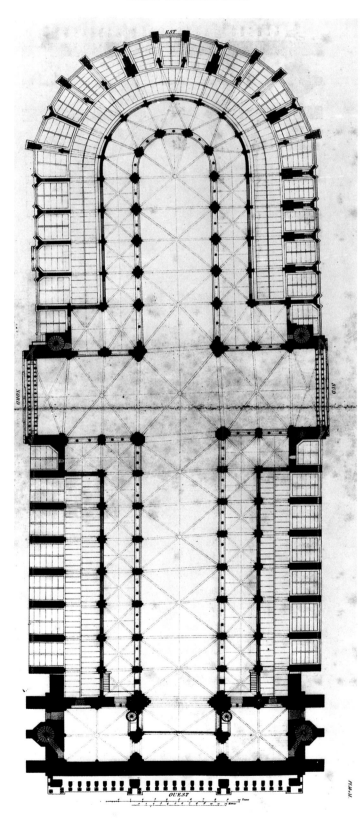

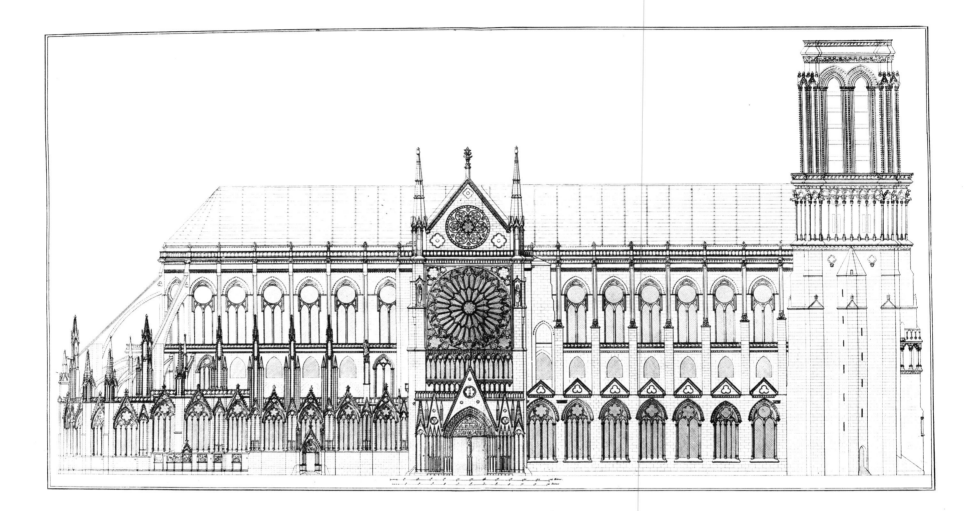

Northern exterior, elevation.
This image reveals the shape of the windows of the
tribune prior to the restoration campaign.

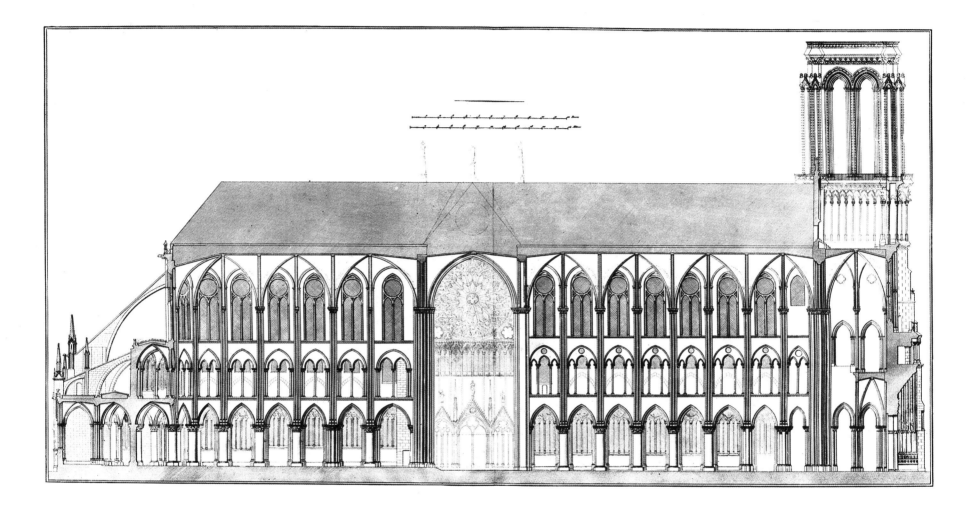

Section facing south.
The clerestory windows shown here are
those of the thirteenth century, except that of the first bay
of the nave, which dates from the twelfth century.

Northern transept extension, elevation and section of the terminal.

Plans and Elevations

Southern transept extension, elevation and section of the terminal.

Coupé de la Charpente sur la Nef

Coupe sur la largeur de la Croisée

Section of the transept facing east,
with section of the wood-frame roof of the nave.

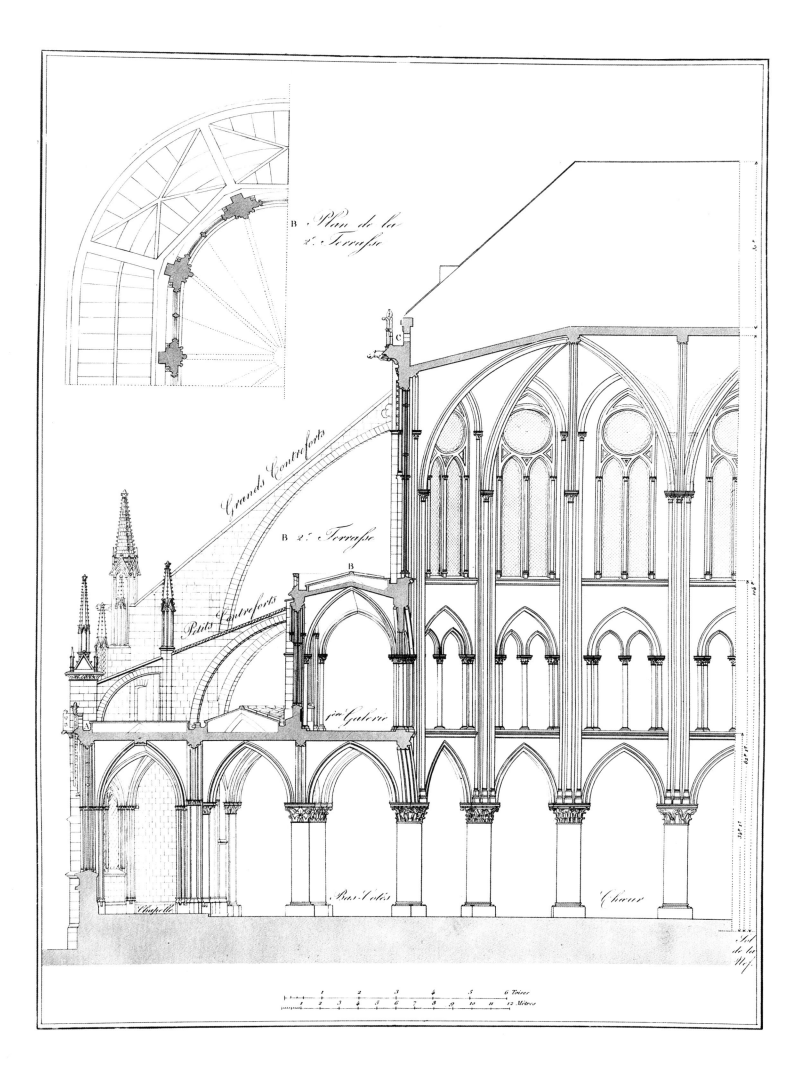

Section of the chancel and ambulatory,
with plan of the terraced roof over the tribune.

Pl. 84

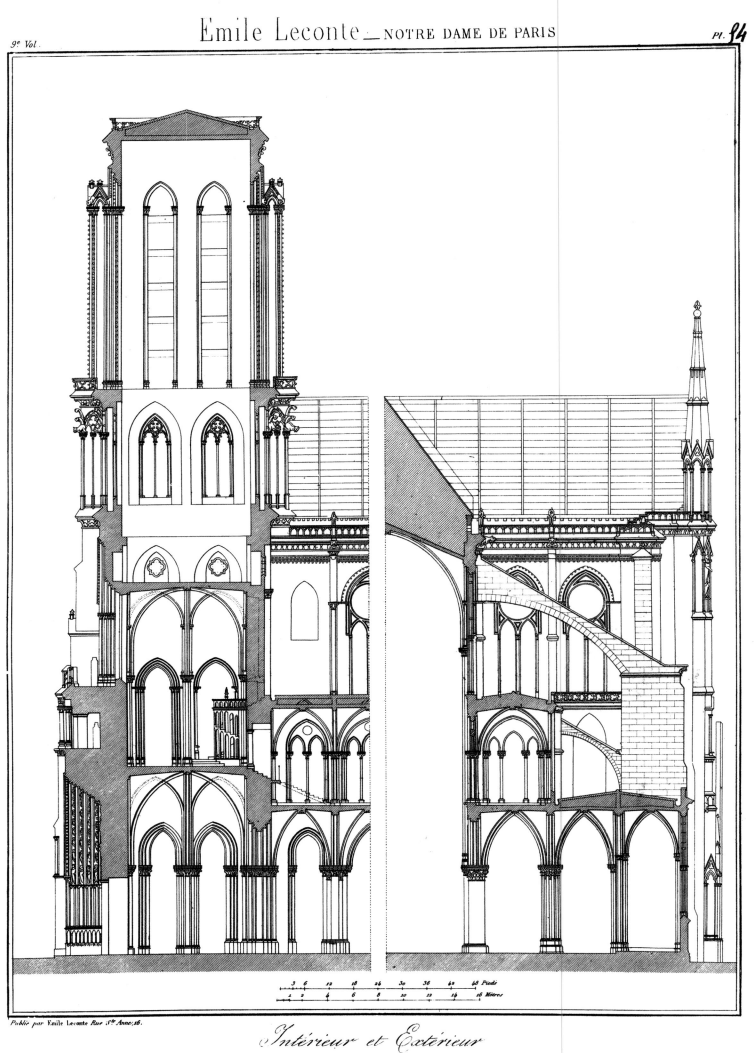

Publié par Emile Leconte Rue St Anne, 16.

Intérieur et Extérieur

Coupes sur la Tour du Midi et sur la Nef.

Section of the south tower and axial section
of the nave facing the southern transept.

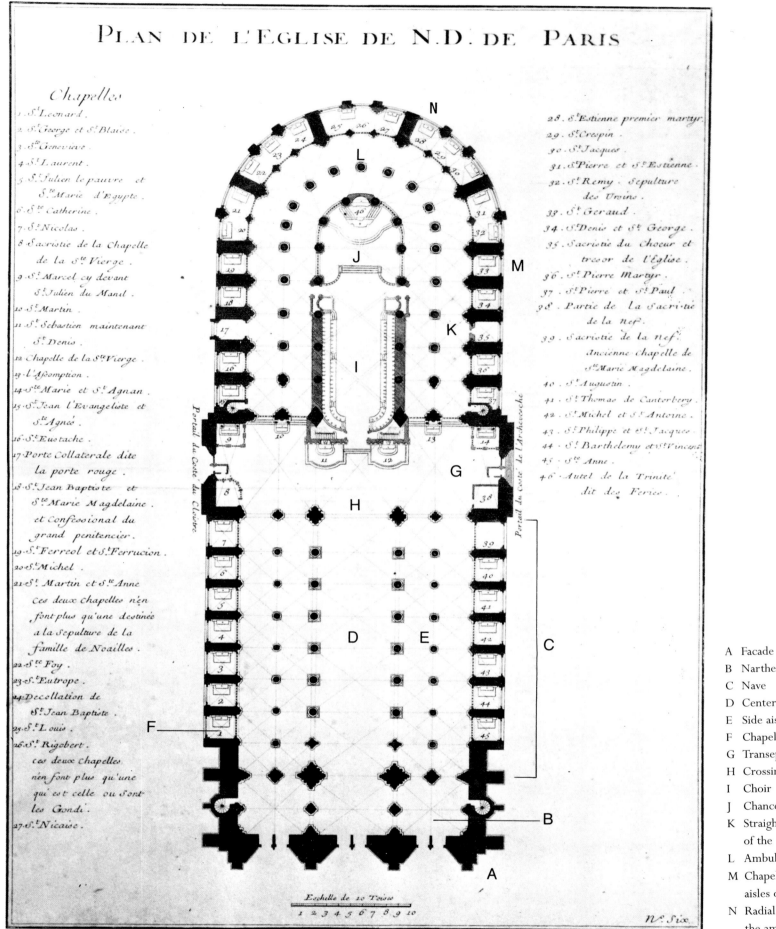

PLAN DE L'EGLISE DE N.D. DE PARIS

Chapelles

1. St Leonard.
2. St George et St Blaise.
3. St Genevieve.
4. St Laurent.
5. St Julien le pauvre et St Marie d'Egypte.
6. St Catherine.
7. St Nicolas.
8. Sacristie de la Chapelle de la Ste Vierge.
9. St Marcel cy devant St Julien du Mauil.
10. St Martin.
11. St Sebastien maintenant St Denis.
12. Chapelle de la Ste Vierge.
13. l'Assomption.
14. Ste Marie et St Agnan.
15. St Jean l'Evangeliste et Ste Agnés.
16. St Eustache.
17. Porte Collaterale dite la porte rouge.
18. St Jean Baptiste et Ste Marie Magdelaine. et Confessional du grand penitencier.
19. St Ferreol et St Ferrucion.
20. St Michel.
21. St Martin et Ste Anne. ces deux chapelles n'en font plus qu'une destinée a la Sepulture de la famille de Noailles.
22. Ste Foy.
23. St Eutrope.
24. Decollation de St Jean Baptiste.
25. St Louis.
26. St Rigobert. ces deux chapelles n'en font plus qu'une qui est celle ou sont les Gondi.
27. St Nicaise.

28. St Estienne premier martyr.
29. St Crespin.
30. St Jacques.
31. St Pierre et St Estienne.
32. St Remy. Sepulture des Ursins.
33. St Geraud.
34. St Denis et St George.
35. Sacristie du Choeur et tresor de l'église.
36. St Pierre Martyr.
37. St Pierre et St Paul.
38. Partie de la Sacristie de la Nef.
39. Sacristie de la Nef. Ancienne chapelle de Ste Marie Magdelaine.
40. St Augustin.
41. St Thomas de Canterbery.
42. St Michel et St Antoine.
43. St Philippe et St Jacques.
44. St Barthelemy et St Vincent.
45. Ste Anne.
46. Autel de la Trinité dit des Feries.

Portail du Coste du Cloistre

Portail du Coste de l'Archevesche

Eschelle de 10 Toises
1 2 3 4 5 6 7 8 9 10

N.º Six

A Facade
B Narthex
C Nave
D Center aisle
E Side aisles
F Chapel
G Transept
H Crossing
I Choir
J Chancel
K Straight side aisles of the choir
L Ambulatory
M Chapels of the side aisles of the choir
N Radial chapels of the ambulatory

Plan specifying the dedications of each chapel, from
François-Philippe Charpentier, *Description historique
et chronologique de l'église métropolitaine de Paris*
(Paris, 1767).

Index

Photograph Credits